Water and the Atmosphere

interactive SCIENCE

SAVVAS
LEARNING COMPANY

AUTHORS

You're an author!

As you write in this science book, your answers and personal discoveries will be recorded for you to keep, making this book unique to you. That is why you are one of the primary authors of this book.

✎ In the space below, print your name, school, town, and state. Then write a short autobiography that includes your interests and accomplishments.

YOUR NAME

SCHOOL

TOWN, STATE

AUTOBIOGRAPHY

Your Photo

ISBN-13: 978-0-13-368486-5
ISBN-10:   0-13-368486-5
24 2021

ON THE COVER
Capturing Wind
Without the wind to move her, this kitesurfer would be stuck. It's a good thing she's surfing off the coast of Queensland, Australia. The trade winds blowing from the southeast will keep her skimming across the water's surface.

Program Authors

DON BUCKLEY, M.Sc.
Information and Communications Technology Director,
The School at Columbia University, New York, New York
Mr. Buckley has been at the forefront of K–12 educational
technology for nearly two decades. A founder of New York City
Independent School Technologists (NYCIST) and long-time chair
of New York Association of Independent Schools' annual IT
conference, he has taught students on two continents and
created multimedia and Internet-based instructional systems
for schools worldwide.

ZIPPORAH MILLER, M.A.Ed.
Associate Executive Director for Professional Programs
and Conferences, National Science Teachers Association,
Arlington, Virginia
Associate executive director for professional programs and
conferences at NSTA, Ms. Zipporah Miller is a former K–12 science
supervisor and STEM coordinator for the Prince George's County
Public School District in Maryland. She is a science education
consultant who has overseen curriculum development and staff
training for more than 150 district science coordinators.

MICHAEL J. PADILLA, Ph.D.
Associate Dean and Director, Eugene P. Moore School of
Education, Clemson University, Clemson, South Carolina
A former middle school teacher and a leader in middle school
science education, Dr. Michael Padilla has served as president of
the National Science Teachers Association and as a writer of the
National Science Education Standards. He is professor of science
education at Clemson University. As lead author of the *Science
Explorer* series, Dr. Padilla has inspired the team in developing a
program that promotes student inquiry and meets the needs of
today's students.

KATHRYN THORNTON, Ph.D.
Professor and Associate Dean, School of Engineering
and Applied Science, University of Virginia,
Charlottesville, Virginia
Selected by NASA in May 1984, Dr. Kathryn Thornton is a veteran
of four space flights. She has logged over 975 hours in space,
including more than 21 hours of extravehicular activity. As an
author on the *Scott Foresman Science* series, Dr. Thornton's
enthusiasm for science has inspired teachers around the globe.

MICHAEL E. WYSESSION, Ph.D.
Associate Professor of Earth and Planetary Science,
Washington University, St. Louis, Missouri
An author on more than 50 scientific publications, Dr. Wysession
was awarded the prestigious Packard Foundation Fellowship and
Presidential Faculty Fellowship for his research in geophysics. Dr.
Wysession is an expert on Earth's inner structure and has mapped
various regions of Earth using seismic tomography. He is known
internationally for his work in geoscience education and outreach.

Instructional Design Author

GRANT WIGGINS, Ed.D.
President, Authentic Education,
Hopewell, New Jersey
Dr. Wiggins is a co-author with
Jay McTighe of *Understanding by Design,
2nd Edition* (ASCD 2005). His approach
to instructional design provides teachers
with a disciplined way of thinking about
curriculum design, assessment, and instruc-
tion that moves teaching from covering
content to ensuring understanding.
   UNDERSTANDING BY DESIGN® and
UbD™ are trademarks of ASCD, and are
used under license.

Planet Diary Author

JACK HANKIN
Science/Mathematics Teacher,
The Hilldale School, Daly City, California
Founder, Planet Diary Web site
Mr. Hankin is the creator and writer of
Planet Diary, a science current events
Web site. He is passionate about bringing
science news and environmental awareness
into classrooms and offers numerous Planet
Diary workshops at NSTA and other events
to train middle and high school teachers.

ELL Consultant

JIM CUMMINS, Ph.D.
Professor and Canada Research Chair,
Curriculum, Teaching and Learning
department at the University of Toronto
Dr. Cummins focuses on literacy
development in multilingual schools and
the role of technology in promoting student
learning across the curriculum. *Interactive
Science* incorporates essential research-
based principles for integrating language
with the teaching of academic content
based on his instructional framework.

Reading Consultant

HARVEY DANIELS, Ph.D.
Professor of Secondary Education,
University of New Mexico,
Albuquerque, New Mexico
Dr. Daniels is an international consultant
to schools, districts, and educational
agencies. He has authored or coauthored
13 books on language, literacy, and
education. His most recent works are
*Comprehension and Collaboration: Inquiry
Circles in Action* and *Subjects Matter:
Every Teacher's Guide to Content-Area
Reading.*

REVIEWERS

Contributing Writers

Edward Aguado, Ph.D.
Professor, Department of Geography
San Diego State University
San Diego, California

Elizabeth Coolidge-Stolz, M.D.
Medical Writer
North Reading, Massachusetts

Donald L. Cronkite, Ph.D.
Professor of Biology
Hope College
Holland, Michigan

Jan Jenner, Ph.D.
Science Writer
Talladega, Alabama

Linda Cronin Jones, Ph.D.
Associate Professor of Science and Environmental Education
University of Florida
Gainesville, Florida

T. Griffith Jones, Ph.D.
Clinical Associate Professor of Science Education
College of Education
University of Florida
Gainesville, Florida

Andrew C. Kemp, Ph.D.
Teacher
Jefferson County Public Schools
Louisville, Kentucky

Matthew Stoneking, Ph.D.
Associate Professor of Physics
Lawrence University
Appleton, Wisconsin

R. Bruce Ward, Ed.D.
Senior Research Associate
Science Education Department
Harvard-Smithsonian Center for Astrophysics
Cambridge, Massachusetts

Content Reviewers

Paul D. Beale, Ph.D.
Department of Physics
University of Colorado at Boulder
Boulder, Colorado

Jeff R. Bodart, Ph.D.
Professor of Physical Sciences
Chipola College
Marianna, Florida

Joy Branlund, Ph.D.
Department of Earth Science
Southwestern Illinois College
Granite City, Illinois

Marguerite Brickman, Ph.D.
Division of Biological Sciences
University of Georgia
Athens, Georgia

Bonnie J. Brunkhorst, Ph.D.
Science Education and Geological Sciences
California State University
San Bernardino, California

Michael Castellani, Ph.D.
Department of Chemistry
Marshall University
Huntington, West Virginia

Charles C. Curtis, Ph.D.
Research Associate Professor of Physics
University of Arizona
Tucson, Arizona

Diane I. Doser, Ph.D.
Department of Geological Sciences
University of Texas
El Paso, Texas

Rick Duhrkopf, Ph.D.
Department of Biology
Baylor University
Waco, Texas

Alice K. Hankla, Ph.D.
The Galloway School
Atlanta, Georgia

Mark Henriksen, Ph.D.
Physics Department
University of Maryland
Baltimore, Maryland

Chad Hershock, Ph.D.
Center for Research on Learning and Teaching
University of Michigan
Ann Arbor, Michigan

Jeremiah N. Jarrett, Ph.D.
Department of Biology
Central Connecticut State University
New Britain, Connecticut

Scott L. Kight, Ph.D.
Department of Biology
Montclair State University
Montclair, New Jersey

Jennifer O. Liang, Ph.D.
Department of Biology
University of Minnesota–Duluth
Duluth, Minnesota

Candace Lutzow-Felling, Ph.D.
Director of Education
The State Arboretum of Virginia
University of Virginia
Boyce, Virginia

Cortney V. Martin, Ph.D.
Virginia Polytechnic Institute
Blacksburg, Virginia

Joseph F. McCullough, Ph.D.
Physics Program Chair
Cabrillo College
Aptos, California

Heather Mernitz, Ph.D.
Department of Physical Science
Alverno College
Milwaukee, Wisconsin

Sadredin C. Moosavi, Ph.D.
Department of Earth and Environmental Sciences
Tulane University
New Orleans, Louisiana

David L. Reid, Ph.D.
Department of Biology
Blackburn College
Carlinville, Illinois

Scott M. Rochette, Ph.D.
Department of the Earth Sciences
SUNY College at Brockport
Brockport, New York

Karyn L. Rogers, Ph.D.
Department of Geological Sciences
University of Missouri
Columbia, Missouri

Laurence Rosenhein, Ph.D.
Department of Chemistry
Indiana State University
Terre Haute, Indiana

Sara Seager, Ph.D.
Department of Planetary Sciences and Physics
Massachusetts Institute of Technology
Cambridge, Massachusetts

Tom Shoberg, Ph.D.
Missouri University of Science and Technology
Rolla, Missouri

Patricia Simmons, Ph.D.
North Carolina State University
Raleigh, North Carolina

William H. Steinecker, Ph.D.
Research Scholar
Miami University
Oxford, Ohio

Paul R. Stoddard, Ph.D.
Department of Geology and Environmental Geosciences
Northern Illinois University
DeKalb, Illinois

John R. Villarreal, Ph.D.
Department of Chemistry
The University of Texas–Pan American
Edinburg, Texas

John R. Wagner, Ph.D.
Department of Geology
Clemson University
Clemson, South Carolina

Jerry Waldvogel, Ph.D.
Department of Biological Sciences
Clemson University
Clemson, South Carolina

Donna L. Witter, Ph.D.
Department of Geology
Kent State University
Kent, Ohio

Edward J. Zalisko, Ph.D.
Department of Biology
Blackburn College
Carlinville, Illinois

Museum of Science.

Special thanks to the Museum of Science, Boston, Massachusetts, and Ioannis Miaoulis, the Museum's president and director, for serving as content advisors for the technology and design strand in this program.

CONTENTS

CHAPTER 1 Fresh Water

? The Big Question 1
How does fresh water cycle on Earth?

    Vocabulary Skill: Latin Word Origins 2
    ⟳ Reading Skills 3

LESSON 1
Water on Earth 4
    ? Unlock the Big Question 4
    do the math! Analyzing Data 6
    △ Inquiry Skill: Observe 9

LESSON 2
Surface Water 10
    ? Unlock the Big Question 10
    △ Inquiry Skill: Form Operational Definitions 14
    ? Explore the Big Question 17
    ? Answer the Big Question 17

LESSON 3
Water Underground 18
    ? Unlock the Big Question 18
    do the math! Read Graphs 21
    △ Inquiry Skill: Predict 21

LESSON 4
Wetland Environments 24
    ? Unlock the Big Question 24
    △ Inquiry Skill: Classify 26

Study Guide & Review and Assessment 30
    ? Review the Big Question 30
    ? Apply the Big Question 32

Science Matters 34
    • A Pearl of a Solution • What Was Fort Miami?

 Enter the Lab zone for hands-on inquiry.

△ **Chapter Lab Investigation:**
• Directed Inquiry: Water From Trees
• Open Inquiry: Water From Trees

△ **Inquiry Warm-Ups:**
• Where Does the Water Come From?
• Mapping Surface Waters • Where Does the Water Go? • Wet or Dry?

△ **Quick Labs:** • Water, Water Everywhere
• Water on Earth • What Is a Watershed?
• Modeling How a Lake Forms • How Can Algal Growth Affect Pond Life? • Soil Percolation • An Artesian Well • Describing Wetlands • A Natural Filter

my science online.com

Go to MyScienceOnline.com to interact with this chapter's content.
Keyword: Fresh Water

> **UNTAMED SCIENCE**
• Water Cyclists

> **PLANET DIARY**
• Fresh Water

> **INTERACTIVE ART**
• Water Cycle • Importance of Wetlands

> **ART IN MOTION**
• How Does Groundwater Collect?

> **REAL-WORLD INQUIRY**
• Water Cycle, Interrupted

CHAPTER 2

The Oceans

The Oceans **36**
What are some characteristics of Earth's oceans?

Vocabulary Skill: Suffixes 38
Reading Skills 39

LESSON 1
Exploring the Ocean 40
Unlock the Big Question 40
Inquiry Skill: Interpret Data 43
Explore the Big Question 45
Answer the Big Question 45

LESSON 2
Wave Action 46
Unlock the Big Question 46
Inquiry Skill: Form Operational Definitions 48

LESSON 3
Currents and Climate 54
Unlock the Big Question 54
Inquiry Skill: Infer 56
do the math! Calculating Density 59
Inquiry Skill: Calculate 59

LESSON 4
Ocean Habitats 60
Unlock the Big Question 60
Inquiry Skill: Predict 61

Study Guide & Review and Assessment 64
Review the Big Question 64
Apply the Big Question 66

Science Matters 68
• Sustainable Shrimp Farms • Aquanauts

 Enter the Lab zone for hands-on inquiry.

Chapter Lab Investigation:
• Directed Inquiry: Modeling Ocean Currents
• Open Inquiry: Modeling Ocean Currents

Inquiry Warm-Ups: • What Can You Learn Without Seeing? • How Do Waves Change a Beach? • Bottom to Top • How Complex Are Ocean Feeding Relationships?

Quick Labs: • Ocean Conditions • The Shape of the Ocean Floor • Making Waves • Modeling Currents • Deep Currents • Designing an Organism

my science online.com

Go to MyScienceOnline.com to interact with this chapter's content.
Keyword: The Oceans

> **UNTAMED SCIENCE**
• Keeping Current in the Ocean

> **PLANET DIARY**
• The Oceans

> **INTERACTIVE ART**
• Features of the Ocean Floor • Water Motion • Ocean Food Web

> **ART IN MOTION**
• El Niño

> **VIRTUAL LAB**
• How Does the Density of Seawater Change?

CONTENTS

CHAPTER 3

The Atmosphere

The Big Question **70**
How does the sun's energy affect Earth's atmosphere?

Vocabulary Skill: Word Origins 72
Reading Skills 73

LESSON 1
The Air Around You **74**
Unlock the Big Question 74
Inquiry Skill: Infer 76

LESSON 2
Air Pressure **78**
Unlock the Big Question 78
Inquiry Skill: Develop Hypotheses 82

LESSON 3
Layers of the Atmosphere **84**
Unlock the Big Question 84
do the math! Read Graphs 87
Inquiry Skill: Interpret Data 87

LESSON 4
Energy in Earth's Atmosphere **90**
Unlock the Big Question 90
Inquiry Skill: Graph 93

LESSON 5
Heat Transfer **96**
Unlock the Big Question 96
Inquiry Skill: Infer 98

LESSON 6
Winds **100**
Unlock the Big Question 100
Inquiry Skill: Draw Conclusions 105
Explore the Big Question 107
Answer the Big Question 107

Study Guide & Review and Assessment **108**
Review the Big Question 108
Apply the Big Question 110

Science Matters **112**
• The Aura Mission • Up, Up, and Away! • Plugging Into the Jet Stream

® **Enter the Lab zone for hands-on inquiry.**

Chapter Lab Investigation:
• Directed Inquiry: Heating Earth's Surface
• Open Inquiry: Heating Earth's Surface

Inquiry Warm-Ups: • How Long Will the Candle Burn? • Does Air Have Mass? • Is Air There? • Does a Plastic Bag Trap Heat? • What Happens When Air Is Heated? • Does the Wind Turn?

Quick Labs: • Breathe In, Breathe Out • What Is the Source of Earth's Energy? • Properties of Air • Soda Bottle Barometer • Effects of Altitude on the Atmosphere • Layers of the Atmosphere • Calculating Temperature Changes • How Does the Sun's Energy Reach Earth? • Measuring Temperature • Temperature and Height • Build a Wind Vane • Modeling Global Wind Belts

my science online.com

Go to MyScienceOnline.com to interact with this chapter's content. Keyword: The Atmosphere

> INTERACTIVE ART
• Measuring Air Pressure • Global Winds

> ART IN MOTION
• Greenhouse Effect

> VIRTUAL LAB
• What Do Temperature and Volume Have to Do With Air Pressure?

Weather

CHAPTER 4

 The Big Question 114
How do meteorologists predict the weather?

Vocabulary Skill: Prefixes 116
Reading Skills 117

LESSON 1
Water in the Atmosphere 118
Unlock the Big Question 118
do the math! Calculate 121
Inquiry Skill: Interpret Data 121

LESSON 2
Clouds 122
Unlock the Big Question 122
Inquiry Skill: Predict 125

LESSON 3
Precipitation 126
Unlock the Big Question 126
Inquiry Skill: Calculate 127, 129

LESSON 4
Air Masses 132
Unlock the Big Question 132
Inquiry Skill: Classify 133, 134, 135, 137, 139

LESSON 5
Storms 140
Unlock the Big Question 140
Inquiry Skill: Infer 143, 149

LESSON 6
Predicting the Weather 150
Unlock the Big Question 150
Inquiry Skill: Predict 153
Explore the Big Question 155
Answer the Big Question 155

Study Guide & Review and Assessment 156
Review the Big Question 156
Apply the Big Question 158

Science Matters 160
• The S'COOL Project • Tracking Hurricanes With Latitude and Longitude

Lab zone® Enter the Lab zone for hands-on inquiry.

Chapter Lab Investigation:
• Directed Inquiry: Reading a Weather Map
• Open Inquiry: Reading a Weather Map

Inquiry Warm-Ups: • Where Did the Water Go? • How Does Fog Form? • How Can You Make Hail? • How Do Fluids of Different Densities Move? • Can You Make a Tornado? • Predicting Weather

Quick Labs: • Water in the Air • Measuring to Find the Dew Point • How Clouds Form • Identifying Clouds • Types of Precipitation • Floods and Droughts • Tracking Air Masses • Weather Fronts • Cyclones and Anticyclones • Where Do Hurricanes Come From? • Storm Safety • Modeling Weather Satellites

my science online.com

Go to MyScienceOnline.com to interact with this chapter's content.
Keyword: Weather

> PLANET DIARY
• Weather

> INTERACTIVE ART
• Water Cycle • Weather Fronts • Different Conditions, Different Storms

> ART IN MOTION
• How Does Precipitation Form?

> REAL-WORLD INQUIRY
• Predicting the Weather

CONTENTS

CHAPTER 5
Climate and Climate Change

 The Big Question **162**
What factors affect Earth's climate?

Vocabulary Skill: High-Use Academic Words **164**
Reading Skills **165**

LESSON 1
What Causes Climate? **166**
Unlock the Big Question **166**
Inquiry Skill: Infer **170**

LESSON 2
Climate Regions **174**
Unlock the Big Question **174**
Inquiry Skill: Communicate **183**

LESSON 3
Changes in Climate **184**
Unlock the Big Question **184**
do the math! Interpret Data **188**
Inquiry Skill: Interpret Data **188**

LESSON 4
Human Activities and Climate Change **190**
Unlock the Big Question **190**
Inquiry Skill: Make Models **194**
Explore the Big Question **195**
Answer the Big Question **195**

Study Guide & Review and Assessment **196**
Review the Big Question **196**
Apply the Big Question **198**

Science Matters **200**
• Tracking Earth's Gases From Space • Bacterial Rainmakers

English/Spanish Glossary, Index **202**

Lab zone® Enter the Lab zone
for hands-on inquiry.

Chapter Lab Investigation:
• Directed Inquiry: Sunny Rays and Angles
• Open Inquiry: Sunny Rays and Angles

Inquiry Warm-Ups: • How Does Latitude
Affect Climate? • How Do Climates Differ?
• What Story Can Tree Rings Tell? • What Is
the Greenhouse Effect?

Quick Labs: • Inferring United States
Precipitation Patterns • Classifying Climates
• Making and Interpreting a Climograph
• Climate Clues • Earth's Movement and
Climate • Greenhouse Gases and Global
Warming

my science online.com

Go to MyScienceOnline.com to
interact with this chapter's content.
Keyword: Climate and Climate Change

> **PLANET DIARY**
• Climate and Climate Change

> **INTERACTIVE ART**
• Continental Drift • Climate Change:
Causes, Effects, Solutions

> **ART IN MOTION**
• Greenhouse Effect

> **VIRTUAL LAB**
• Climate Connections

Untamed Science™

Video Series: Chapter Adventures

Untamed Science created this captivating video series for interactive SCIENCE featuring a unique segment for every chapter of the program.

Featuring videos such as

Water Cyclists
Chapter 1 Feeling thirsty? Join the Untamed Science crew as they explore the many amazing forms of water found on Earth.

Keeping Current in the Ocean
Chapter 2 Surf's up as Jonas hits the beach to find out more about what's going on under the waves.

Gliding Through the Atmosphere
Chapter 3 Join Rob as he embarks on a hang-gliding adventure to explore some of the characteristics of Earth's atmosphere.

Twisted Adventures
Chapter 4 The Untamed Science crew goes storm chasing and learns how meteorologists predict the weather.

Searching for the Perfect Climate
Chapter 5 Trek across the globe with the Untamed Science crew as they take a look at climate change on different continents.

interactive SCIENCE

This is your book.
You can write in it!

HOW CAN WIND KEEP YOUR LIGHTS ON?

What are some of Earth's energy sources?

This man is repairing a wind turbine at a wind farm in Texas. Most wind turbines are at least 30 meters off the ground where the winds are fast. Wind speed and blade length help determine the best way to capture the wind and turn it into power. **Develop Hypotheses** Why do you think people are working to increase the amount of power we get from wind?

Wind energy collected by the turbine does not cause air pollution.

> **UNTAMED SCIENCE** Watch the Untamed Science video to learn more about energy resources.

174 Energy Resources

Get Engaged!

At the start of each chapter, you will see two questions: an Engaging Question and the Big Question. Each chapter's Big Question will help you start thinking about the Big Ideas of Science. Look for the Big Q symbol throughout the chapter!

Untamed Science

Follow the Untamed Science video crew as they travel the globe exploring the Big Ideas of Science.

xii

Interact with your textbook.   Interact with inquiry.   Interact online.

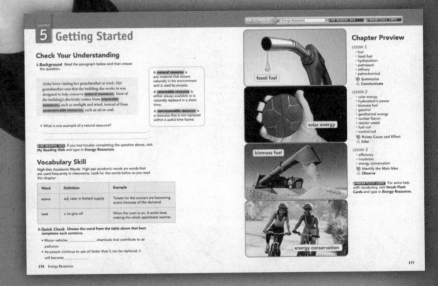

Build Reading, Inquiry, and Vocabulary Skills

In every lesson you will learn new 🔄 Reading and 🔺 Inquiry skills. These skills will help you read and think like a scientist. Vocabulary skills will help you communicate effectively and uncover the meaning of words.

Go Online!

Look for the MyScienceOnline.com technology options. At MyScienceOnline.com you can immerse yourself in amazing virtual environments, get extra practice, and even blog about current events in science.

Explore the Key Concepts.

Each lesson begins with a series of Key Concept questions. The interactivities in each lesson will help you understand these concepts and Unlock the Big Question.

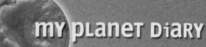

my PLANET DiARY

At the start of each lesson, My Planet Diary will introduce you to amazing events, significant people, and important discoveries in science or help you to overcome common misconceptions about science concepts.

Desertification If the soil i of moisture and nutrients, the advance of desertlike conditio fertile is called **desertification**

One cause of desertificati is a period when less rain tha droughts, crops fail. Without blows away. Overgrazing of g cutting down trees for firewoo

Desertification is a seriou and graze livestock where de people may face famine and s central Africa. Millions of ru cities because they can no lon

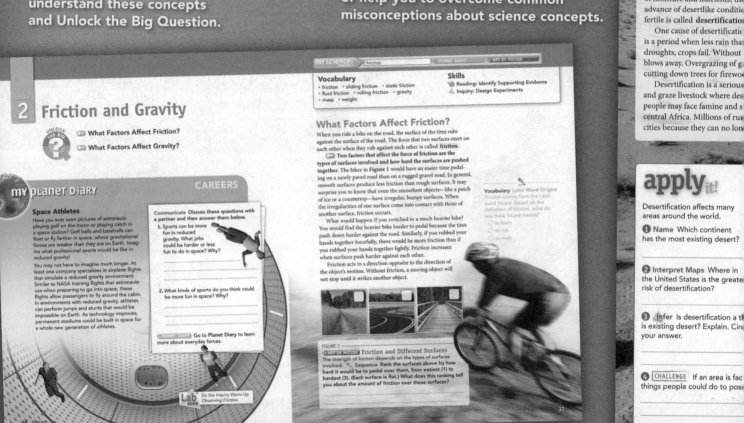

LESSON 2 Friction and Gravity

- What Factors Affect Friction?
- What Factors Affect Gravity?

my PLANET DiARY — CAREERS

Space Athletes

Have you ever seen pictures of astronauts playing golf on the moon or playing catch in a space station? Golf balls and baseballs can float or fly farther in space, where gravitational forces are weaker than they are on Earth. Imagine what professional sports would be like in reduced gravity!

You may not have to imagine much longer. At least one company specializes in airplane flights that simulate a reduced gravity environment. Similar to NASA training flights that astronauts use when preparing to go into space, these flights allow passengers to fly around the cabin. In environments with reduced gravity, athletes can perform jumps and stunts that would be impossible on Earth. As technology improves, permanent stadiums could be built in space for a whole new generation of athletes.

Communicate Discuss these questions with a partner and then answer them below.

1. Sports can be more fun in reduced gravity. What jobs could be harder or less fun to do in space? Why?

2. What kinds of sports do you think could be more fun in space? Why?

▶ PLANET DIARY Go to Planet Diary to learn more about everyday forces.

Lab zone — Do the Inquiry Warm-Up Observing Friction.

36 Forces

my science ▶ Friction ▶ PLANET DIARY ▶ ART IN MOTION

Vocabulary
- friction • sliding friction • static friction
- fluid friction • rolling friction • gravity
- mass • weight

Skills
- Reading: Identify Supporting Evidence
- Inquiry: Design Experiments

What Factors Affect Friction?

When you ride a bike on the road, the surface of the tires rubs against the surface of the road. The force that two surfaces exert on each other when they rub against each other is called **friction**.

Two factors that affect the force of friction are the types of surfaces involved and how hard the surfaces are pushed together. The biker in Figure 1 would have an easier time pedaling on a newly paved road than on a rugged gravel road. In general, smooth surfaces produce less friction than rough surfaces. It may surprise you to know that even the smoothest objects—like a patch of ice or a countertop—have irregular, bumpy surfaces. When the irregularities of one surface come into contact with those of another surface, friction occurs.

What would happen if you switched to a much heavier bike? You would find the heavier bike harder to pedal because the tires push down harder against the road. Similarly, if you rubbed your hands together forcefully, there would be more friction than if you rubbed your hands together lightly. Friction increases when surfaces push harder against each other.

Friction acts in a direction opposite to the direction of the object's motion. Without friction, a moving object will not stop until it strikes another object.

Vocabulary Latin Word Origins Friction comes from the Latin word fricare. Based on the definition of friction, what do you think fricare means?
- to burn
- so rub
- to melt

FIGURE 1
▶ ART IN MOTION **Friction and Different Surfaces**
The strength of friction depends on the types of surfaces involved. Sequence Rank the surfaces above by how hard it would be to pedal over them, from easiest (1) to hardest (3). (Each surface is flat.) What does this ranking tell you about the amount of friction over these surfaces?

37

apply it!

Desertification affects many areas around the world.

❶ **Name** Which continent has the most existing desert?

❷ **Interpret Maps** Where in the United States is the greate risk of desertification?

❸ **Infer** Is desertification a th is existing desert? Explain. Cir your answer.

❹ **CHALLENGE** If an area is fac things people could do to poss

132 Land, Air, and Water Res

Explain what you know.

Look for the pencil. When you see it, it's time to interact with your book and demonstrate what you have learned.

apply it!

Elaborate further with the Apply It activities. This is your opportunity to take what you've learned and apply those skills to new situations.

Lab Zone

Look for the Lab zone triangle. This means it's time to do a hands-on inquiry lab. In every lesson, you'll have the opportunity to do a hands-on inquiry activity that will help reinforce your understanding of the lesson topic.

ile area becomes depleted
come a desert. The
s that previously were
h fih KAY shun).
   For example, a **drought**
s in an area. During
the exposed soil easily
cattle and sheep and
e desertification, too.
eople cannot grow crops
has occurred. As a result,
esertification is severe in
ere are moving to the
themselves on the land.

n areas where there
on the map to support

fication, what are some
s effects?

Land Reclamation   Fortunately, it is possible to replace land damaged by erosion or mining. The process of restoring an area of land to a more productive state is called **land reclamation**. In addition to restoring land for agriculture, land reclamation can restore habitats for wildlife. Many different types of land reclamation projects are currently underway all over the world. But it is generally more difficult and expensive to restore damaged land and soil than it is to protect those resources in the first place. In some cases, the land may not return to its original state.

FIGURE 4 ·····························
Land Reclamation
These pictures show land before and after it was mined.
✎ **Communicate** Below the pictures, write a story about what happened to the land.

💬 Assess Your Understanding

1a. Review Subsoil has (less/more) plant and animal matter than topsoil.

b. Explain What can happen to soil if plants are removed?

c. Apply Concepts
that could prev
land reclama

got it? ·····························

○ I get it! Now I know that soil management is important becau

○ I need extra help with
Go to **MY SCIENCE** 🔍 **COACH** online for help with this subject.

Lab zone — Do the Quick Lab Modeling Soil

got it?

Evaluate Your Progress.

After answering the Got It question, think about how you're doing. Did you get it or do you need a little help? Remember, **MY SCIENCE** 🔍 **COACH** is there for you if you need extra help.

Explore the Big Question.

At one point in the chapter, you'll have the opportunity to take all that you've learned to further explore the Big Question.

Pollution and Solutions

EXPLORE THE BIG ?

What can people do to use resources wisely?

FIGURE 4 ⋯⋯⋯⋯⋯⋯⋯⋯⋯⋯⋯⋯⋯

> **REAL-WORLD INQUIRY** All living things depend on land, air, and water. Conserving these resources for the future is important. Part of resource conservation is identifying and limiting sources of pollution.

✎ **Interpret Photos** On the photograph, write the letter from the key into the circle that best identifies the source of pollution.

Land
Describe at least one thing your community could do to reduce pollution on land.

Air
Describe at least one thing your community could do to reduce air pollution.

Water
Describe at least one thing your community could do to reduce water pollution.

Pollution Sources

A. Sediments
B. Municipal solid waste
C. Runoff from development

Lab zone

🗐 **Assess Your Und...**

1a. Define What are sedimen...

b. Explain How can bacteria... spill in the ocean?

c. 🔎 What can people resources wisely?

d. CHALLENGE Why might a to recycle the waste they would reduce water poll...

got it? ⋯⋯⋯⋯⋯⋯⋯⋯⋯⋯

○ I get it! Now I know th... can be reduced by ⋯⋯⋯⋯

○ I need extra help with ...

Go to MY SCIENCE ⬤ c... with this subject.

ANSWER THE BIG ?

Answer the Big Question.

Now it's time to show what you know and answer the Big Question.

Review What You've Learned.

Use the Chapter Study Guide to review the Big Question and prepare for the test.

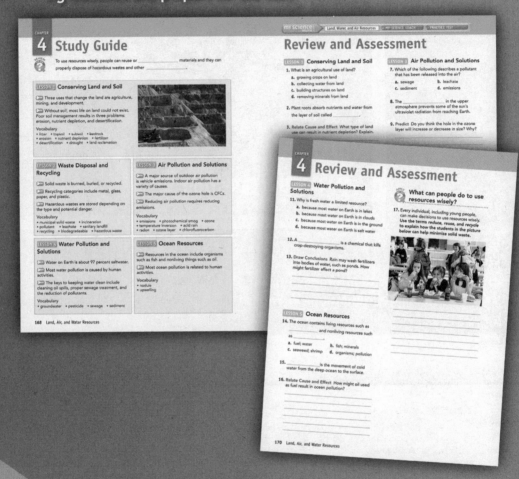

Practice Taking Tests.

Apply the Big Question and take a practice test in standardized test format.

Go to **MyScienceOnline.com** and immerse yourself in amazing virtual environments.

▶ THE BIG QUESTION

Each online chapter starts with a Big Question. Your mission is to unlock the meaning of this Big Question as each science lesson unfolds.

▶ VOCAB FLASH CARDS

Practice chapter vocabulary with interactive flash cards. Each card has an image, definitions in English and Spanish, and space for your own notes.

▶ INTERACTIVE ART

At MyScienceOnline.com, many of the beautiful visuals in your book become interactive so you can extend your learning.

Unit 4 > Chapter 1 > Lesson 1

The Big Question   Unlock the Big Question   Explore the Big Question
The Big Question   Check Your Understanding   Vocabulary Skill

Populations and Communities

Tools

? The Big Question

Unit 2 > Chapter 4 > Lesson 1

Engage & Explore   Explain
Planet Diary

my planet diary

Unit 4 > Chapter 1 > Lesson 1

The Big Question   Unlock the Big Question   Explore the Big Question
The Big Question   Untamed Science   Check Your Understanding   Vocabulary Skill   Vocabulary Flashcards

Vocabulary Flashcards

Tools

Card List   Create-a-Card   10 Cards Left   Test Me
Lesson Cards   My Cards

Birth Rate
Carrying Capacity
Commensalism
Community
Competition
Death Rate
Ecology
Ecosystem
Emigration
Habitat
Host
Immigration
Limiting Factor

Science Vocabulary

Term: Community

Definition: All the different populations that live together in a particular area.

View Spanish

Add Notes

Card 5 of

Unit 6 > Chapter 1 > Less

Engage & Explore
Apply It   Directed Virtual La

Color in Light

Exit

Unit 6 > Chapter 1 > Lesson 1

Engage & Explore   Explain   Elaborate   Evaluate
Apply It   Do the Math   Art in Motion   Interactive Art   Real World Inquiry

The Nebraska Plains

▶ Bald Eagle
Information   Media

Haliaeetus leucocephalus
Bald Eagles are 80-95 cm tall with a wingspan of 180-230 cm. These birds are born with all brown feathers but grow white feathers on their head, neck, and tail.

Layers List   ▲ Show

Next

22 of 22

Back

interactive SCIENCE
GO ONLINE

my science online.com | Populations and Communities > PLANET DIARY > LAB ZONE > VIRTUAL LAB

↻ ＋ 🌐 http://www.myscienceonline.com/

> PLANET DIARY

My Planet Diary online is the place to find more information and activities related to the topic in the lesson.

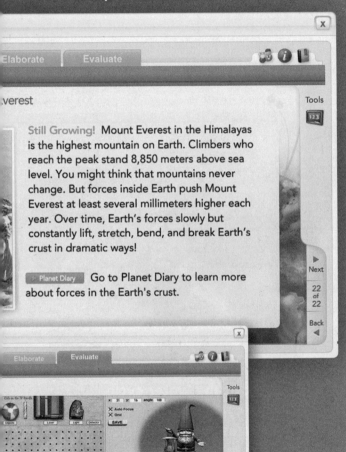

Elaborate | Evaluate

.verest

Tools
123

Still Growing! Mount Everest in the Himalayas is the highest mountain on Earth. Climbers who reach the peak stand 8,850 meters above sea level. You might think that mountains never change. But forces inside Earth push Mount Everest at least several millimeters higher each year. Over time, Earth's forces slowly but constantly lift, stretch, bend, and break Earth's crust in dramatic ways!

▶ Next

22 of 22

Planet Diary Go to Planet Diary to learn more about forces in the Earth's crust.

◀ Back

Elaborate | Evaluate

Tools
123

X Auto Focus
X Grid
SAVE

X Red
X Green
X Blue

Red-Green Colorblind
Blue-Yellow Colorblind

Height Factor:

▶ Next

22 of 22

◀ Back

0:35 / 1:30 🔊

> VIRTUAL LAB

Get more practice with realistic virtual labs. Manipulate the variables on-screen and test your hypothesis.

Find Your Chapter

1 Go to www.myscienceonline.com.

2 Log in with username and password.

3 Click on your program and select your chapter.

Keyword Search

1 Go to www.myscienceonline.com.

2 Log in with username and password.

3 Click on your program and select Search.

4 Enter the keyword (from your book) in the search box.

Other Content Available Online

> UNTAMED SCIENCE Follow these young scientists through their amazing online video blogs as they travel the globe in search of answers to the Big Questions of Science.

> MY SCIENCE COACH Need extra help? My Science Coach is your personal online study partner. My Science Coach is a chance for you to get more practice on key science concepts. There you can choose from a variety of tools that will help guide you through each science lesson.

> MY READING WEB Need extra reading help on a particular science topic? At My Reading Web you will find a choice of reading selections targeted to your specific reading level.

? BIG IDEAS OF SCIENCE

Have you ever worked on a jigsaw puzzle? Usually a puzzle has a theme that leads you to group the pieces by what they have in common. But until you put all the pieces together you can't solve the puzzle. Studying science is similar to solving a puzzle. The big ideas of science are like puzzle themes. To understand big ideas, scientists ask questions. The answers to those questions are like pieces of a puzzle. Each chapter in this book asks a big question to help you think about a big idea of science. By answering the big questions, you will get closer to understanding the big idea.

✎ **Before you read each chapter, write about what you know and what more you'd like to know.**

BIGIDEA

Earth is the water planet.

What do you already know about Earth's fresh water and salty oceans?

✎ **What would you like to know?**

_____

_____

_____

_____

Big Questions

❷ How does fresh water cycle on Earth? Chapter 1 Fresh Water

❷ What are some characteristics of Earth's oceans? Chapter 2 The Oceans

✎ **After reading the chapters, write what you have learned about the Big Idea.**

_____

_____

_____

_____

This waterfall in Iceland is part of the water cycle, the cycle by which water moves continually from Earth's surface to the atmosphere and back again.

BIGIDEA

Earth's land, water, air, and life form a system.

A severe storm, drought, or wildfire could cause changes in Yellowstone National Park that would affect these bison.

What do you already know about how changes in one part of Earth can affect another part?

✏️ **What would you like to know?**

_____

_____

_____

Big Questions

❓ How does the sun's energy affect Earth's atmosphere? Chapter 3 The Atmosphere

❓ How do meteorologists predict the weather? Chapter 4 Weather

✏️ **After reading the chapters, write what you have learned about the Big Idea.**

_____

_____

_____

BIGIDEA

Human activities can change Earth's land, water, air, and life.

The carbon dioxide released as cars burn gasoline is one source of the "greenhouse gases" that scientists think are causing a gradual warming of Earth's atmosphere.

What do you already know about how human activities can affect the atmosphere?

✏️ **What would you like to know?**

_____

_____

_____

Big Question

❓ What factors affect Earth's climate? Chapter 5 Climate and Climate Change

✏️ **After reading the chapter, write what you have learned about the Big Idea.**

_____

_____

_____

WHERE IS THIS WATER GOING?

How does fresh water cycle on Earth?

Watch out below! This river is carrying the kayaker straight down. But where did the water come from in the first place? Where is it going? And why is water important?

Develop Hypotheses Explain where you think the water in the river came from and where it will go next.

_____

_____

_____

_____

_____

_____

_____

> UNTAMED SCIENCE Watch the **Untamed Science** video to learn more about water on Earth.

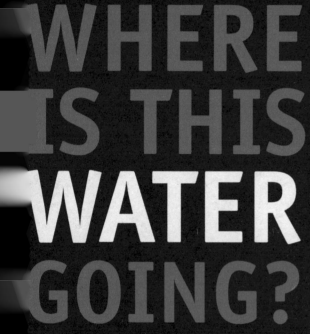

Fresh Water

1 Getting Started

Check Your Understanding

1. Background Read the paragraph below and then answer the question.

> Have you ever sat at a window on a misty day? You might see **condensation** as drops of water form on the glass. These drops form when **water vapor** in the air cools and turns into a liquid. **Gravity** pulls the drops down the windowpane toward Earth's surface.

Condensation occurs when a substance changes from a gas to a liquid.

Water vapor is water in the gaseous state.

Gravity is a force that attracts all objects toward each other.

• How do water drops form on the window?

_____

_____

> **MY READING WEB** If you had trouble completing the question above, visit **My Reading Web** and type in *Fresh Water*.

Vocabulary Skill

Latin Word Origins Many science words come to English from Latin. In this chapter you will learn the term *permeable*. *Permeable* comes from the Latin word parts *per-*, meaning "through"; *meare*, meaning "to go" or "to pass"; and *-bilis*, meaning "capable of."

$$\underset{\text{through}}{per\text{-}} + \underset{\text{go or pass}}{meare} + \underset{\text{capable of}}{\text{-}bilis} = \underset{\text{capable of going through}}{permeable}$$

Learn these Latin word parts to help you remember the vocabulary terms.

Latin Origin	Meaning	Example
trans-	across	transpiration, *n.*
spirare	to breathe	transpiration, *n.*
vapor	steam	evaporation, *n.*
videre	to separate	divide, *v.*

2. Quick Check Use the table to answer the question.

• Based on the table, predict the meaning of *transpiration*.

_____

groundwater

water cycle

divide

tributary

Chapter Preview

LESSON 1
- habitat
- groundwater
- water cycle
- evaporation
- transpiration
- precipitation

🔁 **Identify the Main Idea**
△ **Observe**

LESSON 2
- tributary
- watershed
- divide
- reservoir
- eutrophication

🔁 **Sequence**
△ **Form Operational Definitions**

LESSON 3
- permeable
- impermeable
- unsaturated zone
- saturated zone
- water table
- aquifer
- artesian well

🔁 **Relate Cause and Effect**
△ **Predict**

LESSON 4
- wetland

🔁 **Ask Questions**
△ **Classify**

> **VOCAB FLASH CARDS** For extra help with vocabulary, visit **Vocab Flash Cards** and type in *Fresh Water.*

Water on Earth

UNLOCK
THE BIG
?

🔑 Why Is Water Important?

🔑 Where Is Water Found?

🔑 What Is the Water Cycle?

my planeт Diary

SCIENCE STATS

How Much Water Do You Use?

You take a shower. You brush your teeth. You take a big drink after soccer practice. All day long, you need water! How much water do you use in a day? How much do you think your whole state uses? The graph shows the water used per person in the ten states of the United States with the largest populations. The data include the water used for all purposes, including farming, industry, and electric power.

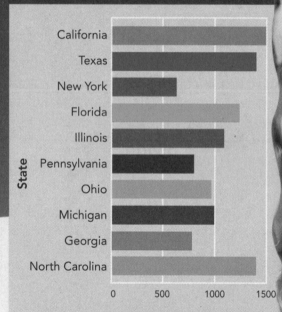

Water Use per Person per Day

Study the graph. Then answer the questions below.

1. In which state is the water use per person greatest? In which state is it least?

_____

_____

2. What do you think might explain the difference in water use between states?

_____

_____

> PLANET DIARY Go to **Planet Diary** to learn more about fresh water on Earth.

Lab zone® Do the Inquiry Warm-Up *Where Does the Water Come From?*

Vocabulary
- habitat • groundwater • water cycle • evaporation
- transpiration • precipitation

Skills
- Reading: Identify the Main Idea
- Inquiry: Observe

Why Is Water Important?

What do you and an apple have in common? You both consist mostly of water! Water makes up nearly two thirds of your body's mass. That water is necessary to keep your body functioning. **All living things need water in order to carry out their body processes. In addition, many living things live in water.**

Body Processes Without water, neither you nor an apple could survive. Water allows organisms to break down food, grow, reproduce, and get and use materials they need from their environments. Animals obtain water by drinking it or by eating foods that contain water. Most animals cannot survive more than a few days without water.

Plants and other organisms that make their own food also need water. Algae and plants use water, along with carbon dioxide and energy from the sun, to make their own food in a process called photosynthesis (foh toh SIN thuh sis). Other organisms get food by eating the plants, or by eating organisms that eat the plants.

Habitats Water provides habitats for many living things. An organism's **habitat** is the place where it lives and obtains all the things it needs to survive. Some organisms cannot live out of water. You are probably familiar with large water-dwelling organisms such as sharks. But most such organisms are microscopic. In fact, aquatic, or water, habitats contain more types of organisms than land habitats do.

FIGURE 1
The Need for Water
Predict Underline the sentence that explains why these animals need the water hole. What would happen if the water hole dried up?

Lab zone — Do the Quick Lab *Water, Water, Everywhere.*

Assess Your Understanding

got it? ....

O I get it! Now I know that living things use water ____

O I need extra help with ____

Go to my science COACH online for help with this subject.

5

Where Is Water Found?

When you turn on the tap, it might seem that an endless supply of fresh water comes out! But Earth's freshwater supply is very limited. 🔑 **Most of Earth's surface water—roughly 97 percent—is salt water found in oceans. Only 3 percent is fresh water.**

Of that 3 percent, about two thirds is frozen in huge masses of ice near the North and South poles. About a third of the fresh water is underground. A tiny fraction of fresh water occurs in lakes and rivers. An even tinier fraction is found in the atmosphere, most of it in the form of invisible water vapor, the gaseous form of water.

Identify the Main Idea

Underline the main idea in each paragraph on this page.

Oceans Find the oceans on the map in **Figure 2**. Pacific, Atlantic, Indian, and Arctic are the names used for the different parts of the ocean. (Some scientists call the area around Antarctica the Southern Ocean.) But the waters are really all interconnected, making up one big ocean. The Pacific Ocean is the largest, covering an area greater than all the land on Earth. The Atlantic Ocean is next largest, though the Indian Ocean is deeper. The Arctic Ocean surrounds the North Pole. Smaller saltwater bodies are called seas.

Ice Much of Earth's fresh water is frozen into sheets of ice. Massive ice sheets cover most of Greenland and Antarctica. Icebergs are floating chunks of ice made of fresh water that break off from ice sheets. You could also find icebergs in the Arctic Ocean and in the North Atlantic.

do the math!

Analyzing Data

These graphs show how much of Earth's water is found in different forms.

❶ Read Graphs Where is most water on Earth found? _____

❷ Read Graphs About what fraction of Earth's fresh water is in the form of ice? _____

❸ Interpret Data How does the total amount of groundwater compare to the total amount of ice?

_____

_____

_____

Salt water in oceans and salt lakes **97%**

Fresh water **3%**

Water vapor **0.04%**

Ice **69%**

Groundwater **30%**

Lakes and rivers **0.26%**

Rivers and Lakes
Look at **Figure 2.** All the rivers and lakes marked on the map contain fresh water, as do many other smaller rivers and lakes. North America's five Great Lakes contain about 20 percent of all the water in the world's freshwater lakes.

Groundwater
To find some of the fresh water on Earth, you have to look underground. When it rains or snows, most water that doesn't evaporate soaks into the ground. This water trickles through spaces between particles of soil and rock. Water that fills the cracks and spaces in underground soil and rock layers is called **groundwater.** Far more fresh water is located underground than in all of Earth's rivers and lakes.

FIGURE 2 ....
Earth's Major Waterways
The map shows Earth's oceans and some major freshwater sources.

✎ **Classify** Circle the names of three saltwater sources. Underline the names of three freshwater sources.

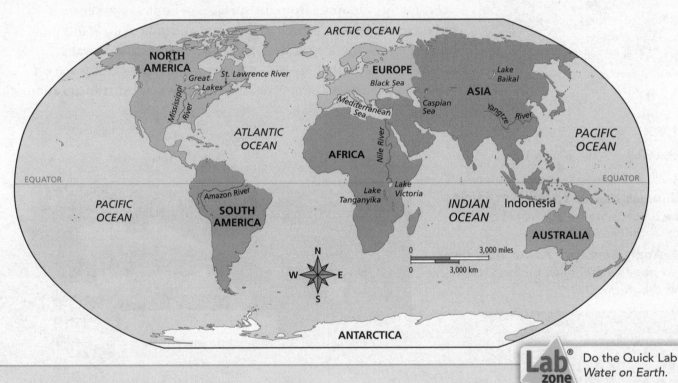

Do the Quick Lab
Water on Earth.

Assess Your Understanding

1a. List What are the four main sources of fresh water on Earth?

_____

_____

b. Make Judgments Which freshwater source do you think is most important to people? Why?

_____

_____

_____

got **it?** ....

○ **I get it!** Now I know that Earth's water is found in _____

_____

○ **I need extra help with** _____

Go to **my science** COACH online for help with this subject.

7

What Is the Water Cycle?

Earth has its own built-in water recycling system: the water cycle. The **water cycle** is the continuous process by which water moves from Earth's surface to the atmosphere and back, driven by energy from the sun and gravity. **In the water cycle, water moves between land, living things, bodies of water on Earth's surface, and the atmosphere.**

Water Evaporates Where does the water in a puddle go when it disappears? It evaporates, becoming water vapor. **Evaporation** is the process by which molecules at the surface of a liquid absorb enough energy to change to a gaseous state. Water constantly evaporates from the surfaces of bodies of water such as oceans and lakes, as well as from soil and your skin. Plants play a role, too, in this step of the water cycle. Plants draw in water from the soil through their roots. Eventually the water is given off through the leaves as water vapor in a process called **transpiration.**

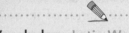

Vocabulary Latin Word Origins The letter e in *evaporation* comes from the Latin word *ex,* meaning "away." *Vapor* is Latin for "water vapor." What do you predict that *evaporation* means?

_____

_____

FIGURE 3 ·····························

▶ INTERACTIVE ART **The Water Cycle**
The diagram below shows the processes of the water cycle.

✎ **Apply Concepts** As you read these two pages, label each process shown in the diagram.

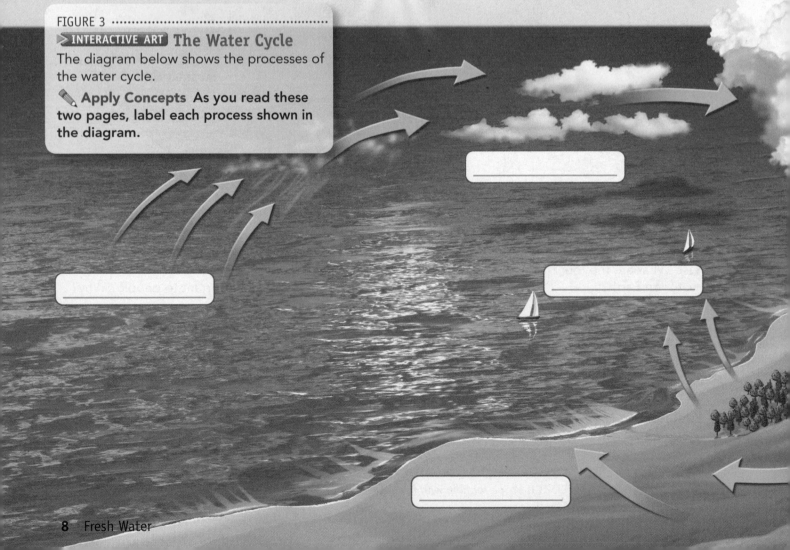

Condensation Forms Clouds

After a water molecule evaporates, warm air can carry the water molecule upward. Air tends to become colder as it rises. Water vapor condenses more easily at lower temperatures, so some water vapor cools and condenses into liquid water. Droplets of liquid water clump around solid particles in the air, forming clouds.

Water Falls as Precipitation

As more water vapor condenses, the water droplets grow larger. Eventually, they become so heavy that they fall back to Earth. Water that falls to Earth as rain, snow, hail, or sleet is called **precipitation.**

Most precipitation falls directly into the ocean. Of the precipitation that falls on land, most evaporates. A small amount of the remaining water runs off the surface into streams and lakes in a process called runoff, but most of it seeps into groundwater. After a long time, this groundwater may flow down to the ocean and evaporate again.

Precipitation is the source of almost all fresh water on and below Earth's surface. For millions of years, the total amount of water cycling through the Earth system has remained fairly constant—the rates of evaporation and precipitation are balanced.

apply it!

❶ **Observe** What water cycle process can you observe here?

_____

❷ **CHALLENGE** What other process or processes can you infer are also taking place?

_____

❸ Give an example of a water cycle process you have seen.

_____
_____

Lab zone® Do the Lab Investigation *Water From Trees.*

🔑 Assess Your Understanding

2a. Identify What are the three major steps in the water cycle?

_____
_____

b. Sequence Start with a puddle on a sunny day. How might water move through the water cycle and eventually fall as rain?

_____
_____
_____
_____
_____

got it? ······················

○ **I get it!** Now I know that the water cycle is _____

_____
_____

○ **I need extra help with** _____

Go to **my science** ⓢ **coach** *online for help with this subject.*

Surface Water

UNLOCK
THE BIG
?

🔑 **What Is a River System?**

🔑 **What Are Ponds and Lakes?**

🔑 **How Can Lakes Change?**

MY PLANET DIARY

FUN FACT

So Near, So Far

In Colorado's mountains, some rain seeps into the Fryingpan River. That river flows into the Colorado River and, more than 2,000 kilometers later, into the Gulf of California. Less than 15 kilometers away, rain seeps into the Arkansas River, which flows 2,350 kilometers until it joins the Mississippi River. Eventually, the Mississippi flows into the Gulf of Mexico. Water that fell less than 15 kilometers apart ends up almost 3,000 kilometers apart, in different oceans!

Use the map and your knowledge of science to answer the following question.

Why do you think the two rivers that start so close together flow to such different locations?

_____

_____

_____

▷ PLANET DIARY Go to **Planet Diary** to learn more about water on Earth's surface.

PACIFIC OCEAN

GULF OF MEXICO

Royal Gorge

Pueblo

John Martin Reservoir

K A N S A S

Great Bend

Wichita

C O L O R A D O

Lab zone® Do the Inquiry Warm-Up *Mapping Surface Waters.*

Vocabulary

- tributary • watershed • divide • reservoir
- eutrophication

Skills

↺ **Reading:** Sequence

△ **Inquiry:** Form Operational Definitions

What Is a River System?

If you were hiking near the beginning of the Fryingpan and Arkansas rivers, you could observe tiny streams of water from melted snow. Gravity causes these tiny streams to flow downhill. As you follow one small stream, you would notice that the stream reaches another stream and joins it, forming a larger stream. That larger stream joins other streams until a small river forms.

Tributaries As you continue following the small river downhill, you might notice more streams joining the river. Eventually, the small river itself flows into a larger river. This river grows as more small rivers flow into it, before finally spilling into the ocean. The streams and smaller rivers that feed into a main river are called **tributaries.** Tributaries flow downward toward the main river, pulled by the force of gravity. 🔑 **A river and all the streams and smaller rivers that flow into it together make up a river system.**

Why is the Arkansas River considered a tributary of the Mississippi River?

_____

_____

_____

FIGURE 1 ⋯⋯⋯⋯⋯⋯⋯⋯⋯⋯⋯⋯⋯⋯⋯⋯⋯⋯⋯⋯⋯⋯⋯⋯⋯

The Arkansas River

✎ **Make Judgments** Put a *K* on the map where you might go kayaking. Put an *F* where you might get water for farming. Put an *M* where you might build a manufacturing plant. Explain why you chose the locations you did.

_____

_____

_____

_____

ARKANSAS

OKLAHOMA

Watersheds Just as all the water in a bathtub flows toward the drain, all the water in a river system drains into a main river. The land area that supplies water to a river system is called a **watershed.** Watersheds are sometimes known as drainage basins.

As you can see in **Figure 2,** the Missouri and Ohio rivers are quite long. Yet they flow into the Mississippi River. When rivers join another river system, the areas they drain become part of the largest river's watershed. The watershed of the Mississippi River covers nearly one third of the United States!

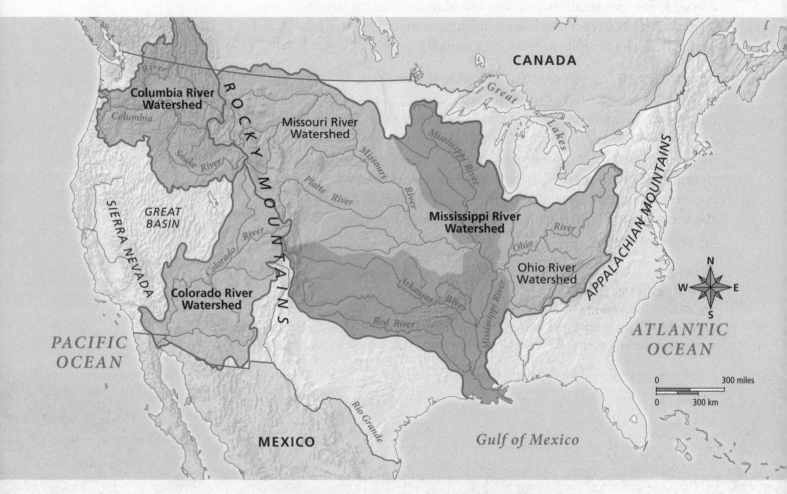

FIGURE 2 ·····························

Major Watersheds of the United States

This map shows watersheds of several large rivers in the United States. ✎ **Interpret Maps** Draw the path that water would take from the Platte River's source to the ocean. Which watersheds would the water pass through?

_____

_____

_____

Divides What keeps watersheds separate? One watershed is separated from another by a ridge of land called a **divide.** Streams on each side of the divide flow in different directions. The Great Divide (also called the Continental Divide) is the longest divide in North America. It follows the line of the Rocky Mountains. West of this divide, water flows toward the Pacific Ocean. Some water is trapped between the Rockies and the Sierra Nevadas, in the Great Basin. Between the Rocky and Appalachian mountains, water flows toward the Mississippi River and into the Gulf of Mexico.

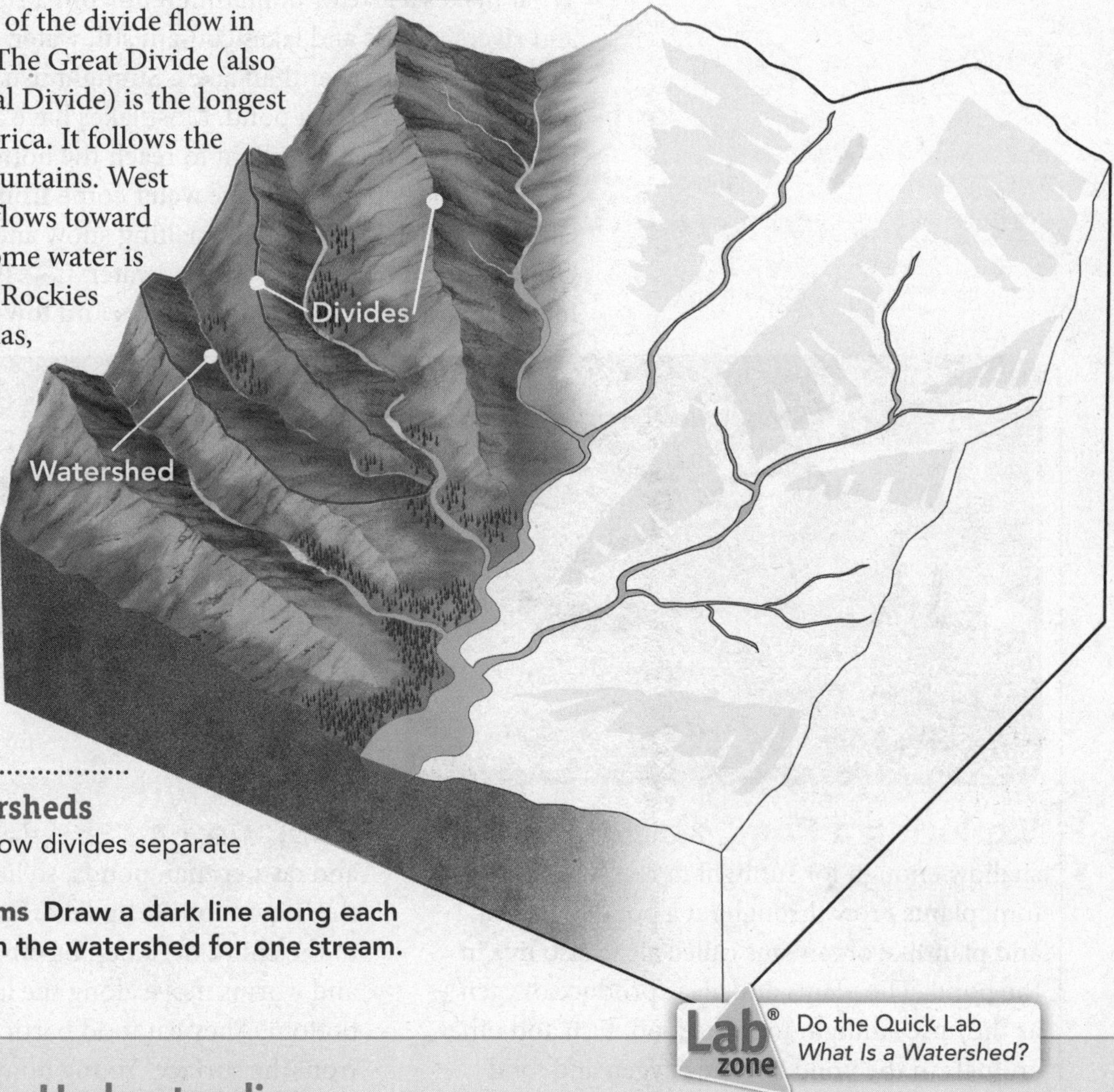

FIGURE 3 ·······························
Divides and Watersheds
The diagram shows how divides separate land into watersheds.

✎ **Interpret Diagrams** Draw a dark line along each divide. Then shade in the watershed for one stream.

Lab zone® Do the Quick Lab
What Is a Watershed?

🗝 **Assess Your Understanding**

1a. Identify A (divide/tributary) separates two watersheds.

b. Summarize How is a watershed related to a river system? _____
_____
_____

c. Make Generalizations How can a stream be part of more than one watershed?
_____
_____
_____
_____
_____

got it? ···

○ **I get it!** Now I know that a river system is _____
_____

○ **I need extra help with** _____

Go to MY SCIENCE ⬤ COACH *online for help with this subject.*

What Are Ponds and Lakes?

What makes a lake or pond different from a river? Unlike streams and rivers, ponds and lakes contain still water. In general, ponds are smaller and shallower than lakes. Sunlight usually reaches to the bottom of all parts of a pond. Most lakes have areas where the water is too deep for much sunlight to reach the bottom.

Where does pond and lake water come from? Some ponds and lakes are supplied by rainfall, melting snow and ice, and runoff. Others are fed by rivers or groundwater. **Ponds and lakes form when water collects in hollows and low-lying areas of land.**

Exploring a Pond Because the water is shallow enough for sunlight to reach the bottom, plants grow throughout a pond. Bacteria and plantlike organisms called algae also live in the pond. The plants and algae produce oxygen as they use sunlight to make food. Fish and other animals in the pond use the oxygen and food provided by plants and algae. Some animals also use these plants for shelter.

Exploring a Lake Lakes are usually larger and deeper than ponds, so little sunlight reaches the bottom of a deep lake. Fewer plants can live in in the chilly, dark depths of such a lake. Mollusks and worms move along the lake's sandy or rocky bottom. They eat food particles that drift down from the surface. Young bony fishes such as pike and sturgeon eat the tiny bottom-dwellers, while the adult fish eat other fish.

apply it!

❶ Complete the Venn diagram to compare and contrast characteristics of lakes and ponds.

❷ **Form Operational Definitions** Based on your answers, write an operational definition for *lake*.

_____

_____

_____

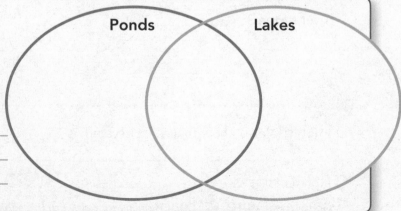

Ponds   Lakes

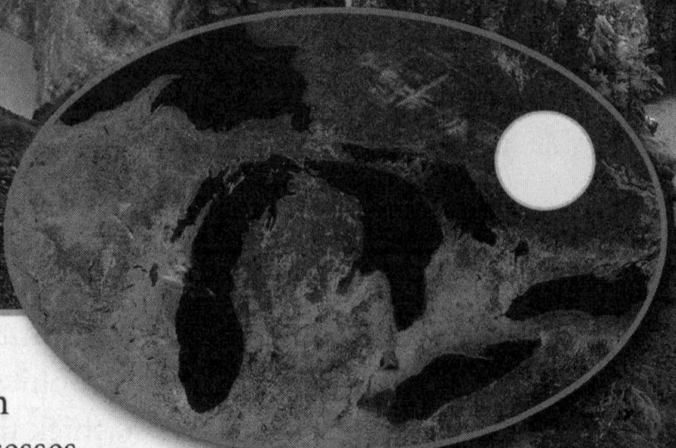

Lake Formation

Lakes can form through several natural processes. A river, for example, may bend and loop as it encounters obstacles in its path. Eventually, a new channel might form, cutting off a loop. The cutoff loop may become an oxbow lake.

Some lakes, such as the Great Lakes, formed in depressions created by ice sheets that melted at the end of the Ice Age. Other lakes were created by movements of Earth's crust that formed long, deep valleys called rift valleys. In Africa, Lake Tanganyika lies in a rift valley. Volcanoes can also form lakes. Lava or mud from a volcano can block a river, forming a lake. Lakes can also form in the empty craters of volcanoes.

People can create a lake by building a dam. A lake that stores water for human use is called a **reservoir.**

FIGURE 4 ···
Types of Lakes
The photos show examples of glacial, volcanic, and rift valley lakes. ✎ **Classify** Write **G** on the glacial lake, **V** on the volcanic lake, and **R** on the rift valley lake.

Do the Quick Lab
Modeling How a Lake Forms.

🔑 Assess Your Understanding

2a. Explain What is one major difference between a lake and a pond?

_____

_____

b. Compare and Contrast How is a reservoir different from other kinds of lakes?

_____

_____

_____

got it?

○ **I get it!** Now I know that lakes and ponds are __

_____

_____

_____

_____

○ **I need extra help with** _____

Go to MY SCIENCE ⓢ COACH *online for help with this subject.*

15

How Can Lakes Change?

If you watch a lake or pond over many years, you will see it change. In time, the lake may shrink and become shallower. 🗝 **Natural processes and human activities can cause lakes to disappear.**

Eutrophication As lake organisms die, bacteria break down the bodies and release nutrients into the water. These nutrients, such as nitrogen and phosphorus, are chemicals that other organisms need. Over time, nutrients can build up in the lake in a process called **eutrophication** (yoo troh fih KAY shun). Algae use these nutrients and spread, forming a layer on the lake's surface.

Figure 5 shows how eutrophication can change a lake. When the algae layer becomes so thick that it blocks sunlight, plants cannot carry out photosynthesis, and they die. Without food and oxygen from the plants, animals die. Decaying material from dead organisms piles up on the bottom, making the lake shallower. As the area fills in, land plants grow in the mud. Eventually, the area fills with plants, and a meadow replaces the former lake.

The Human Role Though eutrophication occurs naturally, human activities can also cause or increase it. For example, fertilizer from farms runs off into ponds and lakes, providing extra nutrients to the algae. The extra nutrients speed up the growth of algae, leading to faster eutrophication.

✏️ **Sequence** Which of the following processes occurs first during eutrophication?

○ Nutrients build up in a lake.

○ A lake is replaced by a meadow.

○ Plants stop carrying out photosynthesis.

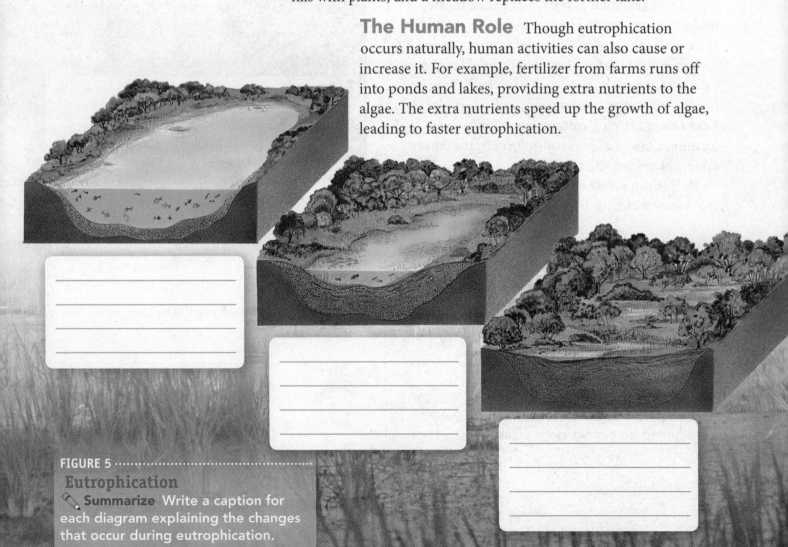

FIGURE 5 ·····
Eutrophication
✏️ **Summarize** Write a caption for each diagram explaining the changes that occur during eutrophication.

An Endless Cycle

How does fresh water cycle on Earth?

FIGURE 6 ....

> REAL-WORLD INQUIRY Make a cycle diagram to show how water cycles. Include the processes listed below.

Processes

Evaporation

Condensation

Transpiration

Precipitation

Runoff

Include examples of:
a river system
a lake or pond
an ocean
groundwater

Lab zone® Do the Quick Lab
How Can Algal Growth Affect Pond Life?

🔑 Assess Your Understanding

3a. Explain Eutrophication occurs when algae block sunlight in a lake or pond and plants cannot _____

b. ANSWER THE BIG ? How does fresh water cycle on Earth?

_____
_____
_____
_____
_____
_____

got it?

○ **I get it!** Now I know that lakes can change due to _____

_____
_____
_____
_____

○ **I need extra help with** _____

_____

Go to **MY SCIENCE** 🔵 **COACH** *online for help with this subject.*

Water Underground

🔑 **How Does Water Move Underground?**

🔑 **How Do People Use Groundwater?**

my planet diary

Looking for Water

How do you know where the water you drink comes from? Saskia Oosting could help you find out! Ms. Oosting works for a company that locates and protects groundwater supplies. She is a project manager, which means she coordinates the work of many other people.

One of her company's jobs is figuring out where the water in a particular well comes from. Scientists and engineers drill other wells near the well they're observing. Then they pump water out of the first well and watch the others to see where the level of groundwater drops. Once they've found the area that contributes water to the well, the company can help people who use that water keep the supply clean.

✏️ **Communicate** With a partner, discuss your answers to these questions.

1. How do engineers find out where the water in a well comes from?

_____

_____

_____

2. What kinds of science skills do you think Ms. Oosting needs to do her job?

_____

_____

_____

_____

> **PLANET DIARY** Go to **Planet Diary** to learn more about groundwater.

 Lab zone® Do the Inquiry Warm-Up *Where Does the Water Go?*

Vocabulary
- permeable • impermeable
- unsaturated zone • saturated zone
- water table • aquifer • artesian well

Skills
↻ Reading: Relate Cause and Effect
△ Inquiry: Predict

How Does Water Move Underground?

Where does underground water come from? Like surface water, underground water generally comes from precipitation. Some precipitation soaks into the ground, pulled by gravity.

If you pour water into a glass full of pebbles, the water flows down around the pebbles until it reaches the bottom of the glass. Then the water begins to fill up the spaces between the pebbles. 🔑 **In the same way, water underground trickles down between particles of soil and through cracks and spaces in layers of rock.**

Effects of Different Materials Different types of rock and soil have different-sized spaces, or pores, between their particles, as shown in **Figure 1.** The size of the pores and the connections between them determine how easily water moves. Because they have large and connected pores, materials such as sand and gravel allow water to pass through, or permeate. They are thus known as **permeable** (PUR mee uh bul) materials.

Other materials have few or no pores or cracks, or the pores are very small. Clay has very small pores and is less permeable than sand. Unless it is cracked, granite is **impermeable,** meaning that water cannot pass through easily.

FIGURE 1 ....
Permeable and Impermeable Materials
Compare how water moves in clay (left) and gravel (right).
✎ **Compare and Contrast** Which material is more permeable? (gravel/clay) **Why?**

_____
_____
_____
_____

19

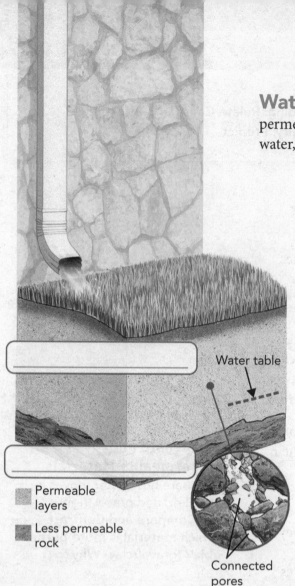

Water Zones Water from precipitation soaks down through permeable rock and soil layers. These layers contain air as well as water, so they are not saturated, or filled, with water. This top layer is thus called the **unsaturated zone.**

However, at some depth, the water reaches a level where the pores in the ground are saturated with water, called the **saturated zone.** The top of the saturated zone is the **water table.** If you know the depth of the water table in your area, you can tell how deep you must dig to reach groundwater.

The saturated zone often reaches deep into Earth, even though the rock becomes less permeable the deeper you go. Sometimes the direction of the water's flow is changed by impermeable layers, which the water has a harder time flowing through.

Water table

Permeable layers

Less permeable rock

Connected pores

FIGURE 2 ·····························

> ART IN MOTION **Groundwater Formation**

Upper areas of the soil contain both air and water, while lower areas, including less permeable rock, are saturated with water.

✏ **Interpret Diagrams** Label the **saturated and unsaturated zones. Shade in the area where water will collect.**

Lab ® Do the Quick Lab
zone *Soil Percolation.*

🔑 Assess Your Understanding

1a. Review Water slows down when it reaches (permeable/impermeable) material.

b. Explain What is the water table?

_____

_____

c. Infer The rock deep within the saturated zone most likely has (large/small) and (connected/unconnected) pores. Explain your answer.

_____

_____

_____

_____

got it? ···

O **I get it!** Now I know that water moves through soil by _____

_____

O **I need extra help with** _____

Go to **MY SCIENCE** 🔵 **COACH** online for help with this subject.

How Do People Use Groundwater?

Suppose you live far from a river, lake, or pond. How could you reach groundwater for your needs? You might be in luck: The water table in your area might be only a few meters underground. In fact, in some places the water table actually meets the surface. Springs can form as groundwater bubbles or flows out of cracks in the rock.

Aquifers Any underground layer of permeable rock or sediment that holds water and allows it to flow is called an **aquifer.** Aquifers can range in size from a small patch to an area the size of several states. The huge Ogallala aquifer lies beneath the plains of the Midwest, from South Dakota to Texas. This aquifer provides water for millions of people, as well as for crops and livestock.

Aquifers are not unlimited sources of water. If people take water from the aquifer faster than the aquifer refills, the level of the aquifer will drop. As you'll see on the next page, this will make it more difficult to reach water in the future.

Vocabulary The Latin root *aqua-* is found in words such as *aquarium* and *aquatic* as well as *aquifer.* What do you think this root means?

do the math!

Uses of Water

The graph shows water use in the United States. Use the graph to answer the questions below.

❶ **Read Graphs** What would be a good title for this graph? _____

_____

❷ **Interpret Data** The two largest categories combine to make up about what percentage of the total water used in the United States? _____

❸ **Predict** How would an increase in the amount of land used for farms affect this graph?

_____

_____

❹ **Calculate** If the total daily usage of water in the United States is 1,280 billion liters, about how many liters are used by power plants?

_____

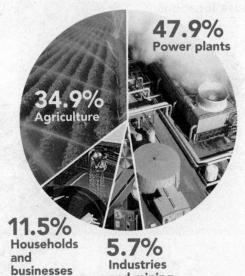

47.9% Power plants

34.9% Agriculture

11.5% Households and businesses

5.7% Industries and mining

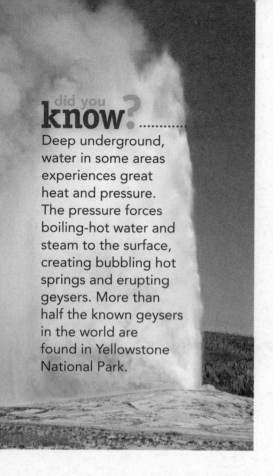

Movement in Aquifers Do you picture groundwater as a large, still pool beneath Earth's surface? In fact, the water is moving, seeping through layers of rock or soil. The rate of motion depends largely on the slope of the water table and the permeability of the rocks. Some groundwater moves only a few centimeters a day. At that rate, the water moves about 10 meters a year. Groundwater may travel hundreds of kilometers and stay in an aquifer for thousands of years before coming to the surface again.

Wells The depth and level of a water table can vary greatly over a small area. Generally, the level of a water table follows the shape of the surface of the land, as shown in **Figure 3.** The level can rise during heavy rains or snow melts, and fall in times of dry weather.

Since ancient times, people have brought groundwater to the surface for drinking and other everyday uses. 🔑 **People can obtain groundwater from an aquifer by drilling a well below the water table.** When the bottom of the well is in a saturated zone, the well contains water. If the water table drops below the bottom of the well, the well will run dry and water cannot be obtained from it.

FIGURE 3 ···

Springs and Wells

Suppose you are a farmer looking for water sources.

✏️ **Make Judgments** Draw lines showing where you would drill a regular well and an artesian well. Explain why you chose those locations.

Spring

Water Table

Aquifer

Using Pumps

Long ago, people dug wells by hand. They used a bucket to bring up the water. People may also have used simple pumps. Today, however, most wells are dug with well-drilling equipment. Mechanical pumps bring up the groundwater.

Pumping water out of an aquifer lowers the water level near the well. If too much water is pumped out too fast, a well may run dry. The owners of the well will have to dig deeper to reach the lowered water table, or wait for rainfall to refill the aquifer.

Relying on Pressure

Another option for bringing up groundwater is an artesian well. In an **artesian well** (ahr TEE zhun), water rises on its own because of pressure within an aquifer.

In some aquifers, groundwater becomes trapped between two layers of impermeable rock or sediment. This water is under great pressure from the water extending back up the aquifer. If the top layer of rock is punctured, the pressure sends water spurting up through the hole. No pump is necessary—in an artesian well, water pressure does the job.

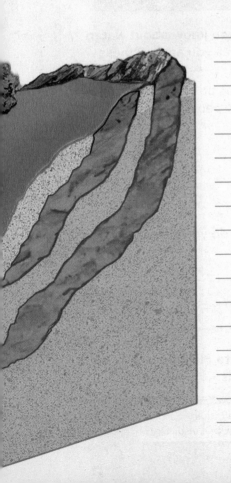

_____
_____
_____
_____
_____
_____
_____
_____
_____
_____
_____
_____

✎

○ **Relate Cause and Effect**
If the water table near a well is (raised/lowered), the well may run dry.

Lab ® Do the Quick Lab
zone *An Artesian Well.*

🔑 Assess Your Understanding

2a. Describe What are three ways people can get water from an aquifer?

_____
_____
_____

b. Infer Use **Figure 3** as a guide. Why is it important to know the depth of an aquifer before drilling a well?

_____
_____
_____

c. Solve Problems During the winter, you draw your water from a well. Every summer, the well dries up. What might be the reason for the change?

_____
_____
_____
_____

got it? ....

○ **I get it!** Now I know that people reach underground water by _____

_____

○ **I need extra help with** _____

Go to MY SCIENCE ⓢ COACH *online for help with this subject.*

23

Wetland Environments

UNLOCK THE BIG ?

🔑 **What Are Wetlands?**

🔑 **Why Are Wetlands Important?**

my planet Diary

PROFILE

Wetland Stories

How much do you know about your school's neighborhood? Students from Exploris Middle School in Raleigh, North Carolina, wanted to know more about the nearby Walnut Creek wetlands. Community groups had worked with the city to stop flooding and protect the wetland area.

The students interviewed people who had lived near the wetlands for decades. They asked about the residents' memories of the area. Students also created a field guide for the wetlands. They included descriptions and drawings of animals found in the area, so others could enjoy the wildlife right in their own city!

Think about what you know about water and wetland areas as you answer these questions.

1. Why did students at Exploris Middle School interview people near Walnut Creek?

_____

_____

_____

2. What questions do you have about wetlands?

_____

_____

_____

> PLANET DIARY Go to **Planet Diary** to learn more about wetlands.

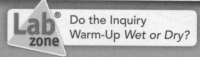

Lab zone Do the Inquiry Warm-Up *Wet or Dry?*

Vocabulary
- wetland

Skills
↻ Reading: Ask Questions
△ Inquiry: Classify

What Are Wetlands?

Imagine coming home from a long trip, only to find that your house has been replaced by a parking lot! Millions of migrating birds have had a similar experience when they tried to return to a wetland. A **wetland** is a land area that is covered with a shallow layer of water during some or all of the year. Human actions have destroyed many wetlands. But now people are beginning to understand the importance of wetlands, to wildlife and to people.

Wetlands help control floods and provide habitats for many species. They form in places where water is trapped in low areas or where groundwater seeps to the surface. Wetlands may be as small as a roadside ditch or cover as much area as a small state. Some wetlands fill up during spring rains, only to dry up during long, hot summers. Others are covered with water year-round.

FIGURE 1 ···

The Everglades

Sometimes called the "River of Grass," the Florida Everglades are a vast wetland that covers more than 10,000 square kilometers. ✎ **Observe** On the notebook below, write at least three observations you can make about the Everglades based on the photograph.

Key
- ▨ Mangrove forests
- — Everglades National Park
- — Rivers and canals

0 ———— 50 miles
0 ———— 50 km

25

Freshwater Wetlands

🔑 **The three common types of freshwater wetlands are marshes, swamps, and bogs.** As shown in **Figure 2,** these wetlands are quite diverse. Marshes are usually grassy areas covered by shallow water or streams. They teem with cattails and other tall, grasslike plants. Swamps look more like flooded forests, with trees and shrubs sprouting from the water. Many swamps are located in warm, humid climates, where trees grow quickly. Bogs are more common in cooler northern areas. They often form in depressions left by pieces of melting ice sheets thousands of years ago. The water in bogs tends to be acidic, and mosses thrive in these conditions. The mosses may form thick mats that cover areas of shallow water.

FIGURE 2 ⋯⋯⋯⋯⋯⋯⋯⋯⋯⋯⋯⋯⋯⋯⋯

Freshwater Wetlands

These photographs show three examples of freshwater wetlands.

△ **Classify** **Based on the descriptions in the text, classify each example as a bog, marsh, or swamp.**

apply it!

The photographs show a kind of freshwater wetland called a pocosin or Carolina bay. Water in pocosins is generally acidic.

❶ **Observe** Describe two features you can observe in the photographs.

_____

_____

❷ △ **Classify** What type of wetland is a pocosin? (bog/swamp)

Coastal Wetlands Wetlands along coasts usually contain both fresh water and salt water. Coastal wetlands include salt marshes and mangrove forests. Salt marshes are found along the east and west coasts of the United States. In salt marshes, grasses grow in the rich mud. Mangrove forests are found along the southeastern coast of the United States. In these forests, short mangrove trees have thick, tangled roots.

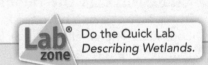

Lab zone® Do the Quick Lab *Describing Wetlands.*

⬤ᗘ Assess Your Understanding

1a. Name What are the three main types of freshwater wetlands?

_____

b. Explain How do coastal wetlands differ from freshwater wetlands?

_____

_____

c. Compare and Contrast How are the three types of freshwater wetlands similar? How are they different?

_____

_____

_____

_____

_____

_____

got it? ....

○ **I get it!** Now I know that wetlands are_____

_____

○ I need extra help with _____

Go to MY SCIENCE ⬤ COACH online for help with this subject.

Why Are Wetlands Important?

If you've ever had cranberry sauce or wild rice, you've eaten plants that grow in wetlands. The layer of water covering a wetland can range from several centimeters to a few meters deep. Dead leaves and other plant and animal materials serve as natural fertilizers. They add nitrogen and other nutrients to the water and soil.

Importance to Wildlife 🔖 **Because of their sheltered waters and rich supply of nutrients, wetlands provide habitats for many living things.** Recall the plants and animals that live in or near ponds. Some of the same organisms live in freshwater wetlands. Insects and fish find food and shelter among wetland plants. Birds, amphibians, and reptiles nest in and around the wetlands, feeding on other organisms. Some larger animals, such as manatees and beavers, also live in the wetlands year-round.

Other animals spend only part of their lives in a wetland. As winter approaches, geese, ducks, and other waterfowl travel from northern areas to warmer climates. They stop at small, shallow marshes along their routes to rest and feed. These migrating birds then spend the winter at large southern marshes.

FIGURE 3 ....

> INTERACTIVE ART **The Importance of Wetlands**
This photo shows a bayou, a kind of swamp found in Louisiana. The smaller photos show some organisms that live in a bayou.

✎ **Apply Concepts** Describe what each of the three organisms obtains from the wetland.

Importance to People

Many people once assumed that wetland areas could not be useful unless they were drained and filled in. Hundreds of thousands of square kilometers of wetlands were developed for farms, homes, and businesses. Beginning in the 1970s, however, the government passed laws to protect wetlands.

What led to these laws? Wetlands serve important functions for people as well as for wildlife. For example, as water moves slowly through a wetland, some waste materials settle out. Other wastes may be absorbed by plants. The thick network of plant roots also traps silt and mud. **In this way, wetlands act as natural water filters. They also help control floods by absorbing extra runoff from heavy rains.** Wetlands are like giant sponges, storing water until it gradually drains or evaporates. When wetlands are destroyed, the floodwaters are not absorbed. Instead, the water runs off the land quickly, worsening flood problems. Wetlands also make climates more moderate. Temperatures are cooler in summer and warmer in winter than they would be without wetlands.

Ask Questions Before you read the paragraphs under Importance to People, write one question you would like answered. After you read, write the answer.

_____
_____
_____
_____
_____

Snowy egret
_____
_____
_____

Bullfrog
_____
_____
_____

Louisiana iris
_____
_____

 Do the Quick Lab *A Natural Filter.*

Assess Your Understanding

2a. Describe Name one way that wetlands benefit wildlife and one way that they benefit people.
_____
_____
_____

b. Develop Hypotheses Without plants, how well would a wetland filter water?
_____
_____
_____
_____

got it?

O **I get it!** Now I know that wetlands are important because _____
_____
_____

O **I need extra help with** _____

Go to my science COACH *online for help with this subject.*

29

REVIEW THE BIG ?

Fresh water on Earth cycles between _____, _____, and the atmosphere.

LESSON 1 **Water on Earth**

🔑 All living things need water in order to carry out their body processes. In addition, many living things live in water.

🔑 Most of Earth's surface water—roughly 97 percent—is salt water found in oceans. Only 3 percent is fresh water.

🔑 In the water cycle, water moves between land, living things, bodies of water on Earth's surface, and the atmosphere.

Vocabulary
• habitat • groundwater • water cycle • evaporation
• transpiration • precipitation

Salt water in oceans and salt lakes **97%** Fresh water **3%**

Water vapor **0.04%**

Ice **69%**

Groundwater **30%**

Lakes and rivers **0.26%**

LESSON 2 **Surface Water**

🔑 A river and all the streams and smaller rivers that flow into it together make up a river system.

🔑 Ponds and lakes form when water collects in hollows and low-lying areas of land.

🔑 Natural processes and human activities can cause lakes to disappear.

Vocabulary
• tributary • watershed • divide
• reservoir • eutrophication

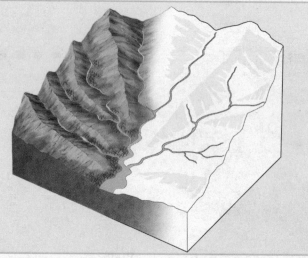

LESSON 3 **Water Underground**

🔑 Water underground trickles down between particles of soil and through cracks and spaces in layers of rock.

🔑 People can obtain groundwater from an aquifer by drilling a well below the water table.

Vocabulary
• permeable • impermeable
• unsaturated zone • saturated zone
• water table • aquifer • artesian well

LESSON 4 **Wetland Environments**

🔑 The three common types of freshwater wetlands are marshes, swamps, and bogs.

🔑 Wetlands provide habitats for many living things.

🔑 Wetlands act as natural water filters and help control floods.

Vocabulary
• wetland

Review and Assessment

LESSON 1 Water on Earth

1. Where is most of Earth's total water supply found?

   a. atmosphere

   b. groundwater

   c. ice sheets

   d. oceans

2. During transpiration, plants _____

_____

_____

3. Sequence Complete the cycle diagram to show one way in which water can move through the water cycle.

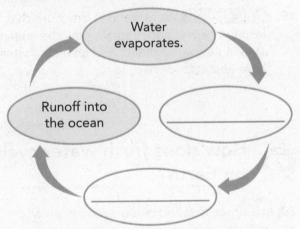

4. Apply Concepts Why is so little of Earth's water available for human use?

_____

_____

_____

5. math! About 3 percent of Earth's water is fresh water. Of that 3 percent, about 69 percent is ice. About what percent of Earth's total water supply is ice?

_____

_____

_____

LESSON 2 Surface Water

6. What is the area that supplies water to a river system called?

   a. reservoir

   b. tributary

   c. watershed

   d. wetland

7. Two watersheds are separated by a(n)

_____

8. Relate Cause and Effect Explain why some rivers experience severe springtime flooding as snow and ice melt along small mountain streams.

_____

_____

_____

_____

_____

_____

9. Compare and Contrast How would the variety of organisms in the center of a pond differ from those in deep water at a lake's center?

_____

_____

_____

10. Classify How can a large river also be a tributary?

_____

_____

_____

_____

_____

31

1 Review and Assessment

Water Underground

11. The top of the saturated zone forms the

    a. artesian well.   **b.** impermeable rock.

    c. unsaturated zone.   **d.** water table.

12. Water can flow through pores or cracks in a _____ material.

Use the diagram to answer Questions 13–15.

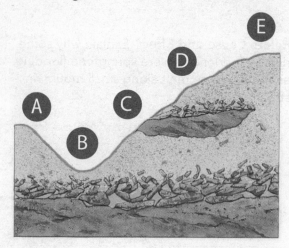

13. Make Judgments Would location D or E be a better place to dig a well? Explain.

_____

_____

_____

14. Infer At which location could you obtain water without using a pump? What is this called?

_____

15. Predict What changes would you expect to see in this area during a very rainy season?

_____

_____

_____

_____

Wetland Environments

16. Wetlands help control floods by absorbing

    a. silt and mud.   **b.** extra runoff.

    c. nutrients.   **d.** bacteria.

17. A wetland is an area that is _____

_____

18. Classify On a walk in a northern state, you come upon an area that is carpeted with mosses. What type of wetland is it likely to be? How do you know?

_____

_____

19. Write About It Write a travel brochure that describes a wetland. Explain how the wetland is valuable for the plants and animals that live there and also for people.

APPLY THE BIG ? How does fresh water cycle on Earth?

20. In a process called cloud seeding, small particles of chemicals such as dry ice are spread into clouds from airplanes. The goal is to provide a place for condensation, causing raindrops to form and fall as precipitation. How would increased condensation affect the other processes of the water cycle?

_____

_____

_____

_____

_____

_____

_____

Standardized Test Prep

Multiple Choice

Circle the letter of the best answer.

1. Use the diagram to answer the question.

Which of the following is a process that occurs in the water cycle?

A condensation   B evaporation
C precipitation   D all of the above

2. Why don't plants normally grow on the bottom of deep lakes?

A The water is too salty.

B The water is too cold.

C There is not enough soil.

D There is not enough sunlight.

3. For a science project, you must build a model of an aquifer. What material would be **best** to use for the layer where the water will accumulate?

A clay

B granite

C gravel

D bedrock

4. How can eutrophication lead to the disappearance of a lake?

A Waste and nutrients build up in the lake.

B The amount of oxygen in the lake increases.

C The lake's water supply dries up.

D Sediment from streams fills up the lake.

5. Which of the following is **most** likely found in a marsh?

A flooded forests

B acidic waters

C shallow streams

D thick mosses

Constructed Response

Use the graph and your knowledge of science to answer Question 6. Write your answer on a separate sheet of paper.

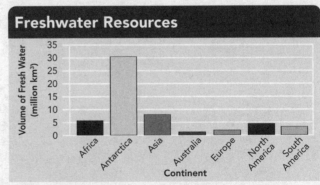

6. The graph shows the total amount of fresh water in all forms found on each continent. Why is so much of Earth's fresh water located in Antarctica? Is that water usable by humans? Explain your answer.

A Pearl of a Solution

▲ Oysters filter nutrients and pollutants from the water in which they feed.

It's hard to say who are the bigger heroes in the Chesapeake Bay—the scientists or the oysters.

The Chesapeake Bay is the world's third-largest estuary. More than 17 million people live within the Chesapeake watershed. For many years, fishing has been an important industry for people in the area. People depend on the bay for food and work. Pollution and habitat loss in the watershed have dramatically reduced marine life in the bay, and people who live and work there have found it more difficult to find food or earn a living.

Now, scientists and volunteers are using oysters to help clean the bay's waters. Oysters get their food by filtering plankton and other nutrients from the water. In this way, oysters help remove pollutants from the water. The oyster population has fallen sharply in recent years, and there are not enough oysters to keep up with the pollution. The Chesapeake Bay Foundation is hoping to restock the bay with 31 million oysters in the next 10 years. If they succeed, other marine life may also return to the bay.

Research It Make a map that shows the Chesapeake Bay watershed and the major rivers that drain into it. On the map, indicate how freshwater pollutants, such as excess fertilizer, enter the bay. Write a paragraph explaining the impact on society if the pollution is allowed to continue.

What Was Fort Miami?

Ohio's 2,000-Year-Old Aqueduct

▲ Archaeologists use computer-generated images to show what the 2,000-year-old irrigation system might have looked like when it was built.

Archaeologists from the University of Cincinnati have made a startling discovery. They had thought that a 2,000-year-old ruin on a hilltop in southwestern Ohio was a fort used by the Shawnee people native to the region to defend their lands from attack. Recently, however, archaeologists have found evidence that the ruin was actually a complex system of dams and canals, stretching almost 6 kilometers! At one spot, the Shawnee constructed a dam nearly 61 meters high!

The Shawnee built the system to collect water from a series of springs and to transport it to farmland, so that they could grow enough food to support their society. Climate records suggest that 2,000 years ago, when the Shawnee built the system, the region was colder and drier than it is now. So moving water from its source to where it was needed for farming would have helped the Shawnee survive.

Design It Find out more about water management systems used by ancient civilizations such as the Maya. Make a presentation that compares how two different civilizations used natural resources. Explain how the climate each group faced may have affected its water management systems.

▲ Archaeologists sift carefully through dirt removed from

WHAT'S GOING ON UNDER THE WAVES?

THE BIG ?

What are some characteristics of Earth's oceans?

Surf's up! This surfer skims over the surface of the ocean as she rides a wave. She needs a board, balance, and the right conditions to surf. Could what's happening below the surface affect the waves above? As the wave's motion propels her forward, she will glide until the wave fades away. **Develop Hypotheses** **What might be happening underneath the ocean's surface?**

_____

_____

_____

_____

_____

> **UNTAMED SCIENCE** Watch the **Untamed Science** video to learn more about Earth's oceans.

2 Getting Started

Check Your Understanding

1. Background Read the paragraph below and then answer the question.

Jon and Vikram weigh a glass of salt water and a glass of fresh water. "Why does the salt water weigh more?" asks Jon. "It has more **mass,**" answers Vikram. "There's more matter, or stuff, in the salt water. This also gives it a higher **density.**" "Okay, so why can we float an egg only in the salt water?" asks Jon. "Salt water provides greater **buoyancy.** It holds the egg up," says Vikram.

Mass is the amount of matter in an object.

Density is the amount of mass in a given volume.

Buoyancy is the force that causes less dense objects to float.

• Why does the salt water weigh more?

_____

_____

▶ MY READING WEB If you had trouble completing the question above, visit **My Reading Web** and type in *The Oceans.*

Vocabulary Skill

Suffixes A suffix is a letter or group of letters added to the end of a word to form a new word with a slightly different meaning. Adding a suffix to a word often changes its part of speech.

Suffix	Meaning	Part of Speech	Example
-al	related to or characterized by	adjective	continental
-ity	condition, state, or quality	noun	density/salinity

2. Quick Check Circle the correct word to complete each sentence.

• Fresh water is less (dense/density) than salt water. Salt water has more mass than fresh water, so it has a higher (dense/density).

salinity

wave

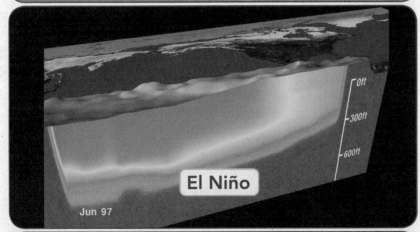

0ft
300ft
600ft

El Niño

Jun 97

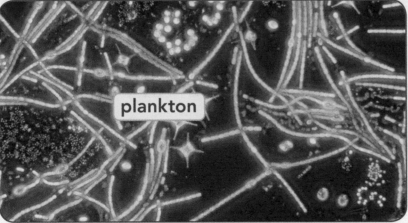

plankton

Chapter Preview

LESSON 1
- salinity • sonar • seamount
- trench • continental slope
- continental shelf • abyssal plain
- mid-ocean ridge
- ↻ **Identify the Main Idea**
- △ **Interpret Data**

LESSON 2
- wave • wavelength • frequency
- wave height • tsunami
- longshore drift • rip current
- groin
- ↻ **Relate Cause and Effect**
- △ **Form Operational Definitions**

LESSON 3
- current • Coriolis effect
- climate • El Niño • La Niña
- ↻ **Compare and Contrast**
- △ **Infer**

LESSON 4
- intertidal zone • neritic zone
- open-ocean zone • plankton
- nekton • benthos • food web
- ↻ **Ask Questions**
- △ **Predict**

> VOCAB FLASH CARDS For extra help
with vocabulary, visit **Vocab Flash
Cards** and type in *The Oceans.*

Exploring the Ocean

UNLOCK
THE BIG
?

🔑 How Do Conditions Vary in Earth's Oceans?

🔑 What Are Some Features of the Ocean Floor?

MY PLANET DIARY   SCIENCE AND TECHNOLOGY

Deep-Sea Escape

You've heard of how parachutes are used for escapes. But have you heard of a special suit that allows people to escape from a submarine 183 meters under water? The suit is designed to help sailors survive very cold temperatures and very high pressure. In an emergency, sailors put on this suit and enter a water-filled rescue chamber. Then the sailors shoot out, rising at two to three meters per second. If the suit tears, they have to exhale all the way to the surface so their lungs don't explode. At the surface, part of the suit inflates to become a life raft.

Discuss these questions with a classmate and write your answers below.

1. What technology was developed to help sailors escape a submarine accident?

_____

_____

2. What would it feel like to escape from a submarine deep under water? How would you help your body adjust to the changing pressure?

_____

_____

▶ PLANET DIARY Go to **Planet Diary** to learn more about characteristics of the ocean.

Lab
zone
Do the Inquiry Warm-Up
What Can You Learn Without Seeing?

How Do Conditions Vary in Earth's Oceans?

People have explored the ocean since ancient times. For centuries, the ocean has provided food and served as a route for trade and travel. Modern scientists have studied the characteristics of the ocean's waters and the ocean floor. 🔑 **The water in Earth's oceans varies in salinity, temperature, and depth.**

Vocabulary

- salinity • sonar • seamount • trench
- continental slope • continental shelf • abyssal plain
- mid-ocean ridge

Skills

↻ Reading: Identify the Main Idea
△ Inquiry: Interpret Data

Salinity

If you've ever swallowed a mouthful of water while you were swimming in the ocean, you know it's pretty salty. But just how salty? If you boiled a kilogram of ocean water in a pot until the water was gone, there would be about 35 grams of salt left in the pot. That's about two tablespoons of salt. **Salinity** is the total amount of dissolved salts in a sample of water. In most parts of the ocean, the salinity is between 34 and 37 parts per thousand.

The substance you know as table salt is sodium chloride. This salt is present in the greatest amount in ocean water. When sodium chloride dissolves in water, it separates into sodium and chloride particles called ions. Ocean water also contains smaller amounts of more than a dozen ions, including magnesium and calcium.

Near the ocean's surface, rain, snow, and melting ice add fresh water, lowering the salinity. Evaporation, on the other hand, increases salinity. Salt is left behind as the water evaporates. Salinity can also be higher near the poles. As the surface water freezes into ice, the salt is left behind in the remaining water.

Effects of Salinity

Salinity affects ocean water in different ways. For instance, fresh water freezes at 0°C. But ocean water doesn't freeze until the temperature drops to about −1.9°C. The salt acts as a kind of antifreeze by interfering with the formation of ice. Salt water also has a higher density than fresh water. That means that the mass of one liter of salt water is greater than the mass of one liter of fresh water. Because its density is greater, seawater lifts, or buoys up, less dense objects floating in it.

> **Vocabulary** Suffixes Circle the correct word to complete the sentence below.
>
> Ocean water has a higher (salinity/saline) than fresh water.

Composition of Ocean Water

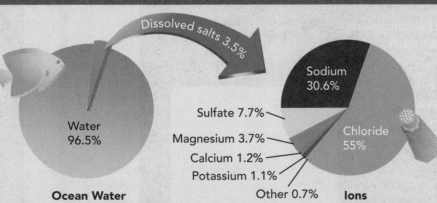

Dissolved salts 3.5%

Water 96.5%

Ocean Water

Sodium 30.6%
Sulfate 7.7%
Magnesium 3.7%
Calcium 1.2%
Potassium 1.1%
Chloride 55%
Other 0.7%

Ions

FIGURE 1 ....

> VIRTUAL LAB **Composition of Ocean Water**
When salts dissolve, they separate into particles called ions.

✎ **Read Graphs** In ocean water, which ion is most common? Which salt?

_____

_____

_____

Identify the Main Idea
Underline the two changes that happen with depth.

Temperature The broad surface of the ocean absorbs energy from the sun. **Like temperatures on land, temperatures at the surface of the ocean vary with location and the seasons.** Near the equator, surface ocean temperatures often reach 25°C, about room temperature. The temperatures drop as you travel away from the equator. Warm water is less dense than cold water, so it doesn't sink. Warm water forms only a thin layer on the ocean surface.

Depth If you could swim from the surface of the ocean to the ocean floor, you would pass through a vertical section of the ocean. This section, shown in **Figure 2**, is referred to as the water column. **As you descend through the ocean, the water temperature decreases.** There are three temperature zones in the water column. The surface zone is the warmest. It typically extends from the surface to between 100 and 500 meters. The average temperature worldwide for this zone is 16.1°C. Next is the transition zone, which extends from the bottom of the surface zone to about 1 kilometer. Temperatures in the transition zone drop very quickly to about 4°C. Below the transition zone is the deep zone. Average temperatures there are 3.5°C in most of the ocean.

Water pressure, the force exerted by the weight of water, also changes with depth. **In the ocean, pressure increases by 1 bar, the air pressure at sea level, with each 10 meters of depth.** Due to the high pressure in the deep ocean, divers can descend safely only to about 40 meters without specialized equipment. To observe the deep ocean, scientists can use a submersible, an underwater vehicle built of materials that resist pressure.

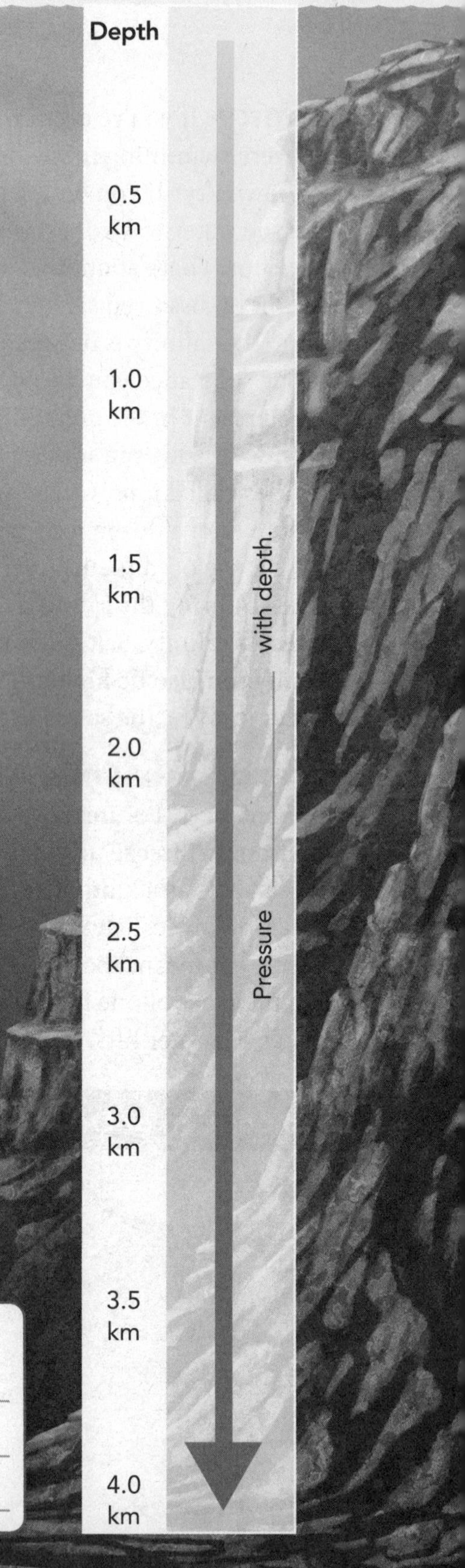

Depth
0.5 km
1.0 km
1.5 km
2.0 km
2.5 km
3.0 km
3.5 km
4.0 km
Pressure ______ with depth.

FIGURE 2

Changes With Depth

The conditions in Earth's oceans change with depth.

1. Shade in each temperature zone in the depth bar and make a key.
2. Fill in the blank in the pressure bar to identify what happens to pressure with depth.

Key

☐ ______________
☐ ______________
☐ ______________

apply it!

Each panel of dials provides information about conditions at various depths in the ocean.

1 ⚠ **Interpret Data** Find the incorrect dial in each panel and correct its reading.

2 Label where in the ocean you might find each set of readings: surface zone, transition zone, or deep zone.

Depth (m) 1000 2000 200 0 3000
Temperature WARM COLD VERY COLD
Pressure LOW MEDIUM HIGH

_____

3 [CHALLENGE] Based on the information in the panels, where is the most dense water in the ocean?

_____
_____
_____

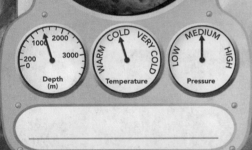

Depth (m) 1000 2000 200 0 3000
Temperature WARM COLD VERY COLD
Pressure LOW MEDIUM HIGH

_____

Depth (m) 1000 2000 200 0 3000
Temperature WARM COLD VERY COLD
Pressure LOW MEDIUM HIGH

_____

Lab zone Do the Quick Lab *Ocean Conditions.*

🗨 Assess Your Understanding

got it? ....

○ **I get it!** Now I know that the water in Earth's oceans varies in _____

○ **I need extra help with** _____

Go to MY SCIENCE ⓢ COACH online for help with this subject.

What Are Some Features of the Ocean Floor?

The ocean is very deep—3.8 kilometers deep on average. That's more than twice as deep as the Grand Canyon. Humans can't survive the darkness, cold temperatures, and extreme pressure of the deep ocean. So scientists have developed technology to study the ocean floor. A major advance in ocean-floor mapping was **sonar**, SOund NAvigation and Ranging. This system uses sound waves to calculate the distance to an object. A ship's sonar system sends out pulses of sound that bounce off the ocean floor. The equipment then measures how quickly the sound waves return to the ship.

Once scientists mapped the ocean floor, they discovered that the deep waters hid mountain ranges bigger than any on land, as well as deep canyons. **Major ocean floor features include trenches, the continental shelf, the continental slope, the abyssal plain, and the mid-ocean ridge. These features have all been formed by the interaction of Earth's plates.** You can see these feaures in **Figure 3**.

FIGURE 3 ....
Ocean Floor
✎ **Relate Text and Visuals**
Match the descriptions below with the ocean floor features in the image. Write the number for each description in the corresponding circles.
(Image not to scale. To show major ocean floor features, thousands of kilometers have been squeezed into one illustration.)

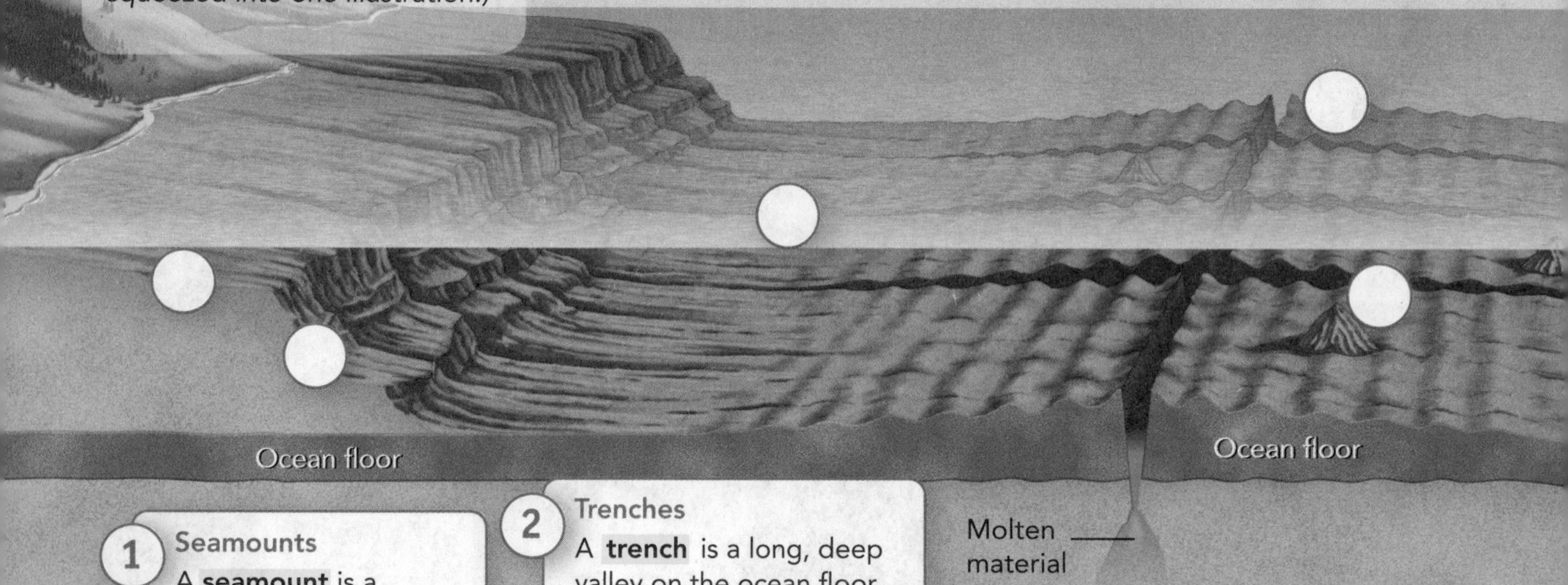

Ocean floor

Ocean floor

Molten material

1 **Seamounts**
A **seamount** is a volcanic mountain rising from the ocean floor that doesn't reach the surface. Seamounts often form near mid-ocean ridges. Some seamounts were once volcanic islands. But they slowly sank because of the movement of the ocean floor toward a trench.

2 **Trenches**
A **trench** is a long, deep valley on the ocean floor through which old ocean floor sinks back toward the mantle. The Marianas Trench in the Pacific Ocean is 11 kilometers deep.

3 **Continental Slope**
At 130 meters down, the slope of the ocean floor gets steeper. The steep edge of the continental shelf is called the **continental slope.**

4 **Continental Shelf**
The **continental shelf** is a gently sloping, shallow area that extends outward from the edge of each continent. Its width varies from a few kilometers to as much as 1,300 kilometers.

LOST AT SEA

FIGURE 4 ······

> INTERACTIVE ART **What are some characteristics of Earth's oceans?**

✏️ **Predict** Your ship has been radioed by a submarine that has lost the use of its navigation instruments. Based on the information in their last transmission, where might the vessel be? What might the conditions of the water be at this depth? Discuss your prediction with a partner.

Last transmission from sub: "Depth reading 3,000 meters; passed over a flat plain...sonar returned waves quickly; possibly approaching mountains."

_____
_____
_____
_____
_____
_____
_____
_____
_____

Lab zone ® Do the Quick Lab *The Shape of the Ocean Floor.*

(5) **Abyssal Plain**
The **abyssal plain** (uh BIHS ul) is a broad area covered with thick layers of mud and silt. It's a smooth, nearly flat region of the ocean.

(6) **Mid-Ocean Ridges**
Mid-ocean ridges are long chains of mountains on the ocean floors. Along the ridges, lava erupts and forms new ocean floor. Because of convection currents inside Earth, the ocean floor slowly moves toward a trench and sinks into the mantle.

🔑 **Assess Your Understanding**

1a. List What are four features of the ocean floor?

_____
_____

b. Explain Why has investigation of the ocean been difficult?

_____

c. ANSWER THE BIG ? What are some characteristics of Earth's oceans?

_____
_____

got it? ······························

⭘ **I get it!** Now I know that the ocean floor has many different features formed by _____

_____

⭘ **I need extra help with** _____

Go to MY SCIENCE ⑤ COACH *online for help with this subject.*

Wave Action

UNLOCK THE BIG ?

🔑 **How Do Waves Form and Change?**

🔑 **How Do Waves Affect the Shore?**

MY PLANET DIARY

DISASTER

Rogue Waves

For hundreds of years, sailors have returned from the sea to tell of 30-meter-high waves that appeared out of nowhere. These waves, they said, plunged the largest ships into the ocean depths. For hundreds of years, these tales were taken no more seriously than the Scottish legend of the Loch Ness monster. Ships were sunk, scientists said, in storms.

Then, in 1995, an oil rig in the North Sea was struck by a rogue wave. Instruments on board measured the wave's height at 26 meters. As a result, the European Union set up a project to study these rogue waves using satellites. What the scientists found was shocking. Within three weeks, they tracked ten different giant waves.

Discuss these questions with a classmate and write your answers below.

1. Why did people begin to believe in rogue waves?

_____

_____

_____

2. How might you track a rogue wave?

_____

_____

> PLANET DIARY Go to **Planet Diary** to learn more about wave action.

Lab® **zone** Do the Inquiry Warm-Up *How Do Waves Change a Beach?*

Vocabulary
- wave • wavelength • frequency • wave height
- tsunami • longshore drift • rip current • groin

Skills
- Reading: Relate Cause and Effect
- Inquiry: Form Operational Definitions

How Do Waves Form and Change?

When you watch a surfer's wave crash onto a beach, you are seeing the last step in the development of a wave. A **wave** is the movement of energy through a body of water. Wave development usually begins with wind. Without the energy of wind, the surface of the ocean would be as smooth as a mirror. 🔑 **Most waves form when winds blowing across the water's surface transmit their energy to the water.**

The size of a wave depends on the strength of the wind and on the length of time it blows. A gentle breeze creates small ripples on the surface of the water. Stronger winds create larger waves. The size of a wave also depends on the distance over which the wind blows. Winds blowing across longer distances build up bigger waves. That's why small ponds have ripples but the Great Lakes have waves you can surf!

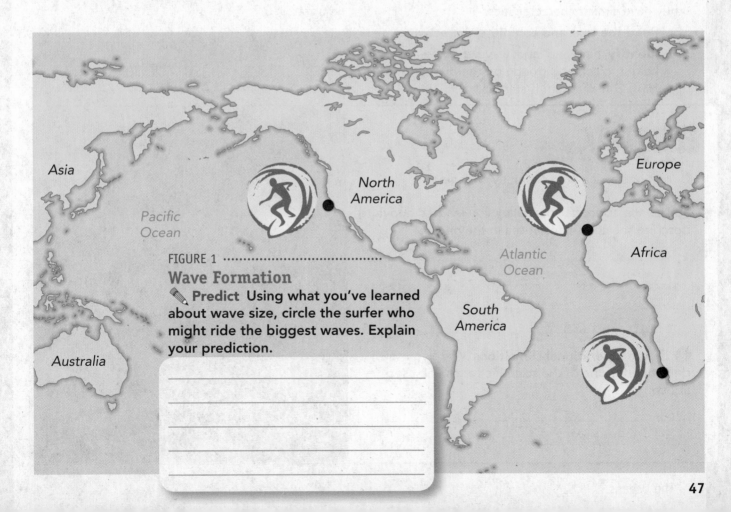

FIGURE 1 ··········

Wave Formation

✎ **Predict** Using what you've learned about wave size, circle the surfer who might ride the biggest waves. Explain your prediction.

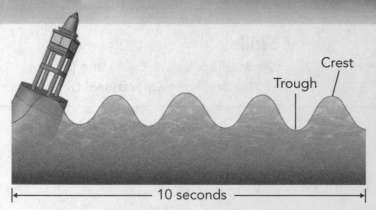

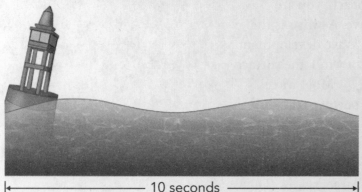

Crest
Trough

|← 10 seconds →|

|← 10 seconds →|

FIGURE 2 ···

Wave Characteristics

There are many different types of waves, but they have similar characteristics.

✎ **Read the text and complete the activity.**

1. **Identify** Find and label wavelength, wave height, crest, and trough on the diagrams. *Hint:* One diagram is started.

Wave Characteristics

Scientists have a vocabulary to describe the characteristics of waves. The name for the highest part of a wave is the crest. The horizontal distance between crests is the **wavelength.** Long, rolling waves with lots of space between crests have long wavelengths. Short, choppy waves have shorter wavelengths. Waves are also measured by their **frequency,** the number of waves that pass a point in a certain amount of time.

As you can see in **Figure 2,** the lowest part of a wave is the trough. The vertical distance from the crest to the trough is the **wave height.** The energy and strength of a wave depend mainly on its wave height. In the open ocean, most waves are between 2 and 5 meters high. During storms, waves can grow much higher and more powerful.

2. **Compare and Contrast** How does the frequency of the waves compare in the two diagrams?

_____

_____

_____

Conditions at sea are constantly changing.

❶ Use the scientific vocabulary you learned above to describe the conditions at sea in the photo.

_____

_____

_____

_____

❷ **Form Operational Definitions** Write your own definition for one of the scientific terms you used above.

_____

_____

Wave Energy

Waves may appear to carry water toward shore, but water doesn't actually move forward in deep water. If it did, ocean water would eventually pile up on the coasts of every continent! The energy of the wave moves toward shore, but the water itself remains in place. You can test this by floating a cork in a bowl of water. Use a spoon to make a wave in the bowl. As the wave passes, the cork lurches forward a little; then it bobs backward. It ends up in almost the same spot where it started.

Water Motion

What happens to the water as a wave travels along? Notice in **Figure 3** that as the wave passes, water particles move in a circular path. They swing forward and down with the energy of the wave, then back up to their original position. Deeper water particles move in smaller circles than those near the surface. At a depth equal to about one half the wavelength, water particles are not affected by the surface wave.

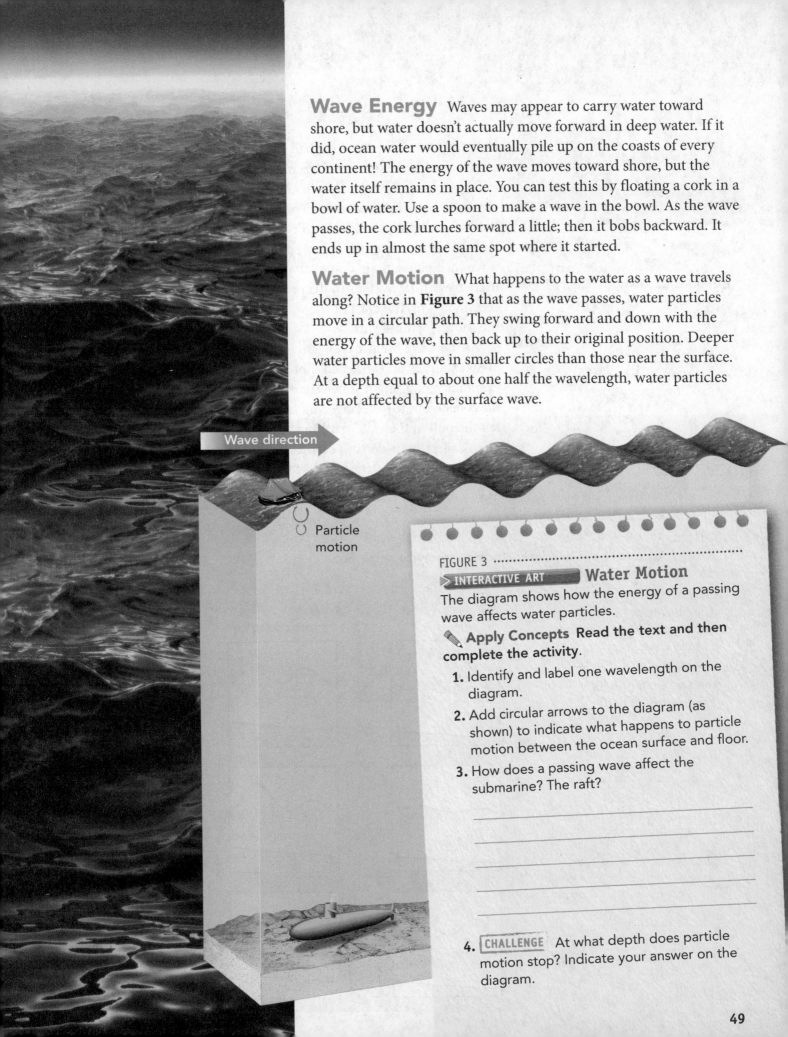

Wave direction

Particle motion

FIGURE 3 ··

> INTERACTIVE ART   **Water Motion**

The diagram shows how the energy of a passing wave affects water particles.

✎ **Apply Concepts** Read the text and then complete the activity.

1. Identify and label one wavelength on the diagram.

2. Add circular arrows to the diagram (as shown) to indicate what happens to particle motion between the ocean surface and floor.

3. How does a passing wave affect the submarine? The raft?

_____

_____

_____

_____

_____

4. [CHALLENGE] At what depth does particle motion stop? Indicate your answer on the diagram.

Breakers

Breakers The white-capped waves that crash onto shore are often called "breakers." In deep water, these waves usually travel as long, low waves called swells. As the waves approach the shore, the water becomes shallower. The bottoms of the waves begin to touch the sloping ocean floor. Friction between the ocean floor and the water causes the waves to slow down. As the speed of the waves decreases, their shapes change. **Near shore, wave height increases and wavelength decreases.** When a wave reaches a certain height, the crest of the wave topples. The wave breaks onto the shore, forming surf.

As the wave breaks, it continues to move forward. At first the breaker surges up the beach. But gravity soon slows it down, eventually stopping it. The water that has rushed up the beach then flows back out to sea. Have you ever stood at the water's edge and felt the pull of the water rushing back out to the ocean? This pull, often called an undertow, carries shells, seaweed, and sand away from the beach. A strong undertow can be dangerous to swimmers.

Relate Cause and Effect
Read the text. Then, underline the cause of breakers and circle the effect.

FIGURE 4 ··

Breakers

After you read about breakers, do the activity to show how waves change shape as they get closer to shore.

1. **Interpret Diagrams** Shade in one drawing in each column to show the sequence of how a wave forms.

2. **Summarize** How does the wave change as it approaches shore?

_____
_____
_____
_____
_____
_____
_____
_____
_____

❶ Deep-water waves

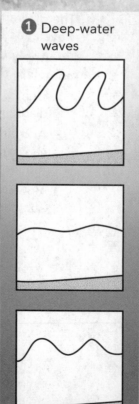

❷ Waves approaching shore

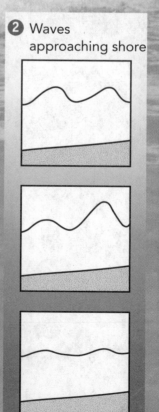

❸ Waves near shore

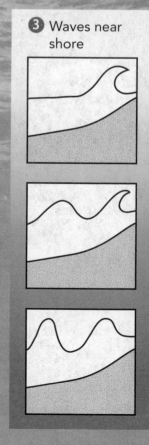

Tsunami So far you've been reading about waves that are caused by the wind. But another kind of wave forms far below the ocean surface. This type of wave, called a **tsunami,** is usually caused by an earthquake beneath the ocean floor. The ocean floor's abrupt movement sends pulses of energy through the water, shown in the diagram below.

Despite the huge amount of energy a tsunami carries, people on a ship at sea may not even realize a tsunami is passing. How is this possible? A tsunami in deep water may have a wavelength of 200 kilometers or more, but a wave height of less than a meter. When the tsunami reaches shallow water near the coast, friction with the ocean floor causes the long wavelength to decrease suddenly. The wave height increases as the water "piles up." Some tsunamis have reached heights of 20 meters or more—taller than a five-story building!

Tsunamis are most common in the Pacific Ocean, often striking Alaska, Hawaii, and Japan. In response, nations in the Pacific have developed a warning system, which can alert them if a tsunami forms. But not all tsunamis occur in the Pacific Ocean. On December 26, 2004, a major earthquake in the Indian Ocean caused tremendous tsunamis that hit 11 nations. Tragically, these tsunamis took the lives of more than 230,000 people. Several nations are now developing a warning system for the Indian Ocean.

FIGURE 5 ·········
Tsunami
✎ **Communicate** Use the diagram below, showing how a tsunami forms, to help you develop a tsunami warning system. Include how you would warn people living in remote areas.

_____
_____
_____
_____
_____
_____
_____
_____

An Indonesian village hit by the 2004 tsunami

Motion of ocean floor

Lab ® Do the Quick Lab
zone Making Waves.

🔑 **Assess Your Understanding**

got it? ···

○ **I get it!** Now I know that waves change as they approach shore because _____

_____

○ **I need extra help with** _____

Go to MY SCIENCE ⓢ COACH *online for help with this subject.*

51

How Do Waves Affect the Shore?

As waves approach and crash onto the shore, the beach can change. Wave direction at sea is determined by the wind. Waves usually roll toward shore at an angle. But as they touch bottom, the shallower water slows the shoreward side of the wave first. The rows of waves gradually turn and become more nearly parallel to the shore.

Longshore Drift As waves come into shore, water washes up the beach at an angle, carrying sand grains, as shown in **Figure 6.** The water and sand then run down the beach. This movement of sand along the beach is called **longshore drift.** ✏️ **As the waves slow down, they deposit the sand they are carrying on the shallow, underwater slope, forming a long ridge called a sandbar.**

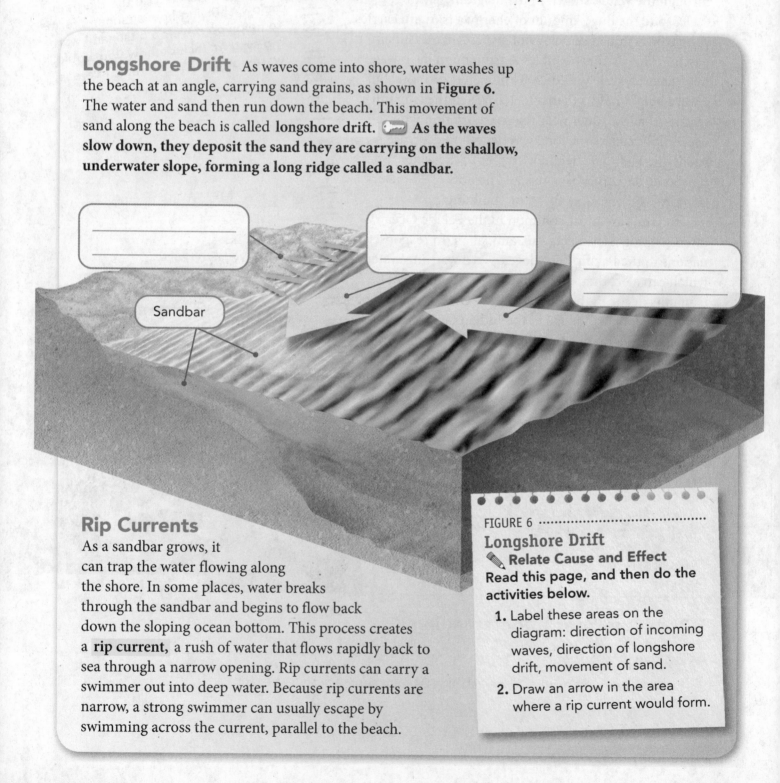

Sandbar

Rip Currents

As a sandbar grows, it can trap the water flowing along the shore. In some places, water breaks through the sandbar and begins to flow back down the sloping ocean bottom. This process creates a **rip current,** a rush of water that flows rapidly back to sea through a narrow opening. Rip currents can carry a swimmer out into deep water. Because rip currents are narrow, a strong swimmer can usually escape by swimming across the current, parallel to the beach.

FIGURE 6 ······················
Longshore Drift
✏️ **Relate Cause and Effect**
Read this page, and then do the activities below.

1. Label these areas on the diagram: direction of incoming waves, direction of longshore drift, movement of sand.

2. Draw an arrow in the area where a rip current would form.

Beach Erosion If you walk on the same beach every day, you might not notice that it's changing. But if you visit a beach just once each year, you might be startled by the changes you see. ▬ **Waves shape a beach by eroding the shore in some places and building it up in others.**

FIGURE 7 ·················

Beach Erosion
✎ **Evaluate the Impact on Society** Your community planning board wants to limit beach erosion. Do you vote to protect the dunes from being built on or to construct a groin instead? Why?

_____
_____
_____
_____
_____
_____
_____

Barrier Beaches Long sand deposits called barrier beaches form parallel to the shore and are separated from the mainland by a shallow lagoon. Waves break against the barrier beach, protecting the mainland from erosion. For this reason, people are working to preserve barrier beaches along the Atlantic coast from Georgia to Massachusetts.

Sand Dunes Hills of windblown sand, called sand dunes, can make a beach more stable and protect the shore from erosion. The strong roots of dune plants hold the sand in place and help slow erosion. Without them, sand dunes can be easily washed away by wave action.

Groins Many people like to live near the ocean, but erosion can threaten buildings near the beach. One way to reduce beach erosion is to build a wall of rocks or concrete, called a **groin,** outward from the beach. Sand carried by the water piles up on one side of the groin instead of moving down shore. However, groins increase erosion farther down the beach.

Lab ® **zone** Do the Quick Lab *Modeling Currents.*

▬ Assess Your Understanding

got it? ···

○ **I get it!** Now I know that waves shape the beach by _____
_____

○ **I need extra help with** _____
Go to **my science** s **COACH** *online for help with this subject.*

Currents and Climate

UNLOCK THE BIG

🔑 **What Causes Surface Currents?**

🔑 **What Causes Deep Currents?**

MY PLANET DIARY   EVERYDAY SCIENCE

Ducky Overboard

What happens when a ship loses its cargo at sea? Is it gone forever? You might think so. One ship traveling from Hong Kong to Tacoma, Washington, lost 29,000 plastic toys. They fell overboard in a storm and were considered lost at sea. But when hundreds of the toys began washing up on distant shores, scientists got excited.

One way scientists study ocean currents is by releasing empty bottles into the ocean. But of 500 to 1,000 bottles released, scientists might only recover 10. That doesn't give them much data. The large number of floating toys could give scientists better data from more data points.

The first toys were spotted off the coast of Alaska. Then beachcombers began finding them in Canada, in Washington, and even as far away as Scotland.

Discuss these questions with a classmate and write your answers below.

1. Why was the plastic toy spill so helpful to scientists studying ocean currents?

_____

_____

_____

2. Have you ever found objects on the beach? What data would scientists need from you for their research?

_____

_____

Lab zone® Do the Inquiry Warm-Up *Bottom to Top.*

> **PLANET DIARY** Go to **Planet Diary** to learn more about ocean currents.

Vocabulary
- current • Coriolis effect
- climate • El Niño • La Niña

Skills
- Reading: Compare and Contrast
- Inquiry: Infer

What Causes Surface Currents?

A **current** is a large stream of moving water that flows through the oceans. Unlike waves, currents carry water from one place to another. Some currents move water at the surface of the ocean. Other currents move water deep in the ocean.

🔑 **Surface currents affect water to a depth of several hundred meters. They are driven mainly by winds.** Surface currents follow Earth's major wind patterns. They move in circular patterns in the five major oceans. Most of the currents flow east or west, then double back to complete the circle, as shown in **Figure 1.**

Coriolis Effect Why do the currents move in these circular patterns? If Earth were standing still, winds and currents would flow in more direct paths between the poles and the equator. But as Earth rotates, the paths of the winds and currents curve. This effect of Earth's rotation on the direction of winds and currents is called the **Coriolis effect** (kawr ee OH lis). In the Northern Hemisphere, the Coriolis effect causes the currents to curve clockwise. In the Southern Hemisphere, the Coriolis effect causes the currents to curve counterclockwise.

FIGURE 1 ·····················
Surface Currents
✏ **Infer** The toys that fell overboard washed up in many places. Two of the locations are marked with ducks below. Circle the currents that you think moved the toys to these spots. Discuss your answer with a classmate.

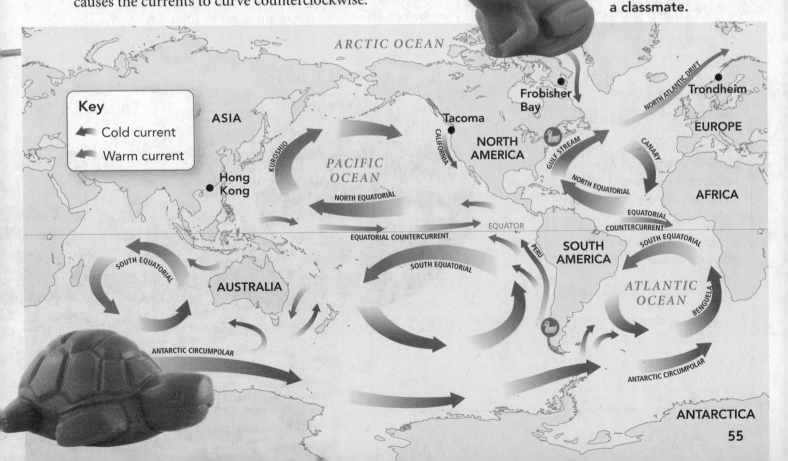

Key
← Cold current
← Warm current

ARCTIC OCEAN

ASIA

KUROSHIO

Hong Kong

PACIFIC OCEAN

NORTH EQUATORIAL

Tacoma

CALIFORNIA

NORTH AMERICA

Frobisher Bay

GULF STREAM

NORTH ATLANTIC DRIFT

Trondheim

EUROPE

CANARY

NORTH EQUATORIAL

AFRICA

EQUATOR

EQUATORIAL COUNTERCURRENT

EQUATORIAL COUNTERCURRENT

SOUTH AMERICA

PERU

SOUTH EQUATORIAL

SOUTH EQUATORIAL

SOUTH EQUATORIAL

AUSTRALIA

ATLANTIC OCEAN

BENGUELA

ANTARCTIC CIRCUMPOLAR

ANTARCTIC CIRCUMPOLAR

ANTARCTICA

55

Compare and Contrast Use the space below to compare and contrast the effects of warm and cold currents on climate.

_____

_____

_____

_____

_____

_____

_____

_____

_____

Gulf Stream

The Gulf Stream is the largest and most powerful surface current in the North Atlantic Ocean. This current is caused by strong winds from the west. It is more than 30 kilometers wide and 300 meters deep. The Gulf Stream moves warm water from the Gulf of Mexico to the Caribbean Sea. It then continues northward along the east coast of the United States. Near Cape Hatteras, North Carolina, it curves eastward across the Atlantic, as a result of the Coriolis effect. When the Gulf Stream crosses the Atlantic it becomes the North Atlantic Drift.

Effects on Climate

The Gulf Stream has a warming effect on the climate of nearby land areas. **Climate** is the pattern of temperature and precipitation typical of an area over a long period of time. The mid-Atlantic region of the United States, including North Carolina and Virginia, has a more moderate climate because of the Gulf Stream. Winters are very mild and summers are humid.

Currents affect climate by moving cold and warm water around the globe. Currents generally move warm water from the tropics toward the poles and bring cold water back toward the equator. **A surface current warms or cools the air above it. This affects the climate of land near the coast.** Winds pick up moisture as they blow across warm-water currents. This explains why the warm Kuroshio Current brings mild, rainy weather to the southern islands of Japan. Cold-water currents cool the air above them. Cold air holds less moisture than warm air. So cold currents tend to bring cool, dry weather to land areas in their path.

apply it!

Trondheim, Norway, and Frobisher Bay, Canada, are shown here in July. They are at roughly the same latitude, but they have very different climates.

Infer Why does Trondheim have a mild climate? _Hint:_ Refer to the map on the previous page.

_____

_____

_____

_____

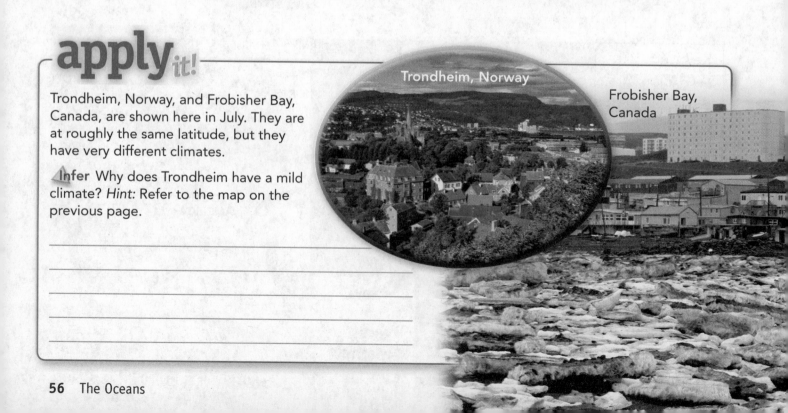

Trondheim, Norway

Frobisher Bay, Canada

El Niño Changes in wind patterns and currents can have a major impact on the oceans and nearby land. One example of such changes is **El Niño,** a climate event that occurs every two to seven years in the Pacific Ocean. El Niño begins when an unusual pattern of winds forms over the western Pacific. This causes a vast sheet of warm water to move east toward the South American coast, as shown in **Figure 2.** This warm water prevents the cold deep water from moving to the surface. El Niño conditions can last for one to two years before the usual winds and currents return.

El Niño causes shifts in weather patterns. This leads to unusual and often severe conditions in different areas. A major El Niño occurred between 1997 and 1998. It caused an especially warm winter in the northeastern United States. It was also responsible for heavy rains, flooding, and mudslides in California, as well as a string of deadly tornadoes in Florida.

La Niña When surface waters in the eastern Pacific are colder than normal, a climate event known as **La Niña** occurs. A La Niña event is the opposite of an El Niño event. La Niña events typically bring colder than normal winters and greater precipitation to the Pacific Northwest and the north central United States.

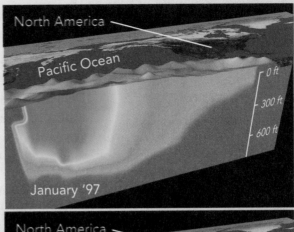

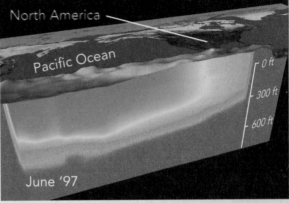

FIGURE 2 ·······································
> ART IN MOTION **Warming Sea Temperature**
The images show what happens to temperature below the surface of the ocean during an El Niño event. Red indicates a warmer sea surface temperature.

✎ **Draw Conclusions** What happened to the the water temperature over six months?

_____

_____

Lab Do the Lab Investigation
zone *Modeling Ocean Currents.*

⌨ Assess Your Understanding

1a. Define What is a current?

_____

_____

b. Describe What causes surface currents?

_____

c. CHALLENGE Why is it helpful to a community to be able to predict an El Niño event?

_____

_____

_____

_____

got it? ·······································

○ **I get it!** Now I know that currents are driven mainly by _____

_____

○ **I need extra help with** _____

Go to MY SCIENCE ⑤ COACH online for help with this subject.

What Causes Deep Currents?

Deep below the ocean surface, another type of current causes chilly waters to creep slowly across the ocean floor. **Deep currents are caused by differences in the density of ocean water.** Recall that cold water is more dense than warm water.

Salinity When a warm surface current moves from the equator toward one of the poles, it gradually cools. As ice forms near the poles, the salinity of the water increases from the salt left behind during freezing. As the water's temperature decreases and its salinity increases, the water becomes denser and sinks. Then, the cold water flows back along the ocean floor as a deep current. Deep currents are affected by the Coriolis effect, which causes them to curve.

Deep currents move and mix water around the world. They carry cold water from the poles toward the equator. Deep currents flow slowly. They may take as long as 1,000 years to circulate between the oceans back to where they started.

Global Ocean Conveyor The simplified pattern of ocean currents in **Figure 3** looks like a conveyor belt, moving water between the oceans. This pattern of ocean currents results from density differences due to temperature and salinity. The currents bring oxygen into the deep ocean that is needed for marine life.

The ocean's deep currents mostly start as cold water in the North Atlantic Ocean. This is the same water that moved north across the Atlantic as part of the Gulf Stream. This cold, salty water, called the North Atlantic Deep Water, is dense. It sinks to the bottom of the ocean and flows southward toward Antarctica. From there it flows northward into both the Indian and Pacific oceans. The deep cold water rises to the surface in the Indian and Pacific oceans, warms, and eventually flows back along the surface into the Atlantic.

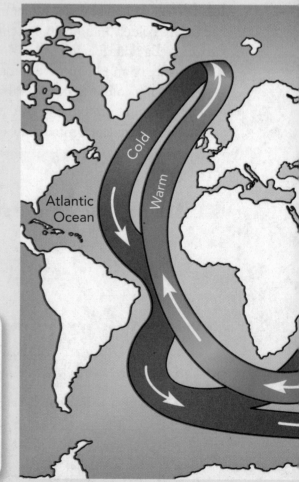

FIGURE 3 ···
Global Conveyor
✎ **Predict** What might happen if the global conveyor stopped?

_____

_____

_____

do the math! Analyzing Data

Calculating Density

Temperature affects the density of ocean water. To calculate the density of a substance, divide the mass of the substance by its volume.

$$\text{Density} = \frac{\text{Mass}}{\text{Volume}}$$

·············· Practice Problem ··············

Calculate Find the density of the following 1-L samples of ocean water. Sample A has a mass of 1.01 kg; Sample B has a mass of 1.06 kg. Which sample is likely to have the higher salinity? Why?

_____

_____

_____

 Do the Quick Lab
Deep Currents.

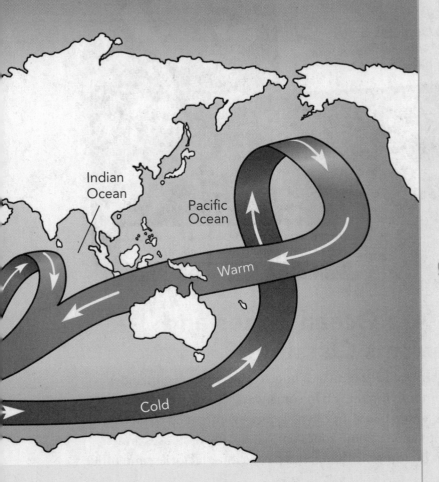

Indian Ocean

Pacific Ocean

Warm

Cold

🔑 Assess Your Understanding

2a. Review What causes deep currents?

_____

_____

b. Explain How does the temperature of ocean water affect its density?

_____

_____

_____

_____

got it? ···

○ **I get it!** Now I know how the global ocean

conveyor moves: _____

_____

_____

○ **I need extra help with** _____

Go to MY SCIENCE ⓢ COACH online for help with this subject.

59

UNLOCK THE BIG ?

🔑 **How Are Ocean Zones and Organisms Classified?**

MY PLANET DIARY

BLOG

Posted by: Dina

Location: St. Louis, Missouri

One of my favorite memories is going to the beach with my brothers and sister. One time we went snorkeling with my father and he took us so far out we could barely see the seashore. I remember looking at the fishes and thinking they were the prettiest things I have ever seen in my life. It was scary at first but the scenery calmed you down. My brother and I would try to see who could go to the bottom and touch the beautiful sand.

After you read, answer the question below.

What did Dina observe on her snorkeling trip?

_____

_____

_____

_____

▷ **PLANET DIARY** Go to **Planet Diary** to learn more about ocean habitats.

Lab zone® Do the Inquiry Warm-Up *How Complex Are Ocean Feeding Relationships?*

How Are Ocean Zones and Organisms Classified?

You can think of the ocean as a huge community that includes living and nonliving things. In some ways, the ocean community resembles a human city or town. Typically, cities and towns are divided into zones. Some zones consist mostly of houses and apartment buildings. Other zones have shops, factories, and offices.

Vocabulary

- intertidal zone • neritic zone • open-ocean zone
- plankton • nekton • benthos • food web

Skills

↻ Reading: Ask Questions

△ Inquiry: Predict

Classifying Ocean Zones The ocean, like cities and towns, can be divided into zones. ☞ **Ocean zones include the intertidal zone, the neritic zone, and the open-ocean zone.** The **intertidal zone** begins at the highest high-tide line on land, as shown in **Figure 1**. From there, the zone stretches out to the point on the continental shelf exposed by the lowest low tide. The **neritic zone** extends from the low-tide line out to the edge of the continental shelf. Beyond the edge of the continental shelf lies the **open-ocean zone.**

Each ocean zone has its own physical conditions that help determine which organisms can live there. For example, light does not penetrate very far beneath the ocean's surface. Organisms that need light for photosynthesis must live near the surface of the ocean. In contrast, in the deep ocean, pressure is high. Organisms that live deep in the ocean must be able to withstand this pressure.

FIGURE 1 ....

Ocean Zones

✎ **Identify** Label the three ocean zones on the diagram and answer the question.

In which ocean zone might physical conditions change the least? Why?

_____

_____

_____

_____

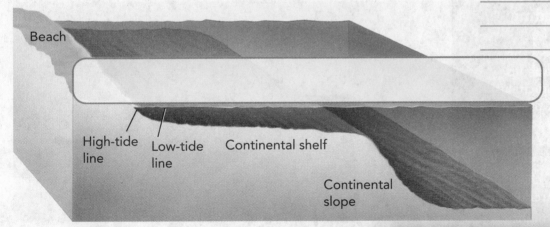

Beach

High-tide line   Low-tide line   Continental shelf

Continental slope

apply it!

Each ocean zone has distinct physical conditions.

△ **Predict** What ocean zone do these mussels live in? How can you tell?

_____

_____

_____

_____

_____

61

Grouping Organisms

On land, most organisms live on or near the surface. The ocean, on the other hand, is inhabited by organisms at every depth. 🔑 **Scientists group marine organisms according to where they live and how they move.**

Plankton Plankton are tiny algae and animals that float in the water and are carried by waves and currents. Algae plankton include geometrically shaped diatoms. Animal plankton include some tiny young fish and microscopic crustaceans, such as copepods.

Nekton Nekton are free-swimming animals that can move throughout the water column. Squid, most fishes, and marine mammals such as whales and seals are nekton.

Benthos Benthos are organisms that inhabit the ocean floor. Some benthos, like crabs, sea stars, octopuses, and lobsters, move from place to place. Others, like sponges and sea anemones, stay in one location.

FIGURE 2 ⋯⋯⋯⋯⋯⋯⋯⋯

▷ INTERACTIVE ART **Feeding Relationships**

✎ Interpret Diagrams The Arctic food web is made up of many different food chains. The arrows represent the flow of energy. They point to the organisms that get the energy by eating plants or animals.

1. Shade in the food chains that involve the Arctic cod.

2. CHALLENGE How might a decrease in Arctic cod affect this Arctic food web?

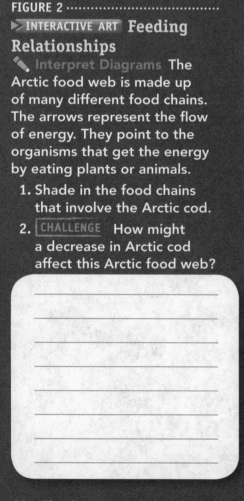

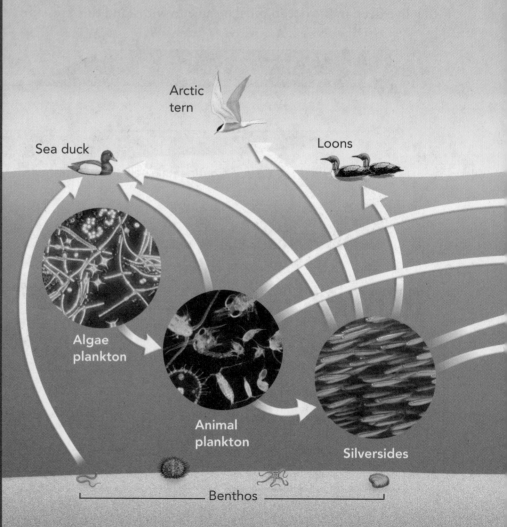

Arctic tern

Sea duck

Loons

Algae plankton

Animal plankton

Silversides

Benthos

Relationships Among Organisms Plankton, nekton, and benthos are all found in most marine habitats. Many plankton and benthos are algae. Like plants, algae use sunlight to produce their own food through photosynthesis. Photosynthetic plankton are called producers. Other plankton and benthos, as well as all nekton, eat algae or other organisms. They are called consumers. Finally, some organisms, including many benthos, break down wastes and the remains of other organisms. They are decomposers.

Ocean Food Webs All the feeding relationships that exist in a habitat make up a **food web.** In **Figure 2,** each organism in this Arctic food web depends directly or indirectly on the algae plankton. Throughout the ocean, plankton are a source of food for organisms of all sizes. In fact, you might be surprised to learn that the biggest sharks of all feed directly on tiny plankton! Many whales, including Earth's largest animal the blue whale, also feed only on plankton.

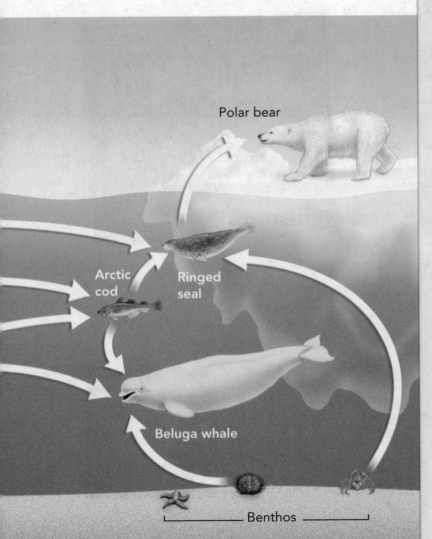

Polar bear

Arctic cod

Ringed seal

Beluga whale

⌐——— Benthos ———⌐

Lab® **zone** Do the Quick Lab
Designing an Organism.

🔋 Assess Your Understanding

1a. Sequence Put the ocean zones in order from deepest to shallowest.

_____

_____

b. Review What characteristics do scientists use to group living organisms?

_____

_____

c. Classify Sea cucumbers are small animals that crawl along the ocean floor. How would you group them and why?

_____

_____

got it?••••••••••••••••••••••••••••••••••••••

○ **I get it!** Now I know that each ocean zone has different _____

○ I need extra help with _____

Go to MY SCIENCE COACH *online for help with this subject.*

63

2 Study Guide

Characteristics of Earth's oceans include _____, _____, _____ , and different ocean floor features.

LESSON 1 Exploring the Ocean

🔑 The water in Earth's oceans varies in salinity, temperature, and depth.

🔑 Like temperatures on land, temperatures at the surface of the ocean vary with location and the seasons. As you descend through the ocean, the water temperature decreases.

🔑 In the ocean, pressure increases by 1 bar with each 10 meters of depth.

🔑 Major ocean floor features include trenches, the continental shelf, the continental slope, the abyssal plain, and the mid-ocean ridge.

Vocabulary
• salinity • sonar • seamount • trench • continental slope • continental shelf
• abyssal plain • mid-ocean ridge

LESSON 2 Wave Action

🔑 Most waves form when winds blowing across the water's surface transmit their energy to the water.

🔑 Near shore, wave height increases and wavelength decreases.

🔑 Waves shape a beach by eroding the shore in some places and building it up in others.

Vocabulary
• wave • wavelength • frequency • wave height
• tsunami • longshore drift • rip current • groin

LESSON 3 Currents and Climate

🔑 Surface currents are driven mainly by winds. A surface current warms or cools the air above it, affecting the climate of the land near the coast.

🔑 Deep currents are caused by differences in the density of ocean water. They move and mix water around the world and carry cold water from the poles toward the equator.

Vocabulary
• current • Coriolis effect • climate
• El Niño • La Niña

LESSON 4 Ocean Habitats

🔑 Ocean zones include the intertidal zone, the neritic zone, and the open-ocean zone.

🔑 Scientists group marine organisms according to where they live and how they move.

Vocabulary
• intertidal zone • neritic zone • open-ocean zone
• plankton • nekton
• benthos • food web

Review and Assessment

Exploring the Ocean

1. Why is ocean water more dense than fresh water at the same temperature?

    a. circular winds   **b.** less pressure

    c. deep currents   **d.** higher salinity

2. The mid-ocean ridge is _____

_____

_____

3. Relate Cause and Effect Name two properties of ocean water affected by depth. How does depth affect each?

_____

_____

_____

_____

4. Apply Concepts Would you expect the salinity of the ocean to be high or low in a rainy region near the mouth of a river?

_____

_____

_____

_____

5. Sequence Put the following parts of the ocean floor in order from least to greatest depth: abyssal plain, continental shelf, mid-ocean ridge, trench, continental slope.

_____

_____

_____

_____

6. **Write About It** In what ways is the ocean at 1,000 meters deep different from the ocean at the surface in the same location?

Wave Action

7. Which describes rolling waves with a large horizontal distance between crests?

    a. long wavelength   **b.** deep trough

    c. great wave height   **d.** high frequency

8. A tsunami is a large wave triggered by

_____

9. Relate Cause and Effect What factors influence the size of a wave?

_____

_____

10. Interpret Diagrams Where will sand pile up against the groins shown in the diagram? Explain.

_____

_____

_____

_____

_____

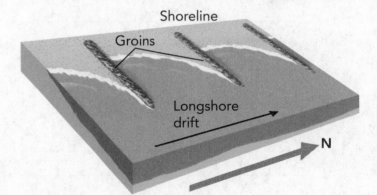

Shoreline

Groins

Longshore drift

N

11. Compare and Contrast How is a wave different when it reaches shore?

_____

_____

_____

_____

65

Currents and Climate

12. What makes winds and currents move in curved paths?

   a. Coriolis effect   **b.** wave height

   c. longshore drift   **d.** ocean trenches

13. Flooding is common during an El Niño, which

is _____

_____

_____

14. Relate Cause and Effect How does the movement of ocean currents explain the mild, wet climate in much of western Europe?

_____

_____

_____

_____

_____

15. Compare and Contrast What causes surface currents? Deep currents?

_____

_____

_____

16. Summarize How does the global ocean conveyor work?

_____

_____

_____

17. math! A 5-liter container of crude oil spills in the ocean. It has a mass of 4.10 kg. What is its density? If 1 liter of ocean water has a density of 1.03 kg, does the crude oil sink or float? Explain.

Ocean Habitats

18. What are free-swimming animals that can move throughout the water column called?

   a. diatoms   **b.** benthos

   c. nekton   **d.** plankton

19. If you travel past the neritic zone, you

reach _____

_____

20. Describe What are the three categories of ocean organisms? How do the organisms in each group move?

_____

_____

_____

_____

APPLY THE BIG

What are some characteristics of Earth's oceans?

21. Compare the conditions of the ocean water and features of the ocean floor in the open-ocean zone with those in the neritic zone.

_____

_____

_____

_____

_____

_____

_____

_____

_____

_____

_____

Standardized Test Prep

Multiple Choice

Circle the letter of the best answer.

1. The diagram below shows different parts of a wave. What is the wave feature W?

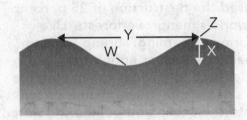

   A wave crest   **B** wave trough
   C wavelength   **D** wave height

2. In which category of ocean organisms do sharks, tuna, killer whales, and squid belong?

   A fishes   **B** plankton
   C benthos   **D** nekton

3. A major warm ocean surface current flows along a coastal area. What type of climate would you most likely find in the area influenced by the current?

   A mild and wet   **B** very cool and wet
   C cool and dry   **D** very hot and dry

4. What is the shallow, gently sloping area of the ocean floor that extends outward from the shoreline?

   A abyssal plain
   B continental shelf
   C continental slope
   D mid-ocean ridge

5. Use your knowledge of ocean zones to infer which adaptation would be most important for organisms in the intertidal zone.

   A ability to withstand changes in pressure from high to low
   B ability to use chemical nutrients in water
   C ability to withstand periods under water and periods exposed to air
   D ability to tolerate low light levels and cold temperatures

Constructed Response

Use the diagram below and your knowledge of science to help you answer Question 6. Write your answer on a separate piece of paper.

Motion of ocean floor

6. What is a tsunami? How does it compare to the breakers you might see crashing on shore at a beach?

Sustainable
Shrimp
Farms

Shrimp—those funny-looking, whiskered marine creatures—are the most popular seafood in the United States. About one quarter of the world's shrimp are raised on shrimp farms, and these farms are often made by cutting down coastal mangrove forests. It is estimated that shrimp farming has caused the destruction of 25 percent of the world's mangrove forests. Like other forms of farming, shrimp farming uses chemicals such as antibiotics, pesticides, and fungicides to increase the numbers of shrimp. These chemicals can drain into the ocean and pollute the water.

Governments and shrimp farmers are working together to solve these problems. For example, farmers are looking into closed production systems. In this kind of farm, the water is filtered and reused, rather than sent back into the ocean. In closed systems, farmers may even be able to raise shrimp organically—without antibiotics. Right now, these high-tech systems are very expensive. But perhaps, with more research, the price tag will come down.

Research It Find out more about the way different shrimp farms work. Compare the economic and ecological impacts of closed production systems with more traditional open systems. Present the costs and benefits and express your opinion in a persuasive essay.

AQUANAUTS

Science has sent people to the moon and robots to Mars. But vast amounts of Earth's surface—the parts that are deep underwater—remain unexplored.

Aquarius, the world's first underwater research station, is located more than 18 meters below the ocean's surface off the southern tip of Florida. The scientists and crew who work in *Aquarius* are called aquanauts.

Aquanauts are marine biologists and oceanographers. While on board *Aquarius*, the aquanauts may study nearby coral reefs or test new technology for marine exploration. *Aquarius* has allowed scientists to study and observe undersea life in ways that were previously impossible. Aquanaut missions are also helping the National Aeronautics and Space Administration (NASA). Because the undersea habitat is similar to a space station, NASA uses *Aquarius* to explore the challenges of living in space.

Design It Find out more about *Aquarius* and the missions it supports. Then write a news article to tell the public about the underwater research station, its missions, and the people who work on it. Remember to write an attention-grabbing headline and exciting lead paragraph.

Warm and dry inside Aquarius, an aquanaut looks out at the ocean. ▼

WHAT KEEPS THIS HANG GLIDER FLYING?

How does the sun's energy affect Earth's atmosphere?

Imagine yourself lazily soaring like a bird above Earth. The quiet, gentle winds and warm sun are so relaxing. No noisy engine, no flapping wings, but wait, what's keeping you aloft? Everyone knows that humans can't fly. **Develop Hypotheses** How does this hang glider fly?

_____

_____

_____

_____

_____

_____

> UNTAMED SCIENCE Watch the **Untamed Science** video to learn more about Earth's atmosphere.

The Atmosphere

3 Getting Started

Check Your Understanding

1. **Background** Read the paragraph below and then answer the question.

Helen blows up a balloon. She adds it to a large garbage bag already full of balloons. Its low **weight** makes the bag easy to carry, but its large **volume** might be a problem fitting it in the car. Capturing air in a balloon makes it easier to understand that air has **mass.**

> **Weight** is a measure of the force of gravity on an object.
>
> **Volume** is the amount of space that matter occupies.
>
> **Mass** is the amount of matter in an object.

• How could the bag's volume make it difficult to fit in the car?

_____

_____

> **MY READING WEB** If you had trouble completing the question above, visit **My Reading Web** and type in *The Atmosphere.*

Vocabulary Skill

Word Origins Many words come to English from other languages. Learning a few common Greek word parts can help you understand new science words.

Greek Word Part	Meaning	Example
-meter	measure	barometer, *n.* an instrument that measures air pressure
thermo-	heat	thermosphere, *n.* the outer layer of Earth's atmosphere

2. **Quick Check** Use the Greek word parts above to write a definition of a thermometer.

_____

_____

atmosphere

aneroid barometer

troposphere

wind

Chapter Preview

LESSON 1
- weather • atmosphere
- water vapor
- ↻ **Summarize**
- △ **Infer**

LESSON 2
- density • air pressure
- barometer • mercury barometer
- aneroid barometer • altitude
- ↻ **Relate Cause and Effect**
- △ **Develop Hypotheses**

LESSON 3
- troposphere • stratosphere
- mesosphere • thermosphere
- ionosphere • exosphere
- ↻ **Identify Supporting Evidence**
- △ **Interpret Data**

LESSON 4
- electromagnetic waves
- radiation • infrared radiation
- ultraviolet radiation • scattering
- greenhouse effect
- ↻ **Ask Questions**
- △ **Graph**

LESSON 5
- temperature • thermal energy
- thermometer • heat
- convection • conduction
- convection currents
- ↻ **Identify the Main Idea**
- △ **Infer**

LESSON 6
- wind • anemometer
- windchill factor • local winds
- sea breeze • land breeze
- global winds • Coriolis effect
- latitude
- ↻ **Identify Supporting Evidence**
- △ **Draw Conclusions**

LESSON

1 The Air Around You

- What Is the Composition of Earth's Atmosphere?

- How Is the Atmosphere a System?

MY PLANET DIARY

VOICES FROM HISTORY

Antoine Lavoisier

French chemist Antoine Lavoisier was determined to solve a puzzle: How could a metal burned to a powder weigh more than the original metal? In his 1772 lab notes he observed, "Sulphur, in burning . . . gains weight." So did mercury. Lavoisier thought a gas in the air was combining with the mercury as it burned, making it heavier. Then he heated the mercury powder to a higher temperature. It turned back to liquid mercury and a gas. Lavoisier observed that a mouse exposed to the gas could breathe it. He named the gas *principe oxygine*. Today we call it oxygen.

Discuss Lavoisier's experiment with a partner and answer the question below.

Why do you think Lavoisier exposed a mouse to the gas he collected from the mercury?

_____

_____

_____

> PLANET DIARY Go to **Planet Diary** to learn more about air.

 Do the Inquiry Warm-Up *How Long Will the Candle Burn?*

What Is the Composition of Earth's Atmosphere?

The sun disappears behind thick, dark clouds. In the distance you see a bright flash. Then you hear a crack of thunder. You make it home just as the downpour begins. The weather changed quickly—that was close!

Weather is the condition of Earth's atmosphere at a particular time and place. But what is the atmosphere? Earth's **atmosphere** (AT muh sfeer) is the envelope of gases that surrounds the planet. **Earth's atmosphere consists of nitrogen, oxygen, carbon dioxide, water vapor, and other gases, as well as particles of liquids and solids.**

Vocabulary
- weather   • atmosphere
- water vapor

Skills
- Reading: Summarize
- Inquiry: Infer

Nitrogen   The most abundant gas in the atmosphere is nitrogen. It makes up a little more than three fourths of the air we breathe. Nitrogen occurs in all living things and makes up about 3 percent of the weight of the human body.

Oxygen   Although oxygen is the second most abundant gas in the atmosphere, it makes up only about 21 percent of the volume. Plants and animals take oxygen directly from the air and use it to release energy from their food.

Oxygen is also involved in many other processes. A fire uses oxygen rapidly as it burns. Without oxygen, a fire will go out. Some processes use oxygen more slowly. Steel in cars and other objects reacts slowly with oxygen to form iron oxide, or rust.

Carbon Dioxide   Carbon dioxide makes up much less than 1 percent of the atmosphere, but it is essential to life. Plants must have carbon dioxide to produce food. The cells of animals break down food and give off carbon dioxide as a waste product.

When fuels like coal and gasoline are burned, they also release carbon dioxide. Burning these fuels increases the amount of carbon dioxide in the atmosphere.

Other Gases   Oxygen and nitrogen together make up 99 percent of dry air. Argon makes up most of the other 1 percent. The remaining gases are called trace gases because only small amounts of them are present.

FIGURE 1 ·······························
Gases in the Air
The atmosphere is a thin layer of gases.

✎ Graph Identify which circle graph shows the correct percentage of gases in the atmosphere. Shade in the key and the graph. Give your graph a title.

Key
☐ Nitrogen
☐ Oxygen
☐ Other gases

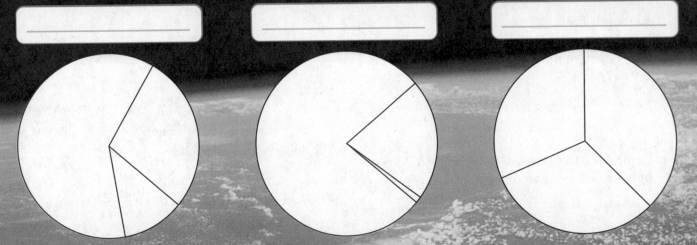

75

apply it!

The amount of water vapor in the air can differ from place to place.

1 There is more water vapor in the (desert/ rain forest) than in the (desert/rain forest).

2 Infer What evidence do you see for your answer to Question 1?

_____

_____

_____

_____

3 CHALLENGE What factors might affect the amount of water vapor in the air?

_____

_____

_____

Water Vapor So far, we've discussed the composition of dry air. But in reality, air is not dry. Air contains **water vapor**—water in the form of a gas. Water vapor is invisible. It is not the same thing as steam, which is made up of tiny droplets of liquid water.

The amount of water vapor in the air varies greatly from place to place and from time to time. Water vapor plays an important role in Earth's weather. Clouds form when water vapor condenses out of the air to form tiny droplets of liquid water or crystals of ice. If these droplets or crystals become heavy enough, they fall as rain or snow.

Particles Pure air contains only gases. But pure air exists only in laboratories. In the real world, air contains tiny solid and liquid particles of dust, smoke, salt, and chemicals. You can see some of these particles in the air around you, but most of them are too small to see.

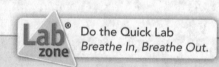
Lab zone
Do the Quick Lab
Breathe In, Breathe Out.

Assess Your Understanding

1a. Define The _____ is the envelope of _____ that surrounds Earth.

b. List What are the four most common gases in dry air?

_____

_____

c. Compare and Contrast What is the difference between wet air and dry air?

_____

_____

got it?

○ I get it! Now I know that the atmosphere is made up of _____

_____

_____

_____

○ I need extra help with _____

_____

Go to MY SCIENCE COACH online for help with this subject.

How Is the Atmosphere a System?

The atmosphere is a system that interacts with other Earth systems, such as the ocean. The atmosphere has many different parts. Some of these parts you can actually see, such as clouds. But most parts of the atmosphere—like air, wind, and energy—you can't see. Instead, you might feel a wind when it blows on you. Or you might feel energy from the sun warming your face on a cool winter day.

At first, the wind that blows and the heat you feel may seem unrelated. But as you'll learn, the different parts of the atmosphere interact with one another. **Events in one part of the atmosphere affect other parts of the atmosphere.**

Energy from the sun drives the motions in the atmosphere. A storm such as the hurricane in **Figure 2,** involves a tremendous amount of energy. The spiraling shape of a hurricane is due in part to forces resulting from Earth's rotation. A hurricane also gains energy from warm ocean water. Since the ocean water is warmed by the sun, a hurricane's energy comes mostly from the sun.

Summarize Write a short summary of the third paragraph.

_____

_____

_____

_____

_____

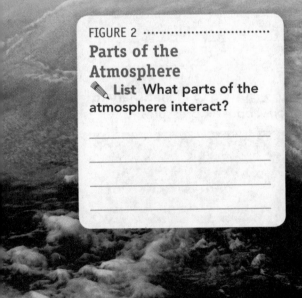

FIGURE 2 ....

Parts of the Atmosphere

✏ **List** What parts of the atmosphere interact?

_____

_____

_____

_____

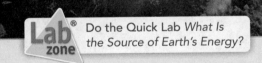

Do the Quick Lab *What Is the Source of Earth's Energy?*

Assess Your Understanding

got it? ....

○ I get it! Now I know that events in one part of the atmosphere _____

_____

○ I need extra help with _____

Go to MY SCIENCE ⓢ COACH online for help with this subject.

Air Pressure

🔑 **What Are Some Properties of Air?**

🔑 **What Instruments Measure Air Pressure?**

🔑 **How Does Altitude Affect Air Pressure and Density?**

MY PLANET DiARY

DISCOVERY

Flying High

Astronauts aren't the only people who go into space. High-altitude pilots who fly above 15,250 meters are in a zone with conditions similar to deep space. At these heights, air pressure is so low that blood can boil. A pilot can also pass out in less than a minute from lack of oxygen. To survive, pilots wear pressure suits. These suits weigh about 16 kilograms and are custom-built for each pilot. They inflate in an emergency, keeping air pressure stable for the pilot. The suits are "very, very restrictive," says pilot David Wright. "But it saves your life, so you're able to put up with that."

Discuss your answer with a classmate.
Pilots wear pressure suits in addition to flying in a pressurized plane. Why do you think this is so?

_____

_____

_____

▶ PLANET DIARY Go to **Planet Diary** to learn more about air pressure.

Lab zone® Do the Inquiry Warm-Up _Does Air Have Mass?_

What Are Some Properties of Air?

How do you know air exists? You can't see it. Instead, you have to understand what air does. It may seem to you that air has no mass. But the air in the atmosphere consists of atoms and molecules, which have mass. 🔑 **Because air has mass, it also has other properties, including density and pressure.**

Vocabulary
- density • air pressure
- barometer • mercury barometer
- aneroid barometer • altitude

Skills
🔁 Reading: Relate Cause and Effect
△ Inquiry: Develop Hypotheses

Density The amount of mass in a given volume of air is its **density.** You calculate the density of a substance by dividing its mass by its volume. If there are more molecules in a given volume, the density is greater. If there are fewer molecules, the density is less.

Pressure The atmosphere is heavy. Its weight exerts a force on surfaces like you. The force pushing on an area or surface is called pressure. **Air pressure** is the result of the weight of a column of air pushing on an area.

As **Figure 1** shows, there is a column of air above you that extends all the way up through the entire atmosphere. In fact, the weight of the column of air above your desk is about the same as the weight of a large school bus. So why doesn't air pressure crush your desk? The reason is that the molecules in air push in all directions—down, up, and sideways. The air pushing down on top of your desk is balanced by the air pushing up on the bottom of your desk.

FIGURE 1 ································
Air Column
The weight of the column of air above you puts pressure on you.

✎ **Answer the questions below.**

1. **Describe** What's an air column?

_____

_____

2. **Apply Concepts** Add arrows to the diagram below to indicate how the pressure from air molecules keeps you from being crushed.

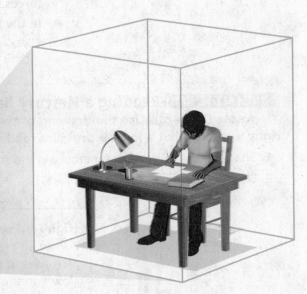

Do the Quick Lab
Properties of Air.

🔑 Assess Your Understanding

got it? ···

○ I get it! Now I know that air has properties such as _____

_____

○ I need extra help with _____

Go to **my science** 🅢 **coach** *online for help with this subject.*

What Instruments Measure Air Pressure?

Air pressure can change daily. A denser substance has more mass per unit volume than a less dense one. So denser air exerts more pressure than less dense air. A **barometer** (buh RAHM uh tur) is an instrument that is used to measure air pressure. ⟐ **The two common kinds of barometers are mercury barometers and aneroid barometers.**

Mercury Barometers Look at **Figure 2** to see a mercury barometer model. A **mercury barometer** consists of a long glass tube that is closed at one end and open at the other. The open end of the tube rests in a dish of mercury. The closed end of the tube is almost a vacuum—the space above the mercury contains very little air. The air pressing down on the surface of the mercury in the dish is equal to the pressure exerted by the weight of the column of mercury in the tube. When the air pressure increases, it presses down more on the surface of the mercury. Greater air pressure forces the column of mercury higher. So, the level of the mercury in the tube shows you the pressure of the air that day.

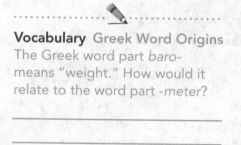

Vocabulary Greek Word Origins The Greek word part *baro-* means "weight." How would it relate to the word part *-meter*?

_____

_____

_____

FIGURE 2 ···

> INTERACTIVE ART **Reading a Mercury Barometer**

✎ **Apply Concepts** Use the drawing of the barometer on the right to show what a low air pressure reading looks like.

1. Shade in the level of the mercury in the tube and in the dish.
2. Describe what is happening.

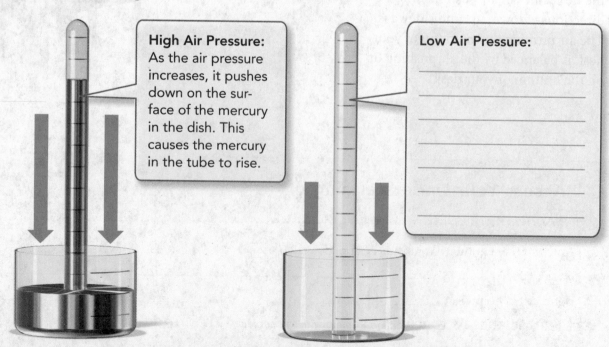

High Air Pressure: As the air pressure increases, it pushes down on the surface of the mercury in the dish. This causes the mercury in the tube to rise.

Low Air Pressure:

_____

_____

_____

_____

_____

Aneroid Barometers

If you have a barometer at home, it's probably an aneroid barometer. The word *aneroid* means "without liquid." An **aneroid barometer** (AN uh royd) has an airtight metal chamber, as shown in **Figure 3**. The metal chamber is sensitive to changes in air pressure. When air pressure increases, the thin walls of the chamber are pushed in. When the pressure drops, the walls bulge out. The chamber is connected to a dial by a series of springs and levers. As the shape of the chamber changes, the needle on the dial moves.

Units of Air Pressure

Weather reports use several different units for air pressure. Most weather reports for the general public use inches of mercury. For example, if the column of mercury in a mercury barometer is 30 inches high, the air pressure is "30 inches of mercury" or "30 inches."

National Weather Service maps indicate air pressure in millibars. The pressure of the atmosphere is equal to one bar. One inch of mercury is about 33.86 millibars, so 30 inches of mercury is equal to about 1,016 millibars.

FIGURE 3 ·······························

Inside an Aneroid Barometer

An aneroid barometer has an airtight metal chamber, shown in red, below.

✎ **Identify** Label the diagram that shows the aneroid barometer under high pressure and the diagram that shows it under low pressure.

Lab zone® Do the Quick Lab
Soda Bottle Barometer.

⊐ Assess Your Understanding

1a. Name What two instruments are commonly used to measure air pressure?

_____

_____

b. Identify What units are used to measure air pressure?

_____

_____

c. CHALLENGE How many millibars are equal to 27.23 inches of mercury?

_____

_____

got it? ···································

○ **I get it!** Now I know that air pressure can be measured _____

_____

○ **I need extra help with** _____

Go to MY SCIENCE ⁵ COACH online for help with this subject.

How Does Altitude Affect Air Pressure and Density?

The higher you hike on a mountain, the more changes you'll notice. The temperature will drop, and the plants will get smaller. But you might not notice another change that is happening. At the top of the mountain, the air pressure is less than the air pressure at sea level—the average level of the oceans. **Altitude,** or elevation, is the distance above sea level. 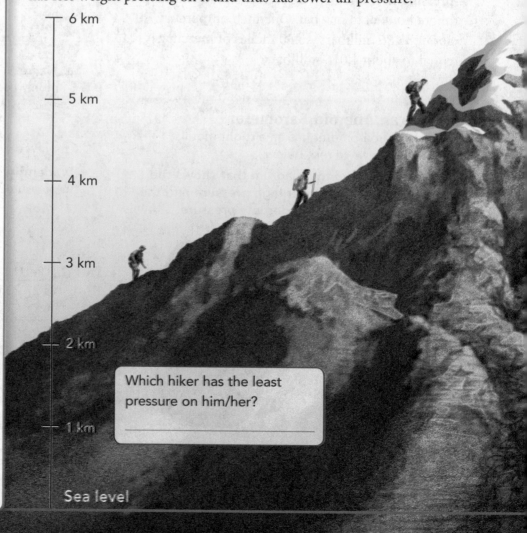 **Air pressure decreases as altitude increases. As air pressure decreases, so does density.**

Altitude Affects Air Pressure Suppose you have a stack of books. Which book has more weight on it, the second book from the top or the book at the bottom? The second book from the top has the weight of only one book on top of it. The book at the bottom of the stack has the weight of all the books pressing on it.

Air at sea level is like the bottom book. Sea-level air has the weight of the whole atmosphere pressing on it. Air near the top of the atmosphere is like the second book from the top. There, the air has less weight pressing on it and thus has lower air pressure.

apply it!

You're back from a high-altitude hike. As you empty your bag, you notice that the two empty bottles you carried down from the mountain look different.

1 Observe What observations can you make about the bottles?

_____

_____

_____

2 Develop Hypotheses What's a possible explanation for your observations?

_____

_____

_____

_____

_____

_____

_____

- 6 km
- 5 km
- 4 km
- 3 km
- 2 km

Which hiker has the least pressure on him/her?

_____

- 1 km

Sea level

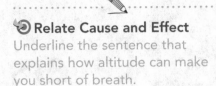

Altitude Also Affects Density

As you go up through the atmosphere, the density of the air decreases. This means the gas molecules that make up the atmosphere are farther apart at high altitudes than they are at sea level. If you were near the top of a tall mountain and tried to run, you would quickly get out of breath. Why? The air contains 21 percent oxygen, whether you are at sea level or on top of a mountain. However, since the air is less dense at a high altitude, each cubic meter of air you breathe has fewer oxygen molecules than at sea level. So you would become short of breath more quickly at a high altitude.

⊃ Relate Cause and Effect
Underline the sentence that explains how altitude can make you short of breath.

FIGURE 4 ....

> VIRTUAL LAB **Effect of Altitude on Pressure and Density**

✎ **Complete the activities below.**

1. **Relate Evidence and Explanation** Draw the air column above each hiker on the mountain. Then answer the question below the hikers.

2. **Make Models** In the empty circles below, draw how densely packed you think the molecules would be at the altitudes shown.

Lab zone ® Do the Quick Lab *Effects of Altitude on the Atmosphere.*

🗝 Assess Your Understanding

2a. Define What is altitude?

_____

b. Summarize How does air pressure change as altitude increases?

_____

_____

c. Predict What changes in air pressure would you expect if you carried a barometer down a mine shaft?

_____

_____

_____

_____

got it? ....

○ I get it! Now I know the properties of air

_____

_____

○ I need extra help with _____

_____

Go to my science ⓢ **COACH** *online for help with this subject.*

LESSON

3 Layers of the Atmosphere

UNLOCK THE BIG **?**

🔑 What Are the Four Main Layers of the Atmosphere?

🔑 What Are the Characteristics of the Atmosphere's Layers?

my planet diary

Earth's Atmosphere

Misconception: The blanket of gases that makes up Earth's atmosphere is thick.

Fact: Earth's atmosphere extends far out into space, at least as far again as the radius of Earth. However, most of the atmosphere is so thin that it would be hard to tell it apart from the vacuum of space. Most of the gas in the atmosphere is found close to Earth's surface. In fact, half of the gas in the atmosphere is found in the bottom 5.5 kilometers—the height of a tall mountain! The rest of the gas extends thinly out into space for thousands of kilometers.

Evidence: The mass of the atmosphere is surprisingly small. In fact, a thin column of air 1 cm² extending out into space for thousands of kilometers has about the same mass as a 1-liter bottle of water.

MISCONCEPTION

Talk about these questions with a classmate and then record your answers.

1. Where is most of the gas in the atmosphere found?

_____

_____

_____

2. Why do you think that people think of the atmosphere as a thick layer around Earth?

_____

_____

▶ PLANET DIARY Go to **Planet Diary** to learn more about layers of the atmosphere.

  Do the Inquiry Warm-Up *Is Air There?*

Vocabulary
- troposphere
- stratosphere
- mesosphere
- thermosphere
- ionosphere
- exosphere

Skills
- Reading: Identify Supporting Evidence
- Inquiry: Interpret Data

What Are the Four Main Layers of the Atmosphere?

Imagine taking a trip upward into the atmosphere in a hot-air balloon. You begin on a warm beach near the ocean, at an altitude of 0 kilometers above sea level.

You hear a roar as the balloon's pilot turns up the burner to heat the air in the balloon. The balloon begins to rise, and Earth's surface gets farther away. As the balloon reaches an altitude of 3 kilometers, you realize the air is getting colder. At 6 kilometers you begin to have trouble breathing. The air is becoming less dense. It's time to go back down.

Six kilometers is pretty high. In fact, it's higher than all but the very tallest mountains. But there are still hundreds of kilometers of atmosphere above you. It may seem as though air is the same from the ground to the edge of space. But air pressure and temperature change with altitude. 🔑 **Scientists divide Earth's atmosphere into four main layers classified according to changes in temperature. These layers are the troposphere, the stratosphere, the mesosphere, and the thermosphere.**

✏️ **Identify Supporting Evidence**
Underline the evidence in the text above that explains how the atmosphere changes as you go up in a hot-air balloon.

Lab zone® Do the Quick Lab *Layers of the Atmosphere.*

🔑 Assess Your Understanding

got it? ....

○ **I get it!** Now I know that the atmosphere has four main layers: _____

_____

○ **I need extra help with** _____

Go to MY SCIENCE 🔵 COACH *online for help with this subject.*

85

What Are the Characteristics of the Atmosphere's Layers?

Unless you become an astronaut, you won't make a trip to the upper atmosphere. But if you could make that journey, what would you see? Read on to learn more about the conditions you would experience in each layer of the atmosphere.

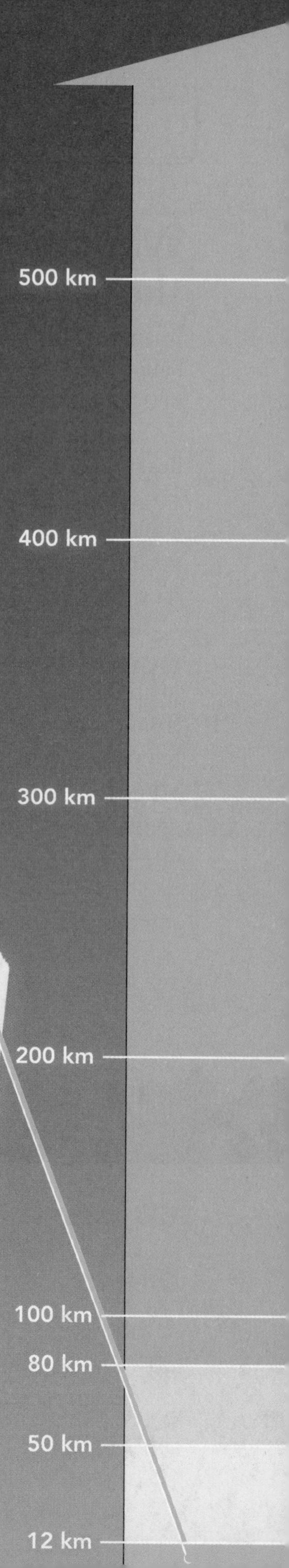

The Troposphere You live in the inner, or lowest, layer of Earth's atmosphere, the **troposphere** (TROH puh sfeer). *Tropo-* means "turning" or "changing." Conditions in the troposphere are more variable than in the other layers. 🔑 **The troposphere is the layer of the atmosphere in which Earth's weather occurs.** The troposphere is about 12 kilometers thick, as you can see in **Figure 1.** However, it varies from 16 kilometers thick above the equator to less than 9 kilometers thick above the North and South poles. Although it's the shallowest layer, the troposphere is the most dense. It contains almost all the mass of the atmosphere.

As altitude increases in the troposphere, the temperature decreases. On average, for every 1-kilometer increase in altitude, the air gets about 6.5°C cooler. At the top of the troposphere, the temperature stops decreasing and stays at about −60°C. Water here forms thin, feathery clouds of ice.

FIGURE 1 ·······································

The Atmosphere Layers
✏️ Observe Use the journal pages in this lesson to record your observations of the layers of the atmosphere.

Altitude _____

Temperature _____
_____

Observations _____
_____
_____
_____

500 km ——

400 km ——

300 km ——

200 km ——

100 km ——
80 km ——

50 km ——

12 km ——

— 500 km

— 400 km

— 300 km

— 200 km

— 100 km

— 80 km

— 50 km

— 12 km

The Stratosphere

The **stratosphere** extends from the top of the troposphere to about 50 kilometers above Earth's surface. *Strato-* means "layer" or "spread out." 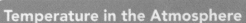 **The stratosphere is the second layer of the atmosphere and contains the ozone layer.**

The lower stratosphere is cold, about –60°C. Surprisingly, the upper stratosphere is warmer than the lower stratosphere. Why is this? The middle portion of the stratosphere has a layer of air where there is much more ozone than in the rest of the atmosphere. Ozone is a form of oxygen that has three atoms in each molecule instead of the usual two. When ozone absorbs energy from the sun, the energy is converted into heat, warming the air. The ozone layer protects living things from ultraviolet radiation from the sun.

Altitude _____

Temperature _____

Observations _____

_____

_____

do the math!

Changing Temperatures

The graph shows how temperatures in the atmosphere change with altitude. Use it to answer the questions below.

1 Read Graphs What is the temperature at the bottom of the stratosphere?

_____

2 Interpret Data What layer of the atmosphere has the lowest temperature?

_____

3 CHALLENGE How does temperature change with altitude in the troposphere?

_____

_____

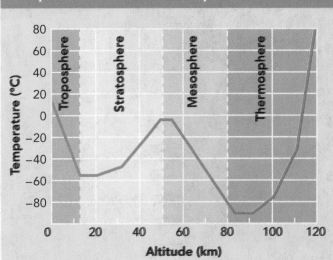

Temperature in the Atmosphere

87

Particles from the sun strike atoms in the ionosphere near the poles. This causes brilliant light displays called auroras.

The Mesosphere

Above the stratosphere, a drop in temperature marks the beginning of the next layer, the **mesosphere.** *Meso-* means "middle," so the mesosphere is the middle layer of the atmosphere. The mesosphere begins 50 kilometers above Earth's surface and ends at an altitude of 80 kilometers. In the upper mesosphere, temperatures approach –90°C.

The mesosphere is the layer of the atmosphere that protects Earth's surface from being hit by most meteoroids. Meteoroids are chunks of stone and metal from space. What you see as a shooting star, or meteor, is the trail of hot, glowing gases the meteoroid leaves behind in the mesosphere as it burns up.

Altitude _____

Temperature _____

_____

Observations _____

500 km

400 km

300 km

200 km

100 km

80 km

50 km

12 km

The Thermosphere

Near the top of the atmosphere, the air is very thin. **The outermost layer of Earth's atmosphere is the thermosphere.** The **thermosphere** extends from 80 kilometers above Earth's surface outward into space. It has no definite outer limit.

Heat in the Thermosphere Sunlight strikes the thermosphere first, making the air very hot, up to 1,800°C. You wouldn't feel warm though. Temperature is the average amount of energy of motion of each molecule of a substance. Gas molecules in this layer move fast, so the temperature is very high. But the molecules are spaced far apart in the thin air, so there aren't enough to collide with you and warm you.

Layers in the Thermosphere The thermosphere has two layers. The lower layer, the **ionosphere** (eye AHN uh sfeer), begins about 80 kilometers above the surface and extends to about 400 kilometers. The **exosphere** is the outer layer. It extends from about 400 kilometers outward for thousands of kilometers.

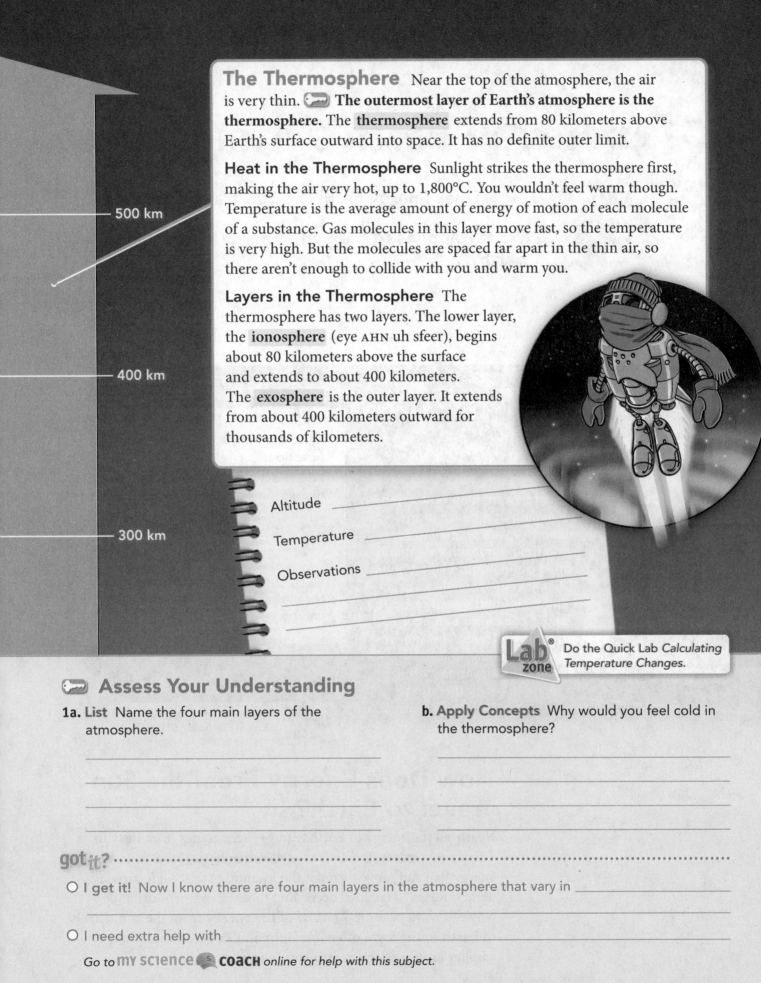

500 km

400 km

300 km

Altitude _____

Temperature _____

Observations _____

_____

_____

Lab® zone Do the Quick Lab *Calculating Temperature Changes.*

Assess Your Understanding

1a. List Name the four main layers of the atmosphere.

_____
_____
_____
_____

b. Apply Concepts Why would you feel cold in the thermosphere?

_____
_____
_____
_____

got it? ....

○ **I get it!** Now I know there are four main layers in the atmosphere that vary in _____
_____

○ I need extra help with _____

Go to MY SCIENCE COACH online for help with this subject.

Energy in Earth's Atmosphere

UNLOCK
THE BIG

🔑 How Does Energy From the Sun Travel to Earth?

🔑 What Happens to the Sun's Energy When It Reaches Earth?

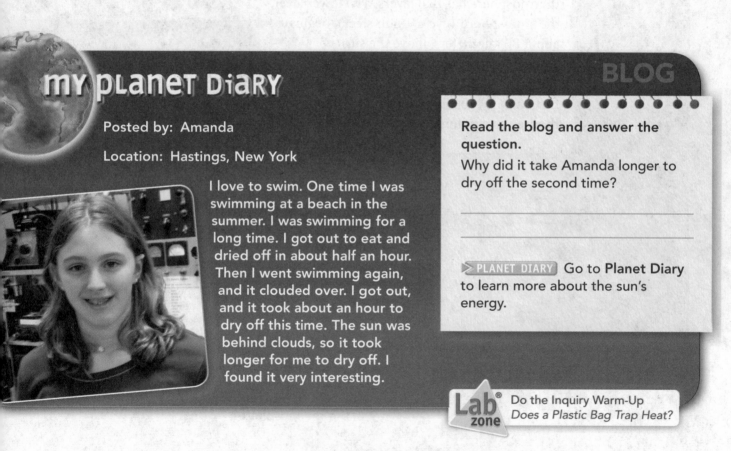

MY PLANET DIARY

BLOG

Posted by: Amanda

Location: Hastings, New York

I love to swim. One time I was swimming at a beach in the summer. I was swimming for a long time. I got out to eat and dried off in about half an hour. Then I went swimming again, and it clouded over. I got out, and it took about an hour to dry off this time. The sun was behind clouds, so it took longer for me to dry off. I found it very interesting.

Read the blog and answer the question.

Why did it take Amanda longer to dry off the second time?

_____

_____

> PLANET DIARY Go to Planet Diary to learn more about the sun's energy.

Lab® Do the Inquiry Warm-Up
zone Does a Plastic Bag Trap Heat?

How Does Energy From the Sun Travel to Earth?

Nearly all the energy in Earth's atmosphere comes from the sun. This energy travels to Earth as **electromagnetic waves,** a form of energy that can move through the vacuum of space. Electromagnetic waves are classified according to wavelength, or distance between wave peaks. 🔑 **Most of the energy from the sun travels to Earth in the form of visible light and infrared radiation. A smaller amount arrives as ultraviolet radiation.**

Vocabulary
- electromagnetic waves
- radiation
- infrared radiation
- ultraviolet radiation
- scattering
- greenhouse effect

Skills
- Reading: Ask Questions
- Inquiry: Graph

Visible Light Visible light includes all of the colors that you see in a rainbow: red, orange, yellow, green, blue, and violet. The different colors are the result of different wavelengths. Red and orange light have the longest wavelengths, while blue and violet light have the shortest wavelengths, as shown in **Figure 1**.

Nonvisible Radiation The direct transfer of energy by electromagnetic waves is called **radiation.** One form of electromagnetic energy, **infrared radiation,** has wavelengths that are longer than wavelengths for red light. Infrared radiation is not visible by humans, but can be felt as heat. The sun also gives off **ultraviolet radiation,** which is an invisible form of energy with wavelengths that are shorter than wavelengths for violet light. Ultraviolet radiation can cause sunburns.

FIGURE 1 ······················

Radiation From the Sun
Energy travels to Earth as electromagnetic waves.

✎ **Identify** Label the types of electromagnetic radiation in the diagram.

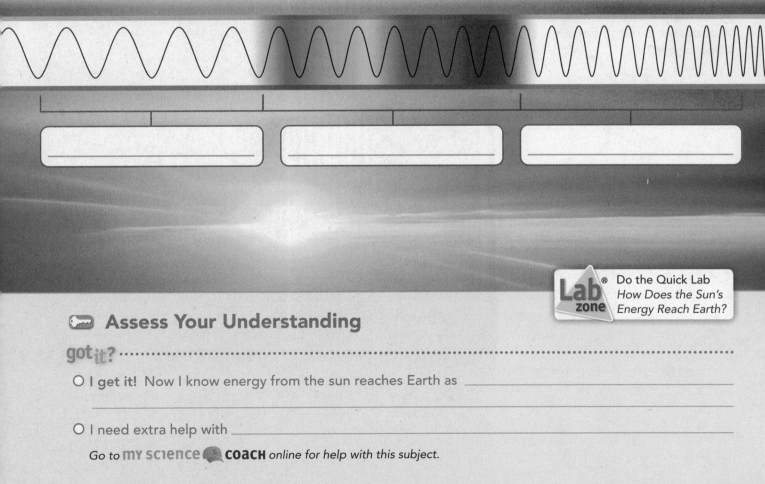

Lab zone ® Do the Quick Lab
How Does the Sun's Energy Reach Earth?

⌕ Assess Your Understanding

got it? ··

○ I get it! Now I know energy from the sun reaches Earth as _____

_____

○ I need extra help with _____

Go to **my science** ⬤ **COACH** online for help with this subject.

What Happens to the Sun's Energy When It Reaches Earth?

Sunlight must pass through the atmosphere before it reaches Earth's surface. The path of the sun's rays is shown in **Figure 2**. 🔑 **Some sunlight is absorbed or reflected by the atmosphere before it can reach the surface. The rest passes through the atmosphere to the surface.**

Upper Atmosphere Different wavelengths of radiation are absorbed by different layers in the atmosphere. For example, some ultraviolet radiation is absorbed by the ozone layer in the stratosphere. Infrared radiation penetrates farther into the atmosphere before some of it is absorbed by water vapor and carbon dioxide.

FIGURE 2 ....

Energy in the Atmosphere
Some wavelengths reach Earth's surface. Other wavelengths are completely or partially absorbed in the atmosphere.

✎ **Compare and Contrast**
What happens to the radiation as it passes through Earth's atmosphere?

_____

_____

_____

_____

_____

_____

_____

_____

_____

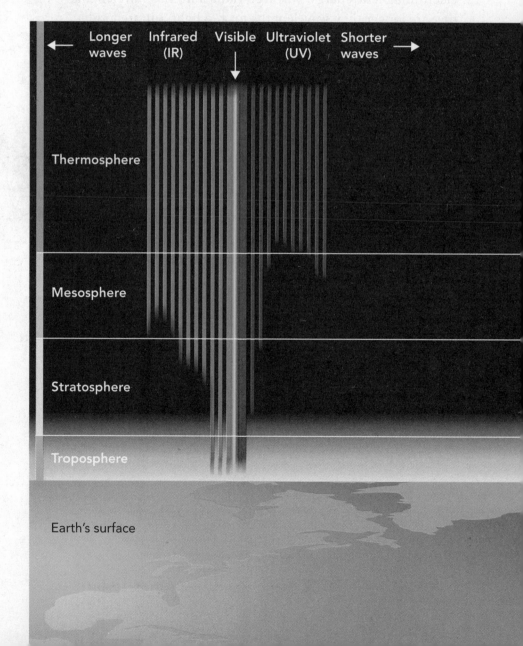

Longer waves ←   Infrared (IR)   Visible   Ultraviolet (UV)   Shorter waves →

Thermosphere

Mesosphere

Stratosphere

Troposphere

Earth's surface

Troposphere Clouds act as mirrors, reflecting sunlight back into space. Dust-size particles and gases in the atmosphere disperse light in all directions, a process called **scattering.** When you look at the sky, the light you see has been scattered by gas molecules in the atmosphere. Gas molecules scatter short wavelengths of visible light (blue and violet) more than long wavelengths (red and orange). Scattered light looks bluer than ordinary sunlight. That's why the clear daytime sky looks blue.

Earth's Surface It may seem like a lot of the sun's energy is absorbed by gases in the atmosphere or reflected by clouds and particles. However, about 50 percent of the energy that reaches Earth's surface is absorbed by land and water and changed into heat. Look at **Figure 3** to see what happens to incoming sunlight at Earth's surface.

⟲ **Ask Questions** Before you read, preview the headings on these two pages. Ask a question you'd like to have answered. After you read, answer your question.

_____

_____

_____

_____

_____

_____

apply it!

The materials at Earth's surface shown below reflect different amounts of energy.

① ⟁ **Graph** Use the higher percentages below to draw a bar graph. Give it a title.

② Based on your graph, which material reflects the most sunlight? Which absorbs the most?

_____

③ **CHALLENGE** Predict what might happen if a forested area was replaced with an asphalt parking lot.

_____

_____

_____

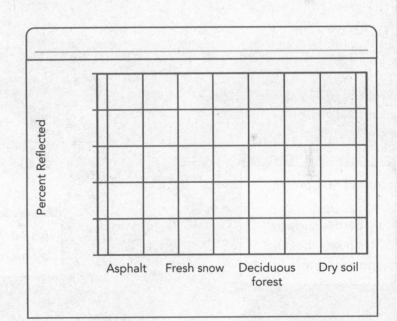

Percent Reflected

Asphalt   Fresh snow   Deciduous forest   Dry soil

Asphalt
5–10% reflected

Fresh snow
80–90% reflected

Deciduous forest
15–20% reflected

Dry soil
20–25% reflected

FIGURE 3

Energy at Earth's Surface

✎ **Identify** What's happening to energy in the lower atmosphere and at Earth's surface? Find out by using the words in the word bank below to complete each sentence.

Word Bank

reflected   absorbed   radiated

Words may be used more than once.

✎ **Draw Conclusions** Using the diagram below, draw a conclusion about energy at Earth's surface.

_____

_____

_____

About 25 percent of incoming sunlight is _____ by clouds, dust, and gases in the atmosphere.

About 50 percent is _____ by Earth's surface. This heats the land and the water.

About 20 percent is _____ by gases and particles in the atmosphere.

Some absorbed energy is _____ back into the atmosphere.

About 5 percent is _____ by the surface back into the atmosphere.

Earth's Energy Budget

What happens to the energy that heats the land and water? Earth's surface radiates some energy back into the atmosphere as infrared radiation. Much of this infrared radiation doesn't immediately travel all the way back into space. Instead, it's absorbed by water vapor, carbon dioxide, methane, and other gases in the air. The energy from the absorbed radiation heats the gases in the air. These gases in turn hold heat in Earth's atmosphere in a process called the **greenhouse effect.**

The greenhouse effect, shown in **Figure 4,** is a natural process. It keeps Earth's atmosphere at a temperature that is comfortable for most living things. Over time, the amount of energy absorbed by the atmosphere and Earth's surface is in balance with the amount of energy radiated into space. In this way, Earth's average temperatures remain fairly constant. But scientists have evidence that human activities may be altering this process.

FIGURE 4 ·······················

> **ART IN MOTION** **Greenhouse Effect**

The greenhouse effect is a natural heat-trapping process.

✎ **Sequence** Number each step in the diagram to show how the greenhouse effect takes place. Discuss the diagram with a partner.

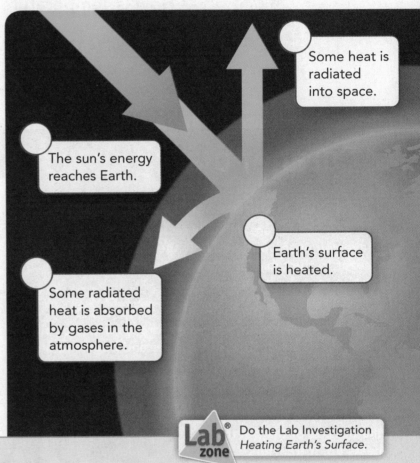

Some heat is radiated into space.

The sun's energy reaches Earth.

Earth's surface is heated.

Some radiated heat is absorbed by gases in the atmosphere.

Lab zone® Do the Lab Investigation *Heating Earth's Surface.*

Assess Your Understanding

1a. Summarize What happens to most of the sunlight that reaches Earth?

_____

b. Interpret Diagrams In **Figure 3,** what percentage of incoming sunlight is reflected by clouds, dust, and gases in the atmosphere?

_____

c. Predict How might conditions on Earth be different without the greenhouse effect?

_____
_____
_____
_____

got**it?** ·······················

○ **I get it!** Now I know some energy _____
_____

○ **I need extra help with** _____

Go to MY SCIENCE ⓢ COACH online for help with this subject.

Heat Transfer

UNLOCK THE BIG ?

🔑 **How Is Temperature Measured?**

🔑 **How Is Heat Transferred?**

my planeT DiaRY

SCIENCE IN THE KITCHEN

From the Freezer to the Table

French fries are on many restaurant menus. But have you ever wondered how they get from the freezer to the table? It takes a little science in the kitchen to make it happen.

First, you heat oil in a fryer until it's around 340°F. Then, the frozen potato slices are dropped in. Hot oil moves from the bottom of the fryer and begins to heat the potatoes. Exposure to so much heat causes the water in the potatoes to boil. This is indicated by bubbles rising to the surface of the oil. As the outside of the potato heats up, it transfers heat to the inside of the potato slice. In a matter of minutes it's crunchy on the outside and soft on the inside.

Answer the following question and discuss it with a partner.

Explain in your own words what happens when the potatoes are exposed to heat.

_____

_____

_____

▷ PLANET DIARY Go to **Planet Diary** to learn more about heat transfer.

Lab zone ® Do the Inquiry Warm-Up What Happens When Air Is Heated?

How Is Temperature Measured?

All substances are made up of tiny particles (atoms and molecules) that are constantly moving. The faster the particles are moving, the more energy they have. **Temperature** is the *average* amount of energy of motion of each particle of a substance. In **Figure 1**, the hot tea in the teapot is the same temperature as the hot tea in the teacup. But do they have the same thermal energy?

Vocabulary
- temperature
- thermal energy
- thermometer
- heat
- convection
- conduction
- convection currents

Skills
- Reading: Identify the Main Idea
- Inquiry: Infer

Thermal energy measures the *total* energy of motion in the particles of a substance. This means that the tea in the pot has more thermal energy than the tea in the cup because it has more mass.

Measuring Temperature
Temperature is an important factor affecting weather. **Air temperature is usually measured with a thermometer.** A **thermometer** is a device that measures temperature. Some thermometers have a thin glass tube with a bulb on one end that holds liquid mercury or colored alcohol. When the air temperature increases, the temperature of the liquid in the bulb increases. This causes the liquid to expand and rise up the column.

Temperature Scales
Temperature is measured in units called degrees. Two temperature scales are the Celsius scale and the Fahrenheit scale. On the Celsius scale at sea level, the freezing point of water is 0°C, while the boiling point is 100°C. On the Fahrenheit scale at sea level, the freezing point of water is 32°F and the boiling point is 212°F. To convert from Farenheit to Celsius, you would use the following formula:

$$\frac{Fahrenheit - 32}{1.8} = Celsius$$

FIGURE 1 ....

Measuring Temperature

✎ Read and then answer the questions.

1. **Review** Circle the correct word in this sentence: The tea in the cup has (the same/less/more) thermal energy than the tea in the pot.

2. **Calculate** If the tea in the cup cooled to 70°F, what would a Celsius thermometer read?

_____

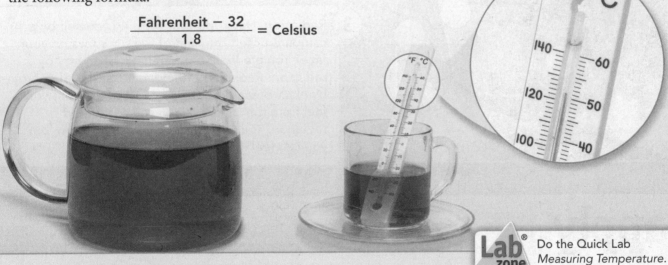

Lab® zone Do the Quick Lab
Measuring Temperature.

🔑 Assess Your Understanding

got it? ....

○ **I get it!** Now I know that temperature and thermal energy are different because _____

_____

○ **I need extra help with** _____

Go to MY SCIENCE ⑤ COACH online for help with this subject.

How Is Heat Transferred?

Heat is thermal energy that is transferred from a hotter object to a cooler one. 🔑 Heat is transferred in three ways: convection, conduction, and radiation.

1 **Convection** In fluids (liquids and gases), atoms and molecules can move easily from one place to another. As they move, their energy moves along with them. The transfer of heat by the movement of a fluid is called **convection.**

2 **Conduction** The transfer of heat between two substances that are in direct contact is called **conduction.** In **Figure 2,** heat is being conducted between the pot and the grate and between the pot and the liquid. When a fast-moving molecule bumps into a slower-moving molecule, the faster molecule transfers some of its energy to the slower one. The closer together the molecules are in a substance, the better they conduct heat. Conduction works well in some solids, such as metals, but not as well in liquids and gases. Air and water do not conduct heat well.

3 **Radiation** Have you ever warmed yourself by a campfire or felt the heat of the sun's rays on your face? You are feeling the transfer of energy by radiation. Radiation is the direct transfer of energy by electromagnetic waves. Most of the heat you feel from the sun travels to you as infrared radiation. You cannot see infrared radiation, but you can feel it as heat.

FIGURE 2 ·····················
Heat Transfer
✏️ Identify Use the numbers provided in the text to identify each type of heat transfer in the photo.

apply it!

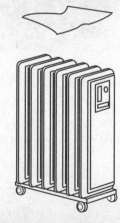

Heat transfer occurs when a warm radiator heats a room.

⚠️ **Infer** What type of heat transfer could keep the paper in the air? Draw arrows on the image to indicate your answer and explain below.

_____

_____

_____

Heating the Troposphere

Heating the Troposphere Radiation, conduction, and convection work together to heat the troposphere. Notice in **Figure 3** how the sun's radiation heats Earth's surface during the day. The land gets warmer than the air. Air doesn't conduct heat well. So only the first few meters of the troposphere are heated by conduction. When ground-level air warms up, its molecules move more rapidly. As they bump into each other they move farther apart, making the air less dense. Cooler, denser air sinks toward the surface, forcing the warmer air to rise. The upward movement of warm air and the downward movement of cool air form convection currents. **Heat is transferred mostly by convection within the troposphere.**

> ✏️ **Identify the Main Idea**
> Underline the main idea in the paragraph at the left.

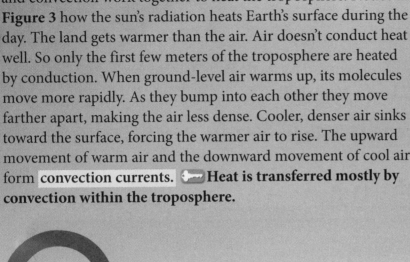

FIGURE 3 ....
Heating the Troposphere
✏️ **Summarize** Describe the process of heat transfer taking place in the diagram at the left.

_____
_____
_____
_____
_____
_____
_____
_____
_____
_____
_____

Lab zone® Do the Quick Lab *Temperature and Height.*

⚷ Assess Your Understanding

1a. Explain Why is convection more important than conduction in the troposphere?

_____
_____
_____

b. Apply Concepts Explain how a convection current can enable a hawk or eagle to soar upward without flapping its wings.

_____
_____
_____
_____

got it? ....

○ **I get it!** Now I know that heat transfer happens in three ways in the atmosphere: _____
_____

○ **I need extra help with** _____
Go to **MY SCIENCE ⑤ COACH** online for help with this subject.

Winds

UNLOCK
THE BIG
?

🔑 **What Causes Winds?**

🔑 **How Do Local Winds and Global Winds Differ?**

my planet diary

Windsurfing

Imagine being able to ride a wave at almost 81 km/h—not in a boat powered by a motor but on a board powered only by the wind. That's what windsurfing is all about.

Windsurfers stand on a sailboard, which is similar to a surfboard. But the sailboard has a mast and a sail that the surfer can control with his or her hands. It uses a sail to capture wind and move the surfer along the surface of the water. Jim Drake, one of the first inventors of windsurfing, points out:

"It's the simplicity of standing up so you can adjust your weight and move quickly, as well as actively participate in transmitting the sail's forces to the board."

EXTREME SPORTS

Discuss these questions with a classmate. Write your answers below.

1. How does wind move the sail?

_____
_____
_____

2. How have you experienced the effects of wind?

_____
_____
_____

▶ **PLANET DIARY** Go to **Planet Diary** to learn more about winds.

Lab® zone   Do the Inquiry Warm-Up *Does the Wind Turn?*

Vocabulary

- wind • anemometer • windchill factor
- local winds • sea breeze • land breeze
- global winds • Coriolis effect • latitude

Skills

↻ Reading: Identify Supporting Evidence

△ Inquiry: Draw Conclusions

What Causes Winds?

Air is a fluid, so it can move easily from place to place. But how does it do that? 🔑 **Differences in air pressure cause the air to move.** Wind is the movement of air parallel to Earth's surface. Winds move from areas of high pressure to areas of lower pressure.

🔑 **Most differences in air pressure are caused by the unequal heating of the atmosphere.** Recall that convection currents form when an area of Earth's surface is heated by the sun's rays. Air over the heated surface expands and becomes less dense. As the air becomes less dense, its air pressure decreases. If a nearby area is not heated as much, the air above the less-heated area will be cooler and denser. The cool, dense air with a higher pressure flows underneath the warm, less dense air. This forces the warm air to rise.

FIGURE 1 ....

Moving Air

Windsurfers need wind in order to move across the water. ✎ **Explain** How do differences in air pressure cause wind?

_____

_____

_____

_____

_____

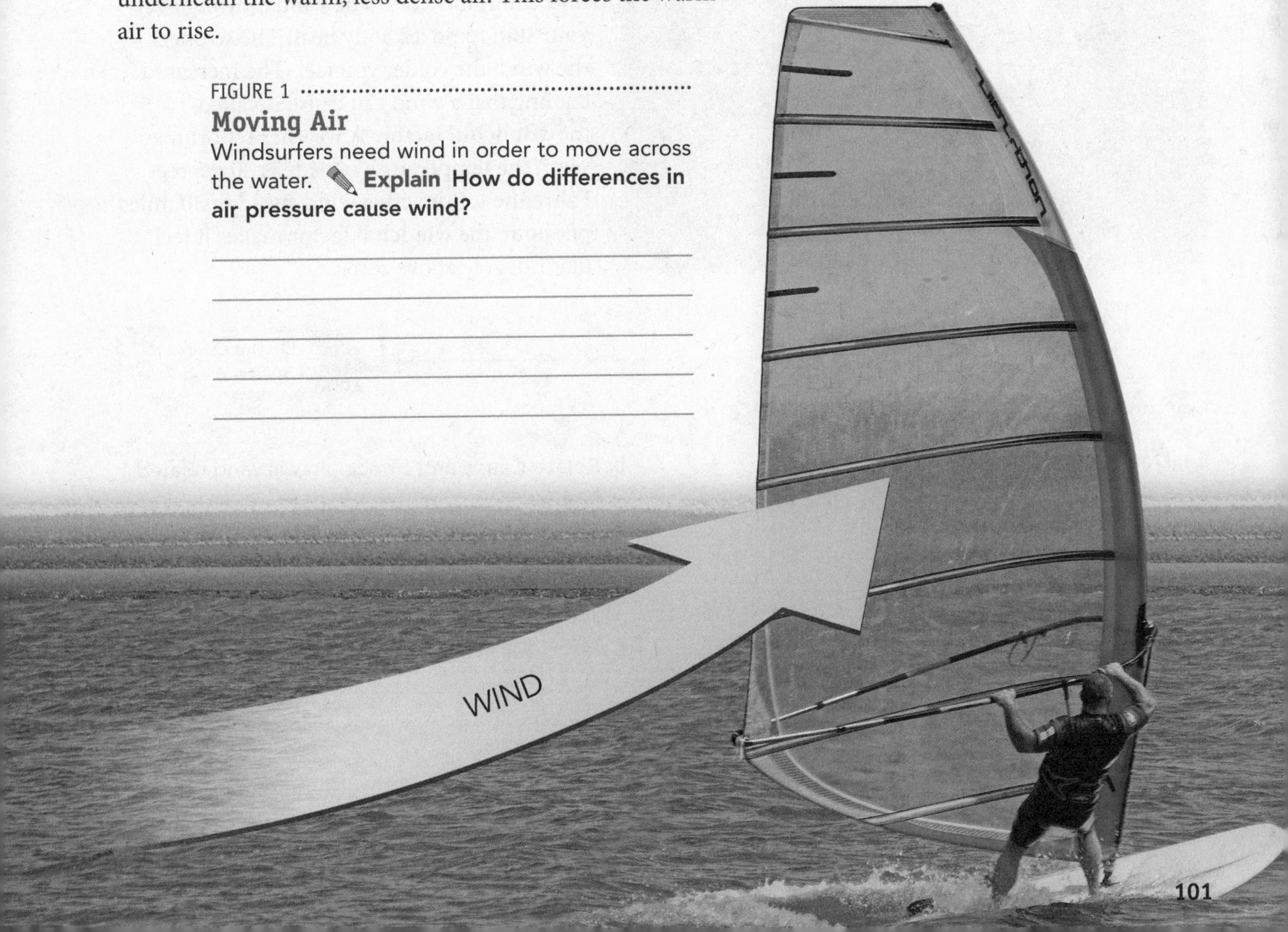

WIND

FIGURE 2 ·····························

Wind Direction and Speed

✏️ **Identify** The short end of the wind vane points into the wind. Based on the direction of the wind vane, which direction would your kite be flying? Indicate your answer by shading in your kite.

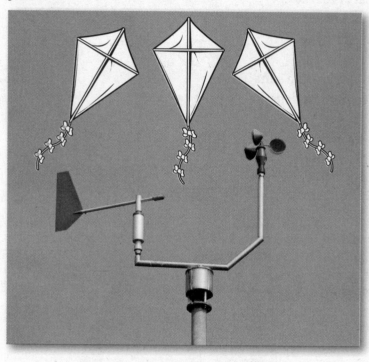

Measuring Wind Winds are described by their direction and speed. Winds can blow from all directions: north, south, east, and west. Wind direction is determined with a wind vane. The wind swings the wind vane so that one end points into the wind. The name of a wind tells you where the wind is coming from. For example, a south wind blows from the south toward the north. A north wind blows to the south.

Wind speed can be measured with an **anemometer** (an uh MAHM uh tur). An anemometer has three or four cups mounted at the ends of spokes that spin on an axle. The force of the wind against the cups turns the axle. A meter connected to the axle shows the wind speed. **Figure 2** shows a wind vane and an anemometer.

Windchill Factor
On a warm day, a cool breeze can be refreshing. But during the winter, the same breeze can make you feel uncomfortably cold. The wind blowing over your skin removes body heat. The stronger the wind, the colder you feel. The increased cooling that a wind can cause is called the **windchill factor.** A weather report may say, "The temperature outside is 20 degrees Fahrenheit. But with a wind speed of 30 miles per hour, the windchill factor makes it feel like 1 degree above zero."

Lab® zone Do the Quick Lab
Build a Wind Vane.

🔑 Assess Your Understanding

1a. Define What is wind?

_____

_____

_____

b. Relate Cause and Effect How is wind related to air pressure and temperature?

_____

_____

_____

_____

got it? ··

○ **I get it!** Now I know that wind is _____

_____

○ **I need extra help with** _____

Go to **MY SCIENCE 🗨 COACH** *online for help with this subject.*

How Do Local Winds and Global Winds Differ?

Have you ever noticed a breeze at the beach on a hot summer day? Even if there is no wind inland, there may be a cool breeze blowing in from the water. This breeze is an example of a local wind.

Local Winds Winds that blow over short distances are called **local winds**. 👈 **The unequal heating of Earth's surface within a small area causes local winds.** These winds form only when large-scale winds are weak. Two types of local winds are sea breezes and land breezes, as shown in **Figure 3**.

FIGURE 3 ·····························

Local Winds

✎ **Relate Text and Visuals** Read about sea breezes. Add arrows to the bottom diagram to indicate how a land breeze develops. Then summarize the process.

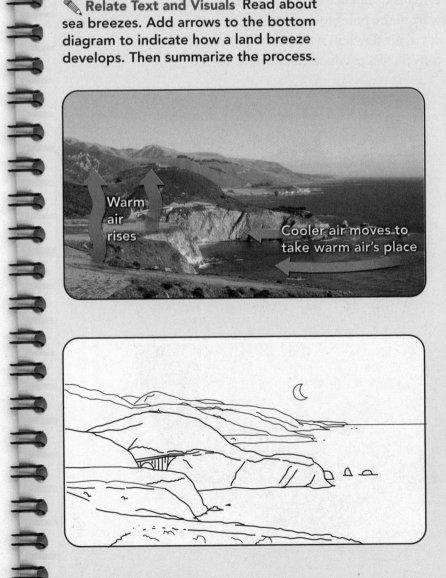

Warm air rises

Cooler air moves to take warm air's place

Sea Breeze During the day, the land warms up faster than the water. The air over the land gets warmer than the air over the water. This warm air is less dense. It expands and rises, creating a low-pressure area. Cool air blows inland from over the water and moves underneath the warm air, causing a sea breeze. A **sea breeze** or a lake breeze is a local wind that blows from an ocean or lake.

Land Breeze At night, the process is reversed. The flow of air from land to a body of water forms a **land breeze**.

_____

_____

_____

_____

_____

Global Winds

Global winds are winds that blow steadily from specific directions over long distances. 🗝 **Like local winds, global winds are created by the unequal heating of Earth's surface. But unlike local winds, global winds occur over a large area.** In **Figure 4,** you can see how the sun's radiation strikes Earth. In the middle of the day near the equator, the sun is almost directly overhead. The direct rays from the sun heat Earth's surface intensely. Near the poles, the sun's rays strike Earth's surface at a lower angle. The sun's energy is spread out over a larger area, so it heats the surface less. As a result, temperatures near the poles are much lower than they are near the equator.

Global Convection Currents How do global winds develop? Temperature differences between the equator and the poles produce giant convection currents in the atmosphere. Warm air rises at the equator, and cold air sinks at the poles. Therefore air pressure tends to be lower near the equator and greater near the poles. This difference in pressure causes winds at Earth's surface to blow from the poles toward the equator. Higher in the atmosphere, however, air flows away from the equator toward the poles. Those air movements produce global winds.

FIGURE 4 ······················

Heating of Earth's Surface

✏ **Interpret Diagrams** The angle of the sun's rays causes temperature differences at Earth's surface.

1. Label the areas where the sun hits Earth most directly (M) and least directly (L).

2. CHALLENGE Draw a convection current in the atmosphere north of the equator.

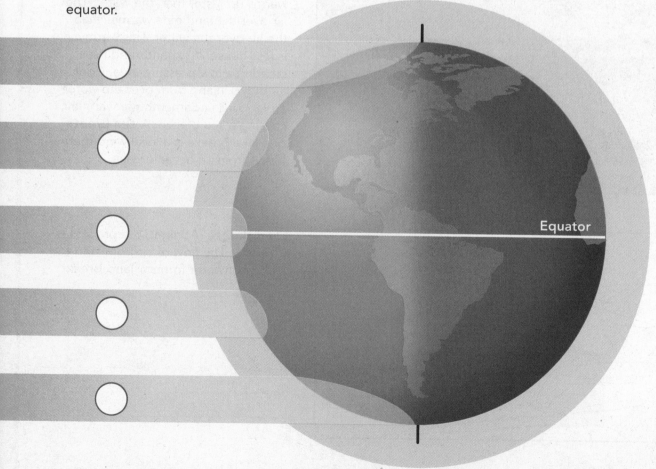

Equator

The Coriolis Effect If Earth did not rotate, global winds would blow in a straight line from the poles toward the equator. Because Earth is rotating, however, global winds do not follow a straight path. As the winds blow, Earth rotates from west to east underneath them, making it seem as if the winds have curved. The way Earth's rotation makes winds curve is called the **Coriolis effect** (kawr ee OH lis). Because of the Coriolis effect, global winds in the Northern Hemisphere gradually turn toward the right. A wind blowing toward the south gradually turns toward the southwest. In the Southern Hemisphere, winds curve toward the left.

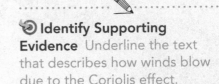

⤵ **Identify Supporting Evidence** Underline the text that describes how winds blow due to the Coriolis effect.

apply it!

The Coriolis effect determines the direction of global winds.

❶ Look at the globe on the left. Shade in the arrows that show the direction the global winds would blow without the Coriolis effect.

❷ Look at the globe on the right. Shade in the arrows that show the direction the global winds blow as a result of the Coriolis effect.

❸ **Draw Conclusions** Based on your last answer, what direction do global winds blow in the Northern Hemisphere? In the Southern Hemisphere?

_____

_____

_____

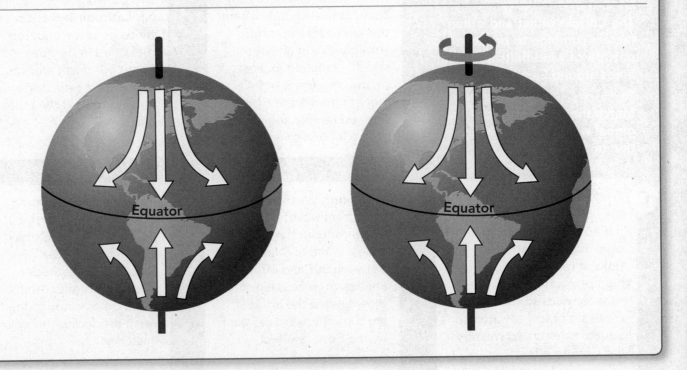

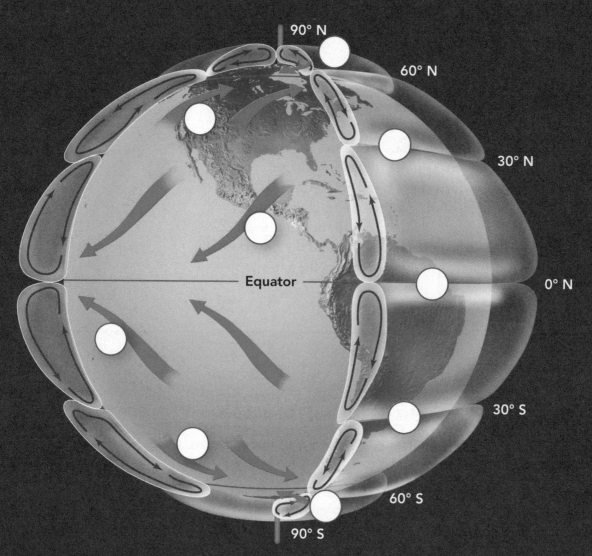

90° N

60° N

30° N

0° N

30° S

60° S

90° S

Equator

FIGURE 5 ·······································

▶ INTERACTIVE ART

Global Wind Belts

The Coriolis effect and other factors combine to produce a pattern of wind belts and calm areas around Earth.

✎ Relate Text and Visuals

Match the descriptions of the global winds with their location on the globe.

A **Doldrums** are a calm area where warm air rises. They occur at the equator where the sun heats the surface strongly. Warm air rises steadily, creating an area of low pressure. Cool air moves into the area, but is warmed rapidly and rises before it moves very far.

B **Horse Latitudes** are two calm areas of sinking air. **Latitude** is the distance from the equator, measured in degrees. At about 30° north and south latitudes, the air stops moving toward the poles and sinks.

C **Trade Winds** blow from the horse latitudes toward the equator. As cold air over the horse latitudes sinks, it forms a region of high pressure. This causes surface winds to blow. The winds that blow toward the equator are turned west by the Coriolis effect.

D **Prevailing Westerlies** blow from west to east, away from the horse latitudes. In the mid-latitudes, between 30° and 60° north and south, winds that blow toward the poles are turned toward the east by the Coriolis effect.

E **Polar Easterlies** blow cold air away from the poles. Air near the poles sinks and flows back toward lower latitudes. The Coriolis effect shifts these polar winds to the west, producing the polar easterlies.

Parts of the Atmosphere

How does the sun's energy affect Earth's atmosphere?

FIGURE 6 ···

Earth's atmosphere is a system made up of many different parts.

✏ **Communicate** In the space below, draw a picture or a diagram that helps you understand the relationship between the concepts in the word bank. Explain your diagram to a classmate.

Word Bank	
atmosphere	air pressure
convection	radiation
global winds	

Lab zone® Do the Quick Lab
Modeling Global Wind Belts.

🔑 Assess Your Understanding

2a. Summarize What causes local winds?

_____

_____

b. Identify What is a global wind?

_____

_____

c. ANSWER THE BIG ? How does the sun's energy affect Earth's atmosphere?

_____

_____

_____

_____

got it? ·····································

○ **I get it!** Now I know that winds blow locally and globally due to _____

_____

○ **I need extra help with**_____

Go to MY SCIENCE 🗨 COACH *online for help with this subject.*

Study Guide

The sun's energy affects Earth's atmosphere by _____ Earth's surface, causing differences in _____ that result in _____ .

LESSON 1 The Air Around You

🔑 Earth's atmosphere consists of nitrogen, oxygen, carbon dioxide, water vapor, and other gases, as well as particles of liquids and solids.

🔑 Events in one part of the atmosphere affect other parts of the atmosphere.

Vocabulary
• weather
• atmosphere
• water vapor

LESSON 2 Air Pressure

🔑 Because air has mass, it also has other properties, including density and pressure.

🔑 Two common kinds of barometers are mercury barometers and aneroid barometers.

🔑 Air pressure decreases as altitude increases. As air pressure decreases, so does density.

Vocabulary
• density   • air pressure   • barometer
• mercury barometer   • aneroid barometer
• altitude

LESSON 3 Layers of the Atmosphere

🔑 Scientists divide Earth's atmosphere into four main layers according to changes in temperature.

🔑 Earth's weather occurs in the troposphere. The stratosphere contains the ozone layer.

🔑 The mesosphere protects Earth from meteoroids. The thermosphere is the outermost layer of Earth's atmosphere.

Vocabulary
• troposphere   • stratosphere   • mesosphere
• thermosphere   • ionosphere   • exosphere

LESSON 4 Energy in Earth's Atmosphere

🔑 The sun's energy travels to Earth as visible light, infrared radiation, and ultraviolet radiation.

🔑 Some sunlight is absorbed or reflected by the atmosphere. Some of the energy Earth absorbs is radiated back out as infrared radiation.

Vocabulary
• electromagnetic waves   • radiation
• infrared radiation   • ultraviolet radiation
• scattering   • greenhouse effect

LESSON 5 Heat Transfer

🔑 Air temperature is usually measured with a thermometer.

🔑 Heat is transferred in three ways: convection, conduction, and radiation.

🔑 Heat is transferred mostly by convection within the troposphere.

Vocabulary
• temperature   • thermal energy   • thermometer
• heat   • convection   • conduction
• convection currents

LESSON 6 Winds

🔑 Winds are caused by differences in air pressure.

🔑 The unequal heating of Earth's surface within a small area causes local winds.

🔑 Global winds are caused by the unequal heating of Earth's surface over a large area.

Vocabulary
• wind   • anemometer   • windchill factor
• local winds   • sea breeze   • land breeze
• global winds   • Coriolis effect   • latitude

Review and Assessment

LESSON 1 The Air Around You

1. Which gas forms less than one percent of the atmosphere, but is essential to life?

   a. carbon dioxide   **b.** oxygen

   c. hydrogen   **d.** nitrogen

2. Weather occurs in Earth's troposphere, which is _____

_____

3. **Draw Conclusions** Why is it difficult to include water vapor in a graph of the percentages of various gases in the atmosphere? How could you solve the problem?

_____

_____

_____

_____

LESSON 2 Air Pressure

4. When density increases, the number of molecules in a volume

   a. increases.   **b.** decreases.

   c. stays the same.   **d.** varies.

5. One force affecting an object is air pressure, which is _____

_____

6. **Apply Concepts** Why can an aneroid barometer measure elevation as well as air pressure?

_____

_____

7. **Write About It** Suppose you're on a hot-air balloon flight. Describe how air pressure and the amount of oxygen would change during your trip. What would the changes feel like?

LESSON 3 Layers of the Atmosphere

8. The layers of the atmosphere are classified according to changes in

   a. altitude.   **b.** air pressure.

   c. distance.   **d.** temperature.

9. **Sequence** List the layers of the atmosphere in order, moving up from Earth's surface.

_____

_____

10. The ozone layer is important because

_____

_____

_____

11. **Infer** Why are clouds at the top of the troposphere made of ice crystals rather than drops of water?

_____

_____

12. **Compare and Contrast** How are the upper and lower parts of the stratosphere different?

_____

_____

_____

13. **Calculate** The table shows the temperature at various altitudes above Omaha, Nebraska, on a January day. Suppose an airplane was 6.8 kilometers above Omaha. What is the approximate temperature at this height?

_____

Altitude (kilometers)	0	1.6	3.2	4.8	6.4	7.2
Temperature (°C)	0	−4	−9	−21	−32	−40

3 Review and Assessment

LESSON 4 Energy in Earth's Atmosphere

14. How does most of the energy from the sun travel to Earth's surface?

   a. convection   **b.** conduction

   c. radiation   **d.** scattering

15. What are three forms of radiation that come from the sun?

_____

16. Relate Cause and Effect Why do people need to wear sunscreen at the beach?

_____

_____

_____

_____

_____

LESSON 5 Heat Transfer

17. What is the main way heat is transferred in the troposphere?

   a. radiation currents   **b.** reflection currents

   c. conduction currents **d.** convection currents

18. Compare and Contrast A pail of lake water is the same temperature as a lake. Compare the thermal energy of the pail of water with the thermal energy of the lake.

_____

_____

_____

_____

19. **Write About It** Describe an example of heat transfer in your daily life.

LESSON 6 Winds

20. The calm areas near the equator where warm air rises are

   a. horse latitudes.   **b.** trade winds.

   c. doldrums.   **d.** polar easterlies.

21. Nights often feature land breezes, which blow

_____

22. Relate Cause and Effect How does the movement of hot air at the equator and cold air at the poles produce global wind patterns?

_____

_____

_____

_____

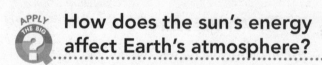

APPLY THE BIG Q How does the sun's energy affect Earth's atmosphere?

23. Imagine you are sailing around the world. What winds would you expect to find on different parts of your route? Explain the role of the sun's energy in creating those winds.

_____

_____

_____

_____

_____

_____

_____

_____

_____

Standardized Test Prep

Multiple Choice

Circle the letter of the best answer.

1. Use trends in the data table to predict how cold the air temperature would feel if the actual temperature was 0°C and the wind speed was 25 km/h.

Windchill Temperature Index				
Wind Speed	**Equivalent Air Temperature (°C)**			
0 km/h	5°	0°	−5°	−10°
10 km/h	2.7°	−3.3°	−9.3°	−15.3°
15 km/h	1.7°	−4.4°	−10.6°	−16.7°
20 km/h	1.1°	−5.2°	−11.6°	−17.9°

A   about 0°C   B   about −15°C
C   about −6°C   D   about 25°C

2. What is the most abundant gas in the atmosphere?

A   ozone
B   water vapor
C   oxygen
D   nitrogen

3. Which device is typically used to measure air pressure?

A   hot-air balloon
B   barometer
C   satellite
D   thermometer

4. Which layer of the atmosphere protects Earth from meteoroids?

A   mesosphere
B   troposphere
C   ionosphere
D   stratosphere

5. Which type of energy causes sunburn?

A   thermal energy
B   infrared radiation
C   the greenhouse effect
D   ultraviolet radiation

Constructed Response

Use the diagram and your knowledge of science to answer Question 6. Write your answer on another sheet of paper.

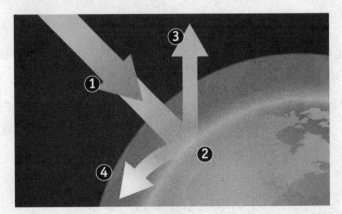

6. Describe the process that results in the greenhouse effect. How does it affect Earth's atmosphere?

When someone mentions the National Aeronautics and Space Administration (NASA), you might think of missions to Mars or Pluto. However, many of NASA's missions help us understand our own planet. In 2004, NASA launched *Aura*, the third satellite in its Earth Observing System (EOS) program. *Aura* helps scientists study the chemistry of the atmosphere.

The *Aura* mission seeks to answer three questions about our atmosphere.

1. Is the ozone layer recovering? *Aura* helps scientists monitor atmospheric gases, such as chlorofluorocarbons (CFCs), that affect the ozone layer. If the ozone layer does not recover, scientists predict that we will need to learn to better protect ourselves from the sun. In the next 10 years, will we need SPF 100 sunscreen?

2. How do pollutants affect air quality? *Aura* monitors levels of ozone, particulate matter, carbon monoxide, nitrogen dioxide, and sulfur dioxide. The data help scientists understand—and predict—the movement of air pollutants. Are attempts to reduce air pollution working?

3. How is Earth's climate changing? *Aura* checks levels of greenhouse gases in the atmosphere to help scientists build more accurate models of climate change. This way, we will have a better idea of how to plan for long-term climate change. Will you need to invest in a really good raincoat?

Research It Research NASA's EOS program. What are the major satellites in this program? Which Earth systems are they designed to monitor? What discoveries has the EOS program made? Make a display with information and pictures to show what you find out.

Up, Up, and Away!

Bobbing along in the sky, hot air balloons look like a fun way to spend a day. Before the invention of satellites or airplanes, though, scientists used hot air balloons to study the atmosphere. Riding in their balloons, scientists recorded air temperatures and humidity, and even gathered information about cosmic rays. For more than 150 years, balloons were cutting-edge atmospheric observatories.

Research It Find out more about the history of ballooning. How did scientific research using balloons contribute to early space missions? Make a timeline showing balloonists' discoveries.

PLUGGING INTO THE JET STREAM

It's windy up there! About 10 kilometers above Earth's surface, the jet stream winds blow constantly. The winds average 80 to 160 km/h, and they can reach 400 km/h. If we could harness just a small fraction of the wind's energy, we could meet the electricity needs of everyone on Earth!

Scientists are testing designs for high-altitude wind farms. They propose that kite-like wind generators flying above Earth could generate electricity. Cables could then transfer the electricity to Earth.

Design It Research the proposed designs for wind farms in the sky. Make a graphic organizer to show the proposed designs, the risks, and the ways scientists are addressing these risks.

WHAT CLUES CAN PREDICT A STORM?

How do meteorologists predict the weather?

This tornado bearing down on this home in Kansas in June of 2004 reached wind speeds of 254–331 km/h. The state of Kansas had 124 tornadoes that year. Although tornadoes can occur anywhere, the United States leads the world with more than 1,000 tornadoes per year. **Observe** **How could you predict a tornado was coming?**

_____

_____

_____

_____

_____

_____

_____

> **UNTAMED SCIENCE** Watch the **Untamed Science** video to learn more about weather.

Check Your Understanding

1. **Background** Read the paragraph below and then answer the question.

"Is that smoke over the baseball field?" Eddie asked Cara in the park. "No," she replied. "It's fog." "Ah, water vapor," Eddie said. "No," Cara said. "If you can see it, it's water droplets suspended in the atmosphere. Water vapor is an invisible gas and can't be seen."

Fog is made up of clouds that form near the ground.

Vapor is water in the form of a gas.

The **atmosphere** is the envelope of gases surrounding Earth.

- What does water vapor in the atmosphere look like?

_____

_____

> **MY READING WEB** If you had trouble completing the question above, visit **My Reading Web** and type in *Weather*.

Vocabulary Skill

Prefixes A prefix is a word part that is added at the beginning of a word to change its meaning. For example, the prefix *anti-* means "against" or "opposed to" and is used frequently in science. In the word *antivenom*, the prefix *anti-* is added to the word *venom* to form *antivenom*, meaning "against poison."

Prefix	Meaning	Example
psychro-	cold	psychrometer, *n.*
alto-	high	altocumulus, *n.*; altostratus, *n.*
anti-	against or opposed to	anticyclone, *n.*

2. **Quick Check** Review the prefixes above. Then predict what the word *altocumulus* means using what you know about the prefix *alto-*. After reading the chapter, revise your definition as needed.

_____

_____

_____

_____

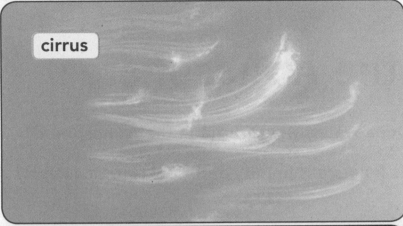

cirrus

precipitation

front

tornado

Chapter Preview

LESSON 1
- water cycle • evaporation
- condensation • humidity
- relative humidity • psychrometer
- ↻ **Sequence**
- △ **Interpret Data**

LESSON 2
- dew point • cirrus • cumulus
- stratus
- ↻ **Summarize**
- △ **Predict**

LESSON 3
- precipitation • rain gauge
- flood • drought
- ↻ **Relate Cause and Effect**
- △ **Calculate**

LESSON 4
- air mass • tropical • polar
- maritime • continental
- jet stream • front • occluded
- cyclone • anticyclone
- ↻ **Relate Text and Visuals**
- △ **Classify**

LESSON 5
- storm • thunderstorm • lightning
- hurricane • storm surge
- tornado • evacuate
- ↻ **Outline**
- △ **Infer**

LESSON 6
- meteorologist • isobar
- isotherm
- ↻ **Compare and Contrast**
- △ **Predict**

> **VOCAB FLASH CARDS** For extra help with vocabulary, visit **Vocab Flash Cards** and type in *Weather.*

Water in the Atmosphere

🗝 How Does Water Move Through the Atmosphere?

🗝 What Is Relative Humidity and How Is It Measured?

MY PLANET DIARY

The Driest Place on Earth

The Atacama Desert in Chile is so dry that there are places where humans have never measured a single drop of rain. But even the Atacama has some moisture in the air. A dense fog along the coastline, known as *camanchaca*, often flows inland from the Pacific Ocean. At one point, the people of the fishing village Chungungo set up nets above the mountains to catch the fog. Water condensed on the nets and then was collected and sent through pipes that brought the water to the village.

Chile
Uruguay
Argentina
Pacific Ocean
Atlantic Ocean

FUN FACT

Write your answers to each question below. Then discuss your answers with a partner.

1. Why did the people of Chungungo need to use nets to catch moisture in the air?

_____

_____

2. What would be one way of collecting water where you live?

_____

▷ **PLANET DIARY** Go to **Planet Diary** to learn more about water in the atmosphere.

Do the Inquiry Warm-Up *Where Did the Water Go?*

How Does Water Move Through the Atmosphere?

During a rainstorm, the air feels moist. On a clear, cloudless day, the air may feel dry. As the sun heats the land and oceans, the sun provides energy to change the amount of water in the atmosphere. Water is always moving between Earth's atmosphere and surface.

The movement of water through Earth's systems, powered by the sun's energy, is the **water cycle**. 🗝 **In the water cycle, water vapor enters the atmosphere by evaporation from the oceans and other bodies of water and leaves by condensation**. **Evaporation** is the process by which molecules of liquid water escape into the air after becoming water vapor. **Condensation** is the process by which water vapor becomes liquid water.

Vocabulary
- water cycle • evaporation • condensation
- humidity • relative humidity • psychrometer

Skills
↻ Reading: Sequence

▲ Inquiry: Interpret Data

Water vapor is also added to the air by living things. Water enters the roots of plants, rises to the leaves, and is released into the air as water vapor. Animals also release water vapor into the air every time they exhale.

As part of the water cycle, shown in **Figure 1,** some of the water vapor in the atmosphere condenses to form clouds. Rain and snow fall from the clouds toward the surface as precipitation. The water then runs off the surface or moves through the ground, back into lakes, streams, and eventually the oceans. Then the water cycle starts all over again with evaporation.

↻ **Sequence** Starting with precipitation, list the order of the steps of the water cycle.

_____

_____

_____

_____

FIGURE 1 ················

▷ **INTERACTIVE ART** **The Water Cycle**
In the water cycle, water moves from plants, lakes, rivers, and oceans into the atmosphere and then falls back to Earth.

✏ **Summarize** Use the word bank to label the parts of the water cycle.

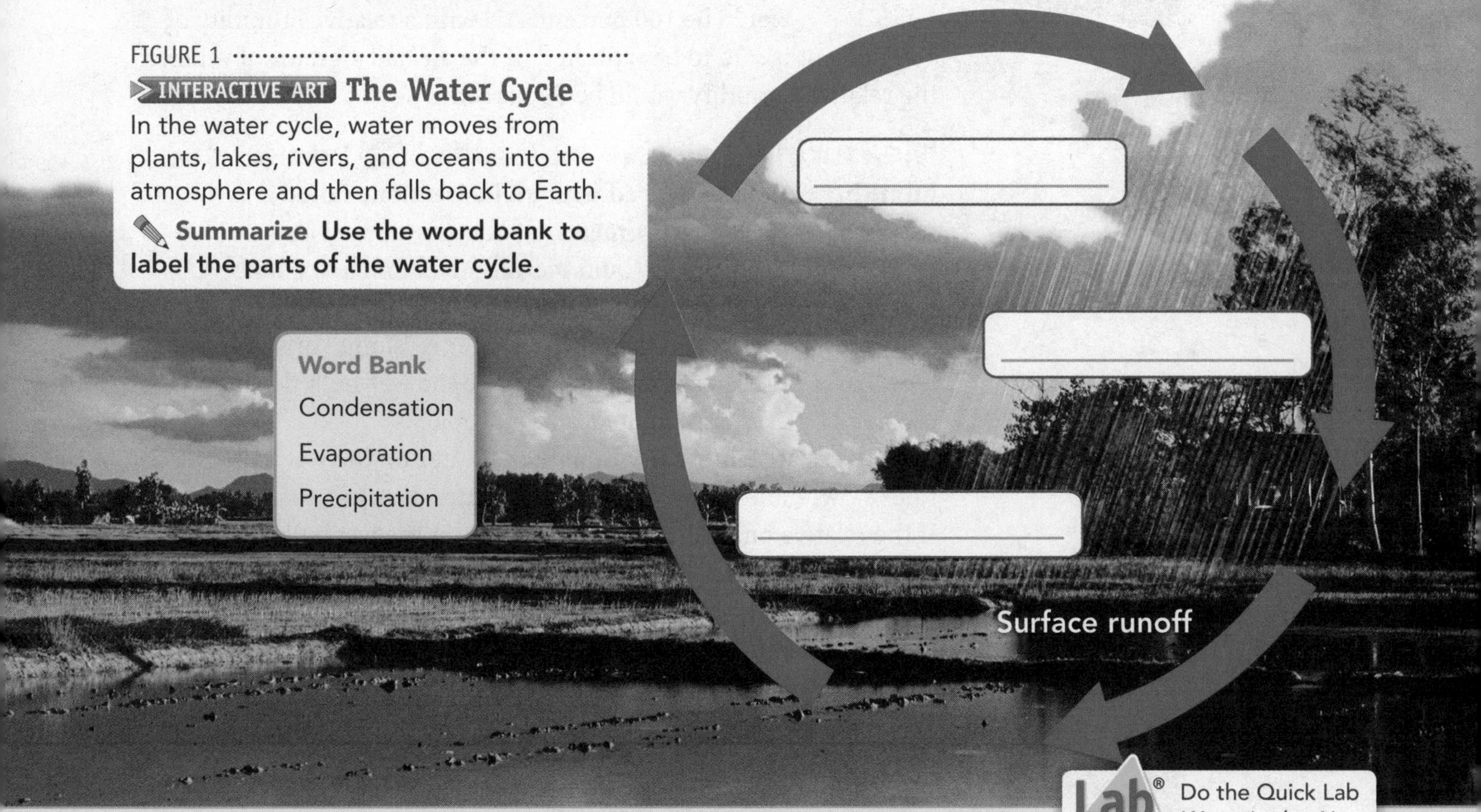

Word Bank

Condensation

Evaporation

Precipitation

Surface runoff

Lab zone ® Do the Quick Lab *Water in the Air.*

🔓 Assess Your Understanding

got it? ················

O **I get it!** Now I know that in the water cycle_____

_____

O **I need extra help with** _____

Go to **my science** 🅂 **coach** *online for help with this subject.*

119

What Is Relative Humidity and How Is It Measured?

How is the quantity of water vapor in the atmosphere measured? **Humidity** is a measure of the amount of water vapor in the air. The ability of air to hold water vapor depends on its temperature. Warm air can hold more water vapor than cool air.

Relative Humidity   Weather reports usually refer to the water vapor in the air as relative humidity. **Relative humidity** is the percentage of water vapor that is actually in the air compared to the maximum amount of water vapor the air can hold at a particular temperature. For example, at 10°C, 1 cubic meter of air can hold at most 8 grams of water vapor. If there were 8 grams of water vapor in the air, then the relative humidity of the air would be 100 percent. Air with a relative humidity of 100 percent is said to be saturated. If the air had 4 grams of vapor, the relative humidity would be 50 percent.

Measuring Relative Humidity   ⊂⊐ **Relative humidity can be measured with an instrument called a psychrometer.** A **psychrometer** (sy KRAHM uh tur) has two thermometers, a wet-bulb thermometer and a dry-bulb thermometer. As shown in **Figure 2,** the wet bulb is covered by a moist cloth. When the psychrometer is "slung," or spun, air blows over both thermometers. Because the wet-bulb thermometer is cooled by evaporation, its reading drops.

If the relative humidity is high, the water on the wet bulb evaporates slowly, and the wet-bulb temperature does not change much. If the relative humidity is low, the water on the wet bulb evaporates rapidly, and the wet-bulb temperature drops by a large amount. The relative humidity can be found by comparing the temperatures of the wet-bulb and dry-bulb thermometers.

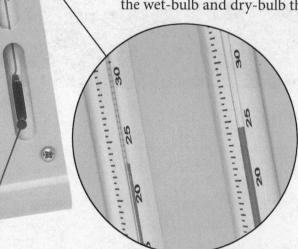

Wet bulb

Dry bulb

FIGURE 2 ·······································

Sling Psychrometer

✎ **Relate Text and Visuals** Read the psychrometer and compare the two Celsius temperatures. Is the relative humidity low or high? How do you know?

_____

_____

_____

_____

do the math!

Relative Humidity

Relative humidity is affected by temperature. Use the data table to answer the questions below. First, find the dry-bulb temperature in the left column of the table. Then find the difference between the wet- and dry-bulb temperatures across the top of the table. The number in the table where these two readings intersect indicates the percentage of relative humidity.

1 Interpret Data At noon the readings on a sling psychrometer are 18°C for the dry bulb and 14°C for the wet bulb. What is the relative humidity?

_____

2 Interpret Data At 5 P.M. the reading on the dry bulb is 12°C and the reading on the wet bulb is 11°C. Determine the new relative humidity.

_____

3 CHALLENGE What was the difference in relative humidity between noon and 5 P.M.? How was the relative humidity affected by air temperature?

_____
_____

Relative Humidity

Dry-Bulb Reading (°C)	Difference Between Wet- and Dry-Bulb Readings (°C)				
	1	2	3	4	5
10	88	76	65	54	43
12	88	78	67	57	48
14	89	79	69	60	50
16	90	80	71	62	54
18	91	81	72	64	56
20	91	82	74	66	58
22	92	83	75	68	60

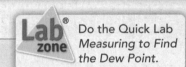

Lab zone Do the Quick Lab *Measuring to Find the Dew Point.*

Assess Your Understanding

1a. Review What is humidity?

_____
_____

b. Calculate Suppose a sample of air can hold at most 10 grams of water vapor. If the sample actually has 2 grams of water vapor, what is its relative humidity?

_____

c. Compare and Contrast How are humidity and relative humidity different?

_____
_____
_____
_____
_____
_____

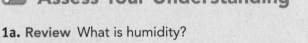

got it? ....

○ **I get it!** Now I know that relative humidity is _____

_____ and it can be measured with _____

○ **I need extra help with** _____

Go to MY SCIENCE ⑤ COACH online for help with this subject.

Clouds

UNLOCK THE BIG ?

🔑 How Do Clouds Form?

🔑 What Are the Three Main Types of Clouds?

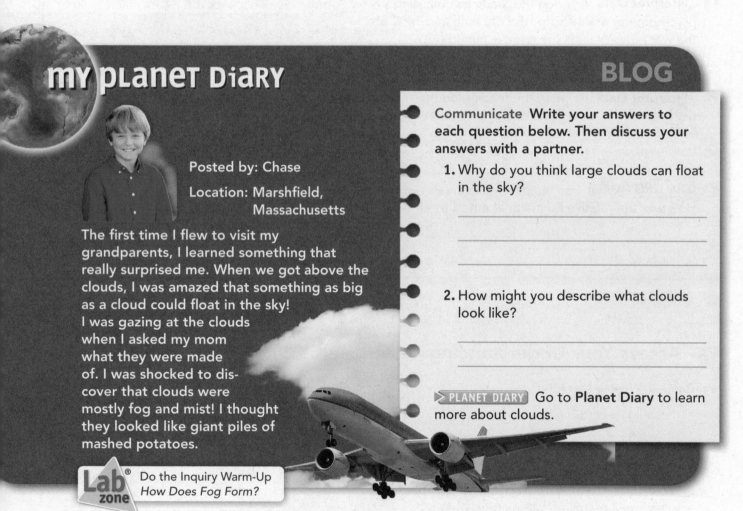

my planet DiaRY

BLOG

Posted by: Chase

Location: Marshfield, Massachusetts

The first time I flew to visit my grandparents, I learned something that really surprised me. When we got above the clouds, I was amazed that something as big as a cloud could float in the sky! I was gazing at the clouds when I asked my mom what they were made of. I was shocked to discover that clouds were mostly fog and mist! I thought they looked like giant piles of mashed potatoes.

Communicate Write your answers to each question below. Then discuss your answers with a partner.

1. Why do you think large clouds can float in the sky?

_____

_____

_____

2. How might you describe what clouds look like?

_____

_____

> PLANET DIARY Go to **Planet Diary** to learn more about clouds.

Lab zone Do the Inquiry Warm-Up *How Does Fog Form?*

How Do Clouds Form?

When you look at a cloud, you are seeing millions of tiny water droplets or ice crystals. 🔑 **Clouds form when water vapor in the air condenses to form liquid water or ice crystals.** Molecules of water vapor in the air become liquid water in a process called condensation. How does water in the atmosphere condense? Two conditions are required for condensation: cooling of the air and the presence of particles in the air.

Vocabulary
- dew point • cirrus
- cumulus • stratus

Skills
- Reading: Summarize
- Inquiry: Predict

The Role of Cooling As you have learned, cold air holds less water vapor than warm air. As air cools, the amount of water vapor it can hold decreases. The water vapor condenses into tiny droplets of water or ice crystals. The temperature at which condensation begins is called the **dew point.** If the dew point is above freezing, the water vapor forms droplets. If the dew point is below freezing, the water vapor may change directly into ice crystals.

The Role of Particles For water vapor to condense and form clouds, tiny particles must be present in the atmosphere so that the water has a surface on which to condense. Most of these particles are salt crystals, dust from soil, or smoke. Water vapor also condenses on solid surfaces, such as blades of grass or window panes. Liquid water that condenses from the air onto a cooler surface is called dew. Ice deposited on a surface that is below freezing is called frost.

Summarize What is the difference between dew and frost?

_____

_____

_____

_____

_____

FIGURE 1 ························

How Clouds Form
Clouds form when warm, moist air rises and cools.

✎ **Interpret Diagrams** Fill in the blanks to complete the sentences about cloud formation.

❸ Water vapor condenses on tiny _____ in the air.

❶ Warm, moist air rises from the surface. As air rises, it _____

❷ At a certain height, air cools to the dew point and _____ begins.

Lab zone ® Do the Quick Lab How Clouds Form.

🔑 Assess Your Understanding
got it? ·······················

○ I get it! Now I know that clouds form when _____

_____

○ I need extra help with _____

  Go to MY SCIENCE ⑤ COACH online for help with this subject.

What Are the Three Main Types of Clouds?

🔑 **Scientists classify clouds into three main types based on their shape: cirrus, cumulus, and stratus. Clouds are further classified by their altitude.** Each type of cloud is associated with a different type of weather.

(km)

13

12

11

10

9

8

7

6

5

4

3

2

1

Cirrus

Cumulonimbus

Altocumulus

Altostratus

Cumulus

Fog

Cirrus Clouds

Wispy, feathery clouds are called **cirrus** (SEER us) clouds. *Cirrus* comes from a word meaning "a curl." Cirrus clouds form at high altitudes, usually above 6 km, and at low temperatures. They are made of ice crystals and indicate fair weather.

Altocumulus and Altostratus

Clouds that form between 2 and 6 km above Earth's surface have the prefix *alto-*, which means "high." The two main types of these clouds are altocumulus and altostratus. These are "medium-level" clouds that are higher than regular cumulus and stratus clouds, but lower than cirrus clouds. These clouds indicate precipitation.

Fog

Clouds that form near the ground are called fog. Fog can form when the ground cools at night after a humid day. CHALLENGE **What happens to fog after sunrise?**

Cumulus Clouds

Clouds that look like cotton are called **cumulus** (KYOO myuh lus) clouds. The word *cumulus* means "heap" in Latin. Cumulus clouds form less than 2 km above the ground, but they may extend upward as much as 18 km. Short cumulus clouds usually indicate fair weather. Towering clouds with flat tops, or cumulonimbus clouds, often produce thunderstorms. The suffix *-nimbus* means "rain."

FIGURE 2 ···

Cloud Types

There are many different types of clouds.

Predict Read about clouds in the text. Then fill in the table to predict the weather that you would expect with each type of cloud.

Cloud	Weather
Cirrus	_____
Cirrocumulus	_____
Cumulus	_____
Cumulonimbus	_____
Stratus	_____
Nimbostratus	_____

Cirrocumulus

Cirrocumulus Clouds

Cirrocumulus clouds, which look like cotton balls, often indicate that a storm is on its way.

Stratus Clouds

Clouds that form in flat layers are known as **stratus** (STRAT us) clouds, from the Latin word *strato*, meaning "spread out." Stratus clouds usually cover all or most of the sky and are a dull, gray color. As stratus clouds thicken, they may produce drizzle, rain, or snow. They are then called *nimbostratus* clouds.

Nimbostratus   **Stratus**

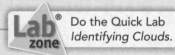

apply it!

❶ **Observe** Look out your window and identify the clouds you see. What kind of clouds are they? Circle a cloud on the page that looks most like one of the clouds you see.

_____

_____

❷ **Predict** From what you know about this type of cloud, what sort of weather would you expect over the next 24 hours? Why?

_____

_____

Lab zone Do the Quick Lab *Identifying Clouds.*

🔑 Assess Your Understanding

1a. Describe Briefly describe the shapes of the three main types of clouds.

_____

_____

_____

b. Classify Classify each of the following cloud types as low-level, medium-level, or high-level.

Altocumulus _____

Altostratus _____

Cirrocumulus _____

Cirrus _____

Cumulus _____

Nimbostratus _____

Stratus _____

got it? ·····································

○ **I get it!** Now I know that the three main types of clouds are _____

_____

○ **I need extra help with** _____

Go to **my science coach** online for help with this subject.

Precipitation

UNLOCK
THE BIG
?

🔑 **What Are the Common Types of Precipitation?**

🔑 **What Are the Causes and Effects of Floods and Droughts?**

MY PLANET DIARY

Cloud Seeding

Is that a space weapon you see in this photo? Not at all. This scientist in China is launching tiny crystals of silver iodide into the air to make rain. Clouds often contain water droplets that have cooled below 0°C. But the droplets do not freeze unless they can condense onto solid particles. When the silver iodide crystals reach the clouds, the droplets can condense onto them. Once that happens, the droplets can fall as rain.

Some scientists think that cloud seeding can increase rainfall by 10 percent. Others think that this is unlikely. In the United States, several western states are trying cloud seeding. Dry states, such as Wyoming and Utah, need as much rainfall as they can get.

TECHNOLOGY

Write your answer to each question below. Then discuss your answers with a partner.

1. Why would scientists want to find a way to make it rain?

_____

_____

_____

_____

2. Name a situation when you would want it to rain.

_____

_____

> **PLANET DIARY** Go to **Planet Diary** to learn more about precipitation.

Lab® Do the Inquiry Warm-Up
zone *How Can You Make Hail?*

Vocabulary
- precipitation • rain gauge
- flood • drought

Skills
- Reading: Relate Cause and Effect
- Inquiry: Calculate

What Are the Common Types of Precipitation?

Suppose you could control the weather. If you wanted it to rain, you would have to get the water from somewhere.

Water evaporates from every water surface on Earth and eventually falls back to the surface. **Precipitation** is any form of water that falls from clouds and reaches Earth's surface. It is a vital part of the water cycle. In warm climates, precipitation is almost always rain. In colder regions, it may fall as snow or ice. **Common types of precipitation include rain, sleet, freezing rain, snow, and hail.**

Rain The most common kind of precipitation is rain. As shown in **Figure 1,** drops of water are called rain if they are at least 0.5 millimeters in diameter. Precipitation made up of smaller drops of water is called drizzle. Precipitation of even smaller drops is called mist.

Measuring Rain What if scientists need to measure how much rain has fallen? An open-ended tube that collects rain is called a **rain gauge.** The amount of rain is measured by dipping a ruler into the water or by reading a scale. For rainfall to be measured more accurately, a rain gauge may have a funnel at the top that collects ten times as much rain as the tube alone would without it. The depth is easier to measure. To get the actual depth of rain, it is necessary to divide by ten.

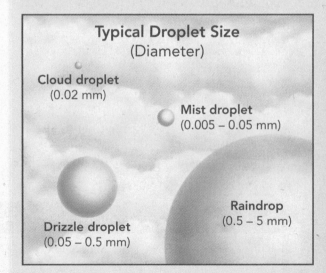

FIGURE 1 ·······························
Water Droplets
Cloud droplets condense to become larger droplets.

Calculate **Determine how many times larger the diameter of a large (5 mm) raindrop is than the diameter of a cloud droplet.**

_____

_____

Typical Droplet Size
(Diameter)

Cloud droplet
(0.02 mm)

Mist droplet
(0.005 – 0.05 mm)

Drizzle droplet
(0.05 – 0.5 mm)

Raindrop
(0.5 – 5 mm)

FIGURE 2 ·······························
Rain Gauge
The rain gauge, measuring in centimeters, collects ten times the actual depth of rain that falls.

Calculate **How much rain has fallen so far?**

_____

Freezing Rain

On a cold day, raindrops can sometimes fall as liquid water but freeze when they touch a cold surface. This kind of precipitation is called freezing rain.

Snow

You probably know that snow-flakes have an endless number of different shapes and patterns, many with six sides or branches. A snowflake forms when water vapor in a cloud is converted directly into ice crystals. Snow-flakes often join together into large clumps of snow in which the crystals are hard to see.

FIGURE 3 ·······················

▶ ART IN MOTION **Freezing Precipitation**

There are four types of freezing precipitation: freezing rain, snow, sleet, and hail.

✎ Review Circle the temperature range in the air and on the ground for which you would expect each kind of precipitation. In some cases, more than one choice may be correct.

Precipitation	Air Temperature	Ground Temperature
Rain	Above 0 °C / At or below 0 °C	Above 0 °C / At or below 0 °C
Freezing rain	Above 0 °C / At or below 0 °C	Above 0 °C / At or below 0 °C
Sleet	Above 0 °C / At or below 0 °C	Above 0 °C / At or below 0 °C
Snow	Above 0 °C / At or below 0 °C	Above 0 °C / At or below 0 °C
Hail	Above 0 °C / At or below 0 °C	Above 0 °C / At or below 0 °C

Hail

A hailstone is a round pellet of ice larger than 5 millimeters in diameter. If you cut a hailstone in half, you would see layers of ice, like the layers of an onion. Hail forms only inside cumulonimbus clouds during thunderstorms. A hailstone starts as an ice pellet inside a cold region of a cloud. Strong updrafts carry the hailstone up through the cold region many times. Each time the hailstone goes through the cold region, a new layer of ice forms around it. Eventually the hailstone becomes heavy enough to fall to the ground. Because hailstones can grow large, hail can cause damage to crops, buildings, and vehicles.

Sleet

Sometimes raindrops fall through a layer of air that is below 0°C, the freezing point of water. As they fall, the raindrops freeze into solid particles of ice. Ice particles smaller than 5 millimeters in diameter are called sleet.

Measuring Snow Rain is not the only kind of precipitation meteorologists measure. Have you ever walked through a large snowstorm and wanted to know exactly how much snow had fallen?

Snowfall is usually measured in two ways: by using a simple measuring stick or by melting collected snow and measuring the depth of water it produces. On average, 10 centimeters of snow contains about the same amount of water as 1 centimeter of rain. However, light, fluffy snow contains far less water than heavy, wet snow does.

apply it!

A rain gauge with a wide funnel collects ten times the actual depth of rain that falls. After the rain ends, the water level is at 15 centimeters.

1 How much rain actually fell?

_____

2 Calculate If snow had fallen instead, how deep would that snow have been?

_____

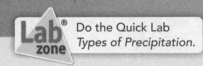 Do the Quick Lab *Types of Precipitation.*

🔑 Assess Your Understanding

1a. Define What is precipitation?

_____

_____

_____

b. Draw Conclusions What factors determine if precipitation falls as freezing rain or as sleet?

_____

_____

_____

got it? ....

○ **I get it!** Now I know that the common types of precipitation are _____

_____

○ **I need extra help with** _____

Go to MY SCIENCE 🔵 COACH *online for help with this subject.*

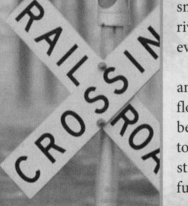

What Are the Causes and Effects of Floods and Droughts?

In September 2008, just three years after Hurricane Katrina, Hurricane Gustav blasted the coasts of Louisiana and Mississippi. Lakes and rivers overflowed. The result was severe flooding.

Floods A **flood** is an overflowing of water in a normally dry area. The floods caused by Gustav fortunately were not as devastating as those caused by Katrina. Because of the flooding caused by Katrina, more than 100,000 homes and businesses were destroyed, along with many bridges and highways.

Causes and Effects of Floods Not all floods are as severe as those caused by a hurricane. 🔑 **Small or large, many floods occur when the volume of water in a river increases so much that the river overflows its channel.** As rain and melting snow add more water, a river gains speed and strength. A flooding river can uproot trees and pluck boulders from the ground. It can even wash away bridges and buildings.

People who live near rivers try to control floods with dams and levees. A dam is a barrier across a river that may redirect the flow of the river to other channels or store floodwaters so they can be released slowly. A levee is an embankment built along a river to prevent flooding of the surrounding land. People sometimes strengthen levees with sandbags or stones and concrete. But powerful floodwaters can sometimes break through dams and levees.

FIGURE 4 ·······································

Flooding Caused by Hurricane Gustav
Hurricane Gustav hit the Gulf Coast in September 2008, causing severe flooding. ✏️ **Answer the questions below.**

1. **Infer** What sort of damage would you expect to your home if this flood took place in the area where you live?

_____

_____

2. CHALLENGE A "100-year flood" is the flooding elevation that has a 1% chance of happening each year. Why is the name misleading?

_____

_____

FIGURE 5

Drought in Texas

In July 1998, a drought hit Wharton County, Texas. This farmer lost about 50 percent of his normal cereal crop to the drought.

Droughts

If you went away for a month and no one was around to water your plants, what would happen to them? They would probably die from lack of water. A long period of scarce rainfall or dry weather is known as a **drought** (drowt). A drought reduces the supplies of groundwater and surface water. A drought can result in a shortage of water for homes and businesses.

Causes and Effects of Droughts

Droughts are usually caused by dry weather systems that remain in one place for weeks or months at a time. Long-term droughts can devastate a region. Droughts can cause crop failure. A drought can even cause famine in places where people must grow their own food. Streams and ponds dry up, and people and animals suffer.

People can prepare for droughts in several ways. When dry conditions first occur, people can begin conserving water. Farmers can grow drought-resistant plants that have been bred to withstand dry conditions. By practicing water and soil conservation, people can ensure that when droughts do occur, people will be prepared for their effects.

✏️ **Relate Cause and Effect**
What causes a flood? A drought?

_____
_____
_____
_____
_____
_____

Lab zone Do the Quick Lab *Floods and Droughts.*

🔑 Assess Your Understanding

2a. Explain What are two ways to help reduce the dangers of floods?

_____

b. Make Judgments Your community is considering building a dam on a nearby river to reduce flooding. Would you support this proposal? Explain.

_____
_____
_____
_____
_____
_____
_____
_____
_____

got it?

⭕ **I get it!** Now I know that floods are caused by _____ and droughts are caused by _____

⭕ **I need extra help with** _____

Go to MY SCIENCE 🔊 COACH *online for help with this subject.*

131

Air Masses

UNLOCK THE BIG ?

🔑 **What Are the Major Air Masses?**

🔑 **What Are the Main Types of Fronts?**

🔑 **What Weather Do Cyclones and Anticyclones Bring?**

my PLaNeT DiaRY

Cyclones and Tornadoes

Misconception: A cyclone is another name for tornado.

Fact: Both cyclones and tornadoes are spinning storm systems. Both rotate around an area of low pressure. However, tornadoes cover a much smaller area than cyclones do. And tornado winds reach much higher speeds.

Evidence: Outside the tropics, cyclones can be 1,000 to 4,000 kilometers across. Tropical cyclones, which are powerful hurricanes, are smaller, ranging from 100 to 1,000 kilometers across. But tornadoes are smaller still. Tornadoes range in size from a few meters to 1,600 meters across. Tornado winds are the fastest known winds on Earth. They can reach speeds of 480 km/h, but are usually much slower. Cyclone winds are strong, but do not move as fast as the fastest tornado winds. Tropical cyclone winds rarely reach more than 320 km/h.

MISCONCEPTION

Think about the cyclones and tornadoes you have heard about as you answer the following questions.

1. Which kind of storm do you think would cause damage over a larger area, a cyclone or a tornado? Why?

   _____

   _____

   _____

2. Have you ever seen water swirl down a drain? How is it related to a tornado?

   _____

   _____

> **PLANET DIARY** Go to **Planet Diary** to learn more about violent weather.

 Lab ® **zone** Do the Inquiry Warm-Up *How Do Fluids of Different Densities Move?*

Vocabulary
- air mass
- tropical
- polar
- maritime
- continental
- jet stream
- front
- occluded
- cyclone
- anticyclone

Skills
- Reading: Relate Text and Visuals
- Inquiry: Classify

What Are the Major Air Masses?

When you have a certain type of weather taking place outside, that's because a certain type of air mass is influencing the weather. An **air mass** is a huge body of air in the lower atmosphere that has similar temperature, humidity, and air pressure at any given height. Scientists classify air masses according to temperature and humidity. **Four major types of air masses influence the weather in North America: maritime tropical, continental tropical, maritime polar, and continental polar.**

As shown in **Figure 1,** the characteristics of an air mass depend on the temperatures and moisture content of the region over which the air mass forms. Remember that temperature affects air pressure. Cold, dense air has a higher pressure, while warm, less-dense air has a lower pressure. **Tropical,** or warm, air masses form in the tropics and have low air pressure. **Polar,** or cold, air masses form north of 50° north latitude and south of 50° south latitude. Polar air masses have high air pressure.

Whether an air mass is humid or dry depends on whether it forms over water or land. **Maritime** air masses form over oceans. Water evaporates from the oceans, so the air can become very humid. **Continental** air masses form over land. Continental air masses have less exposure to large amounts of moisture from bodies of water. Therefore, continental air masses are drier than maritime air masses.

	Wet	Dry
Warm	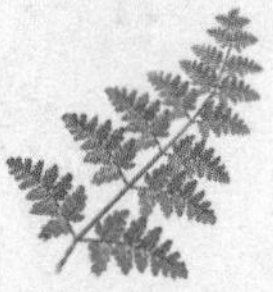 ______ ______	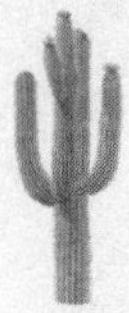 ______ ______
Cool	______ ______	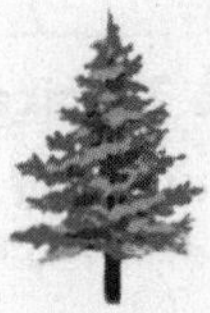 ______ ______

FIGURE 1

Types of Air Masses

Air masses can be classified according to temperature and humidity.

Classify Fill in the table. Classify each type of air mass as *maritime* or *continental* and as *tropical* or *polar.*

FIGURE 2

North American Air Masses

Air masses can be warm or cold, and humid or dry. **Classify Identify the two unlabeled air masses on the page by their descriptions.**

Maritime Polar

Cool, humid air masses form over the icy cold North Atlantic ocean. These air masses are often pushed out to sea by westerly winds.

Continental Polar

Large air masses form over Canada and Alaska and can bring bitterly cold weather with low humidity. Storms may occur when these air masses move south and collide with maritime tropical air masses moving north.

Cool, humid air masses form over the icy cold North Pacific ocean. Even in summer, these air masses often cool the West Coast.

✎ **Type of air mass:** _____

PACIFIC OCEAN

ATLANTIC OCEAN

Gulf of Mexico

Warm, humid air masses form over the Gulf of Mexico and the Atlantic Ocean. They can bring thunderstorms, heavy rain, or snow.

✎ **Type of air mass:** _____

Continental Tropical

Hot, dry air masses form mostly in summer over dry areas of the Southwest and northern Mexico. They can bring hot, dry weather to the southern Great Plains.

Maritime Tropical

Warm, humid air masses form over the Pacific Ocean. In summer, they usually bring hot, humid weather, summer showers, and thunderstorms. In winter, they can bring heavy rain or snow.

↻ **Relate Text and Visuals** According to the map and the text, which two of the following air masses form over water?
- ○ Maritime tropical
- ○ Maritime polar
- ○ Continental tropical
- ○ Continental polar

How Air Masses Move
When an air mass moves into an area and interacts with other air masses, it causes the weather to change, sometimes drastically. In the continental United States, air masses are commonly moved by the prevailing westerlies and jet streams.

Prevailing Westerlies The prevailing westerlies, the major wind belts over the continental United States, generally push air masses from west to east. For example, maritime polar air masses from the Pacific Ocean are blown onto the West Coast, bringing low clouds and showers.

Jet Streams Embedded within the prevailing westerlies are jet streams. Jet streams are bands of high-speed winds about 10 kilometers above Earth's surface. As jet streams generally blow from west to east, air masses are carried along their tracks.

Fronts As huge masses of air move across the land and the oceans, they collide with each other, but do not easily mix. Think about a bottle of oil and water. The less-dense oil floats on top. Something similar happens when two air masses of different temperature and humidity collide. They do not easily mix. The boundary where the air masses meet becomes a front. Storms and changeable weather often develop along fronts like the one in **Figure 3**.

FIGURE 3 ·····································
How a Front Forms
The boundary where unlike air masses meet is called a front. A front may be 15 to 600 km wide and extend high into the troposphere.

Relate Text and Visuals What kind of weather would develop along the front shown in the photo?

_____

_____

Direction of moving front

Warm air mass

Cold air mass

Do the Quick Lab
Tracking Air Masses.

Assess Your Understanding

1a. Review What two characteristics are used to classify air masses?

_____

_____

b. Apply Concepts What type of air mass would form over the northern Atlantic Ocean?

_____

c. Classify Classify the four major types of air masses according to moisture content.

_____

_____

_____

_____

got it? ··

O **I get it!** Now I know that the four major types of air masses are _____

_____

O **I need extra help with** _____

Go to MY SCIENCE COACH online for help with this subject.

What Are the Main Types of Fronts?

When you leave school in the afternoon, you may find that the weather is different from when you arrived in the morning. That might be because a front has just recently passed through the area. 🔑 **Colliding air masses can form four types of fronts: cold fronts, warm fronts, stationary fronts, and occluded fronts.** The kind of front that develops depends on the characteristics of the air masses and the direction in which they move.

FIGURE 4 ·······························

▶ **INTERACTIVE ART** **Types of Fronts**

✏ **Infer** Identify the type of weather brought by each front as it passes through an area.

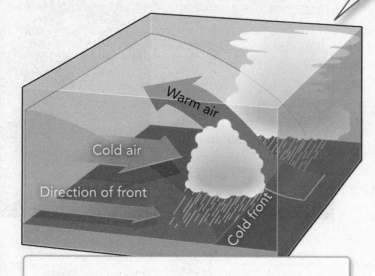

Cold Fronts

Cold air is dense and tends to sink. Warm air is less dense and tends to rise. When a faster cold air mass runs into a slower warm air mass, the denser cold air slides under the lighter warm air. The warm air is pushed upward along the leading edge of the colder air. A cold front forms.

As the warm air rises, it expands and cools. The rising air soon reaches the dew point, the temperature at which water vapor in the air condenses. Clouds form. Heavy rain or snow may fall.

Cold fronts tend to arrive quickly, because their leading edges move along the ground. They can cause abrupt weather changes, including thunderstorms. After a cold front passes, colder, drier air moves in, often bringing clear skies, a shift in wind direction, and lower temperatures.

Warm Fronts

Clouds and precipitation also accompany warm fronts. At a warm front, a fast-moving warm air mass overtakes a slower cold air mass. Because cold air is denser than warm air, the warm air moves over the cold air. If the warm air is humid, light rain or snow falls along the front. If the air is dry, scattered clouds form. Because warm fronts arrive slowly, the weather may be rainy or cloudy for several days. After a warm front passes, the weather tends to be warmer and humid.

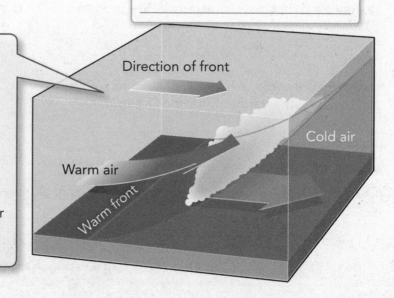

Occluded Fronts

The most complex weather situation occurs at an occluded front, where a warm air mass is caught between two cooler air masses. The denser cool air masses move underneath the less dense warm air mass and push the warm air upward. The two cooler air masses meet in the middle and may mix. The temperature near the ground becomes cooler. The warm air mass is cut off, or **occluded,** from the ground. As the warm air cools and its water vapor condenses, the weather may turn cloudy and rain or snow may fall.

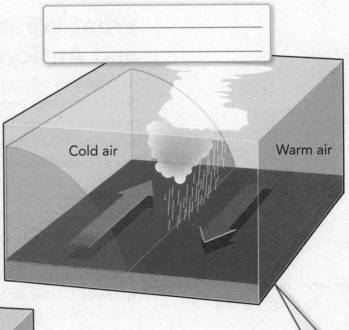

Cold air   Warm air

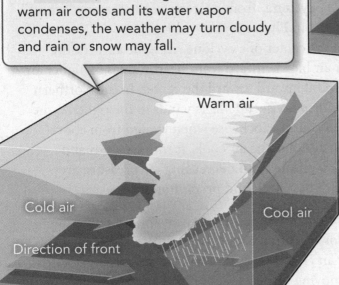

Warm air

Cold air   Cool air

Direction of front

Stationary Fronts

Sometimes cold and warm air masses meet, but neither one can move the other. In this case, the front is called a stationary front. Where the warm and cool air meet, water vapor in the warm air condenses into rain, snow, fog, or clouds. But if a stationary front stalls, it may bring many days of clouds and precipitation.

Do the Quick Lab
Weather Fronts.

🔑 Assess Your Understanding

2a. Define What is a front?

_____

_____

b. Describe What type of weather occurs as a warm front moves through an area?

_____

_____

c. Classify What types of fronts would cause several days of rain and clouds?

_____

_____

got it?

○ **I get it!** Now I know that the four main types of fronts are _____

_____

_____

_____

○ **I need extra help with** _____

_____

_____

Go to my science ⑤ coach online for help with this subject.

137

What Weather Do Cyclones and Anticyclones Bring?

As air masses collide to form fronts, the boundary between the fronts sometimes becomes distorted. This distortion can be caused by surface features, such as mountains, or strong winds, such as the jet stream. When this happens, the air begins to swirl. The swirling air can cause a low-pressure center to form.

Cyclones A circled *L* on a weather map stands for "low," and indicates an area of relatively low air pressure. A swirling center of low air pressure is a **cyclone**, from a Greek word meaning "wheel." You can see a cyclone in **Figure 5**.

As warm air at the center of a cyclone rises, the air pressure decreases. Cooler air blows inward from nearby areas of higher air pressure. Winds spiral inward toward the center. In the Northern Hemisphere, the Coriolis effect deflects winds to the right. So the cyclone winds spin counterclockwise when viewed from above.

As air rises in a cyclone, the air cools, forming clouds and precipitation. ▭ **Cyclones and decreasing air pressure are associated with clouds, wind, and precipitation.**

Anticyclones As its name suggests, an anticyclone is the opposite of a cyclone. **Anticyclones** are high-pressure centers of dry air, shown by an *H* on a weather map. Winds spiral outward from the center, moving toward areas of lower pressure. Because of the Coriolis effect, winds in an anticyclone spin clockwise in the Northern Hemisphere. As air moves out from the center, cool air moves downward from higher in the troposphere. The cool air warms up, so its relative humidity drops. ▭ **The descending air in an anticyclone generally causes dry, clear weather.**

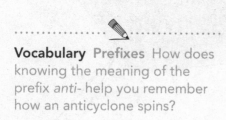

Vocabulary **Prefixes** How does knowing the meaning of the prefix *anti-* help you remember how an anticyclone spins?

_____

_____

_____

_____

FIGURE 5 ································

Cyclones and Anticyclones
✎ **Interpret Diagrams** Label each diagram as either a cyclone or an anticyclone. In each circle, draw an arrow to show the direction of air motion for the system as it would be seen from above.

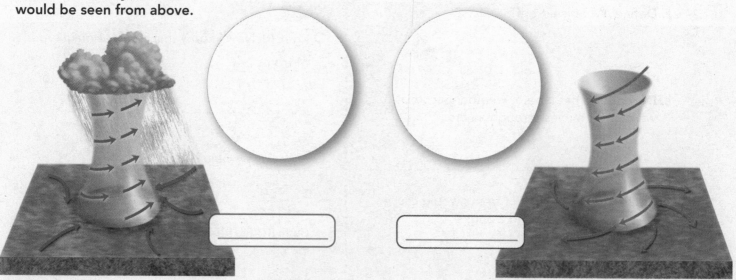

apply it!

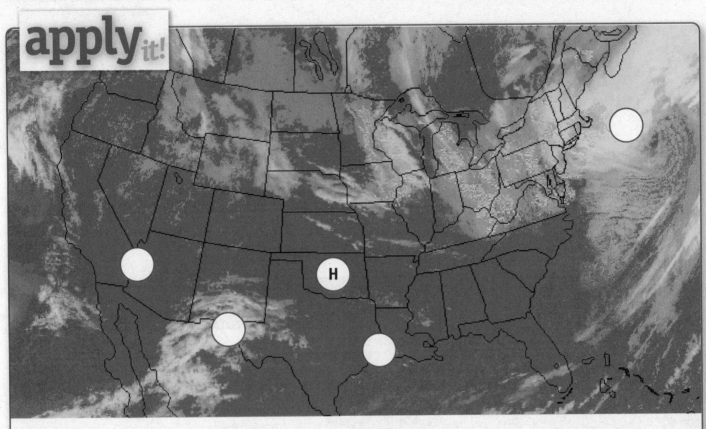

1 Classify Fill in the empty circles with either *L* for a low-pressure center or *H* for a high-pressure center.

2 CHALLENGE What information on the map helped you decide if an area's air pressure was low or high?

_____

_____

 Do the Quick Lab
Cyclones and Anticyclones.

🔑 Assess Your Understanding

3a. Identify What is a cyclone?

_____

b. 🔄 Relate Text and Visuals How does air move in a cyclone?

_____

_____

c. Compare and Contrast What kind of weather is associated with a cyclone? What kind of weather is associated with an anticyclone?

_____

_____

_____

got it? ·

○ **I get it!** Now I know that cyclones cause _____

and anticyclones cause _____

○ **I need extra help with** _____

Go to **my science** 💬 **coach** online for help with this subject.

Storms

UNLOCK
THE BIG
?

🔑 **How Do the Different Types of Storms Form?**

🔑 **How Can You Stay Safe in a Storm?**

my pLaneT DiaRY

DISASTERS

The Blizzard of 1978

In February 1978, a huge blizzard hit the northeastern United States. Weather stations recorded hurricane-force winds, and many cities received record-breaking amounts of snow. The storm hovered over New England, and heavy snow fell for almost 33 hours without letting up.

In Massachusetts, people driving on highways abandoned their cars when the snow became too deep to drive through. Rescuers used cross-country skis and snowmobiles to help evacuate the roads. Stranded drivers returned home any way they could. The governor of Massachusetts declared a state of emergency. He called in the National Guard to clear the roads of snow. It took almost a week until the roads opened again.

Communicate Write your answers to each question below. Then discuss your answers with a partner.

1. What do you think made the blizzard so dangerous?

_____

_____

_____

2. Besides the hurricane-force winds and the roads filling with snow, what other hazards do you think the blizzard caused?

_____

_____

▷ PLANET DIARY Go to **Planet Diary** to learn more about strong storms.

Lab zone® Do the Inquiry Warm-Up *Can You Make a Tornado?*

Vocabulary
- storm • thunderstorm • lightning
- hurricane • storm surge • tornado • evacuate

Skills
- ⟳ Reading: Outline
- △ Inquiry: Infer

How Do the Different Types of Storms Form?

The Blizzard of 1978 was one of the most intense storms ever to hit the northeastern United States. A **storm** is a violent disturbance in the atmosphere. Storms involve sudden changes in air pressure, which cause rapid air movements. There are several types of severe storms: winter storms, thunderstorms, hurricanes, and tornadoes.

Winter Storms In the winter in the northern United States, a large amount of precipitation falls as snow. ⟶ **All year round, most precipitation begins in clouds as snow. If the air is colder than 0°C all the way to the ground, the precipitation falls as snow.** Heavy snow can block roads, trapping people in their homes and delaying emergency vehicles. Extreme cold can damage crops and cause water pipes to burst.

Some places, including Buffalo and Rochester in upstate New York, get a lot more snow than others. In an average winter, nearly three meters of snow fall on these cities due to lake-effect snow, as shown in **Figure 1.** Buffalo is located east of Lake Erie. Rochester is located south of Lake Ontario. In the fall and winter, the land near these lakes cools much more rapidly than the water in the lakes. When a cold, dry air mass moves southeast across one of the lakes, it picks up water vapor and heat. As soon as the air mass reaches the other side of the lake, the air rises and cools again. The water vapor condenses and falls as snow.

FIGURE 1 ·······························

Lake-Effect Snow
As cold, dry air moves across the warmer water, it becomes more humid as water vapor evaporates from the lake surface. When the air reaches land and cools, lake-effect snow falls.

✏️ **Interpret Maps** Circle the cities that receive lake-effect snow. In the box on the map, name a city that does not get it and explain why.

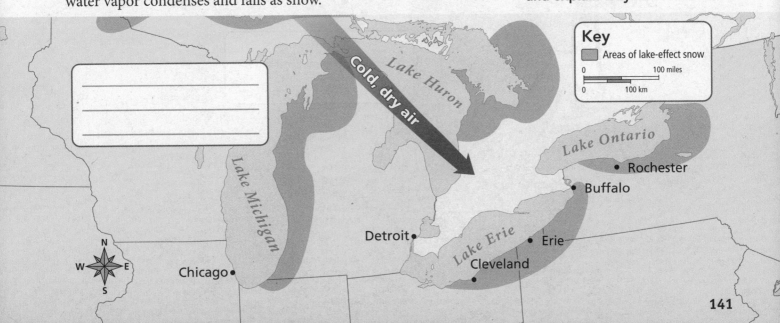

Key
Areas of lake-effect snow
0   100 miles
0   100 km

Lake Huron
Cold, dry air
Lake Ontario
• Rochester
Lake Michigan
Buffalo
Detroit •
Lake Erie
• Erie
Cleveland
Chicago •

N W E S

141

Thunderstorms

Do you find thunderstorms frightening? Exciting? As you watch the brilliant flashes of lightning and listen to long rolls of thunder, you may wonder what causes them.

How Thunderstorms Form A **thunderstorm** is a small storm often accompanied by heavy precipitation and frequent thunder and lightning. **Thunderstorms form in large cumulonimbus clouds, also known as thunderheads.** Most cumulonimbus clouds form on hot, humid afternoons or evenings. They also form when warm air is forced upward along a cold front. In both cases, the warm, humid air rises rapidly, as shown in **Figure 2.** The air cools, forming dense thunderheads with water condensing into rain droplets. Heavy rain falls, sometimes along with hail. Within the thunderhead are strong upward and downward winds known as updrafts and downdrafts. Many thunderstorms form in the spring and summer in southern states or on the western plains.

FIGURE 2 ···

How Thunderstorms Form

A thunderstorm forms when warm, humid air rises rapidly within a cumulonimbus cloud.

✎ **Interpret Diagrams** Fill in the captions noting the direction of the warm, humid air and the cold air.

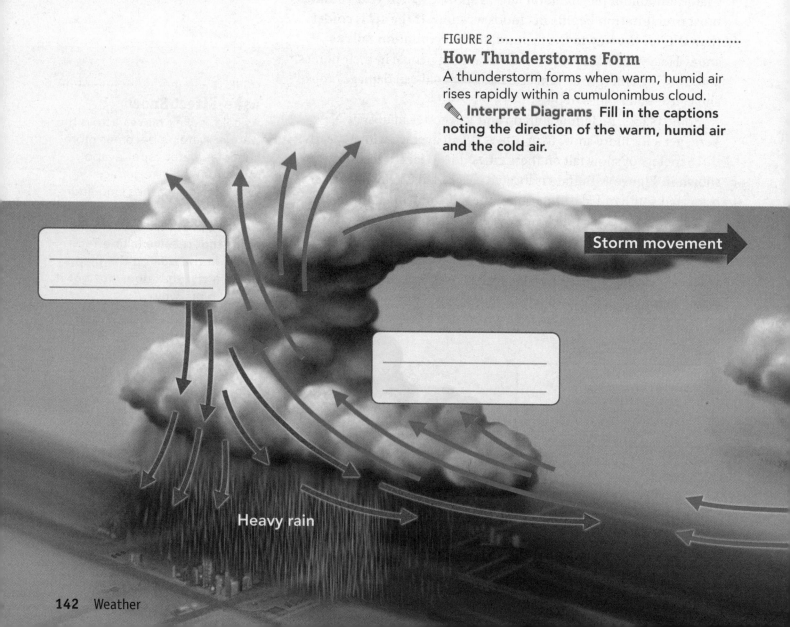

Storm movement

Heavy rain

Lightning and Thunder During a thunderstorm, areas of positive and negative electrical charges build up in the storm clouds. **Lightning** is a sudden spark, or electrical discharge, as these charges jump between parts of a cloud, between nearby clouds, or between a cloud and the ground. Lightning is similar to the shocks you sometimes feel when you touch a metal object on a very dry day. Because lightning is electricity, it is easily conducted by metal.

What causes thunder? A lightning bolt can heat the air near it to as much as 30,000°C, much hotter than the sun's surface. The rapidly heated air expands explosively. Thunder is the sound of the explosion. Because light travels faster than sound, you see lightning before you hear thunder.

Thunderstorm Damage Thunderstorms can cause severe damage. The heavy rains associated with thunderstorms can flood low-lying areas. Lightning can also cause damage. When lightning strikes the ground, the hot, expanding air can shatter tree trunks or start forest fires. When lightning strikes people or animals, it acts like a powerful electric shock. Lightning can cause unconsciousness, serious burns, and heart failure.

Floods A major danger during severe thunderstorms is flooding. Some floods occur when so much water pours into a stream or river that its banks overflow, covering the surrounding land with water. In urban areas, floods can occur when the ground is already saturated by heavy rains. The water can't soak into the water-logged ground or the many areas covered with buildings, roads, and parking lots. A flash flood is a sudden, violent flood that occurs shortly after a storm.

FIGURE 3 ·······················

Lightning Damage

Lightning can cause fires, serious damage, and injuries. **Infer** Which is more likely to be hit by lightning, a metal or a wooden boat? Why?

_____

_____

................✏.................

⟲ **Outline** After reading the text on this page, complete the outline by adding details about how a hurricane forms.

I. Hurricanes
  A. How a Hurricane Forms

   1._____
   _____
   _____
   _____
   2._____
   _____
   _____
   3._____
   _____
   _____

Hurricanes A **hurricane** is a tropical cyclone with winds of 119 km/h or higher. A typical hurricane is about 600 kilometers across. Hurricanes form in the Atlantic, Pacific, and Indian oceans. In the western Pacific, they are called typhoons. In the Indian ocean, they are simply called cyclones.

How Hurricanes Form A typical hurricane that strikes the United States forms in the Atlantic Ocean north of the equator in August, September, or October. 🔑 **A hurricane begins over warm ocean water as a low-pressure area, or tropical disturbance.** If the tropical disturbance grows in size and strength, it becomes a tropical storm, which may then become a hurricane.

Look at **Figure 4** to see how a hurricane forms. A hurricane draws its energy from the warm, humid air at the ocean's surface. As this air rises and forms clouds, more air is drawn into the system. Inside the storm are bands of very high winds and heavy rains. Winds spiral inward toward the area of lowest pressure at the center. The lower the air pressure at the center of a storm, the faster the winds blow toward the center. Hurricane winds may be as strong as 320 km/h.

Hurricane winds are strongest in a narrow band around the storm's center. At the center is a ring of clouds, called the eyewall, that encloses a quiet "eye." The wind gets stronger as the eye approaches. When the eye arrives, the weather changes suddenly. The air grows calm and the sky may clear. After the eye passes, the storm resumes, but the wind blows from the opposite direction.

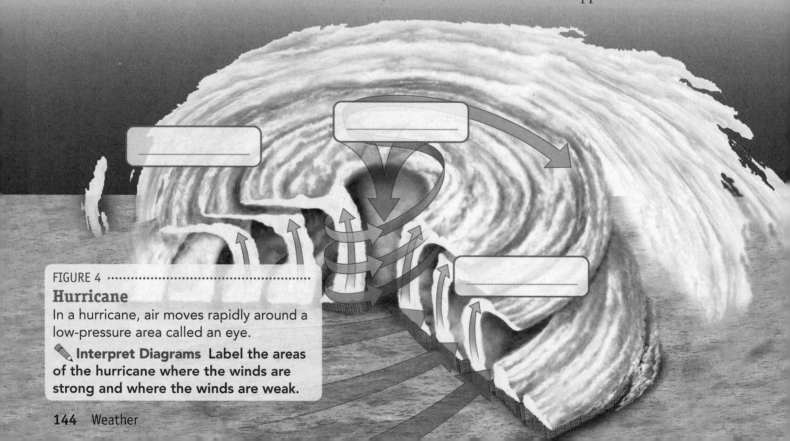

FIGURE 4 ·····················
Hurricane
In a hurricane, air moves rapidly around a low-pressure area called an eye.

✎ **Interpret Diagrams** Label the areas of the hurricane where the winds are strong and where the winds are weak.

August 24, 2005: Katrina approaches Florida.

August 26, 2005: Hurricane Katrina picks up strength over the Gulf of Mexico.

August 29, 2005: Hurricane Katrina hits the Gulf Coast.

How Hurricanes Move Hurricanes can last longer than other storms—a week or more. During that period, they can travel thousands of kilometers. Hurricanes that form in the Atlantic Ocean are steered by easterly trade winds toward the Caribbean islands and the southeastern United States. After a hurricane passes over land, it no longer has warm, moist air to draw energy from. The hurricane gradually weakens, although heavy rainfall may continue for several days.

Hurricane Damage When a hurricane comes ashore, it brings high waves and severe flooding, as well as wind damage. The low pressure and high winds of the hurricane over the ocean raise the level of the water as much as 6 meters above normal sea level. The result is a **storm surge,** a "dome" of water that sweeps across the coast where the hurricane lands. Storm surges can cause great damage, washing away beaches, destroying coastal buildings, and eroding the coastline.

FIGURE 5 ···

Hurricane Katrina
The picture shows the path of Hurricane Katrina.

✎ **Predict** On the picture, draw lines showing the possible paths the hurricane could have taken after reaching land. What happens to a hurricane after it reaches land?

Tornadoes

A tornado is one of the most frightening and intense types of storms. A **tornado** is a rapidly spinning column of air that reaches down from a thunderstorm to touch Earth's surface. If a tornado occurs over a lake or ocean, the storm is called a waterspout. Tornadoes are usually brief, but can be deadly. They may touch the ground for 15 minutes or less and be only a few hundred meters across. But an intense tornado's wind speed may approach 500 km/h.

How Tornadoes Form Tornadoes can form in any situation involving severe weather. 🔑 **Tornadoes most commonly develop in thick cumulonimbus clouds—the same clouds that bring thunderstorms.** Tornadoes often occur when thunderstorms are likely—in spring and early summer, late in the afternoon when the ground is warm.

Tornado Alley Tornadoes occur in nearly every part of the United States. However, the Great Plains often have the kind of weather pattern that is likely to create tornadoes: A warm, humid air mass moves north from the Gulf of Mexico into the lower Great Plains, and a cold, dry air mass moves south from Canada. When the air masses meet, the cold air moves under the warm air, forcing it to rise. A line of thunderstorms called a squall line is likely to form, with storms traveling northeast. A single squall line can produce ten or more tornadoes.

FIGURE 6 ·······································
▶ INTERACTIVE ART **Tornado Formation**
About 1,200 tornadoes occur in the United States every year. Weather patterns on the Great Plains result in a "tornado alley."

✏️ **Interpret Maps Pick a state on the map (or your home state) and indicate whether its risk of tornadoes is low or high.**

_____

_____

_____

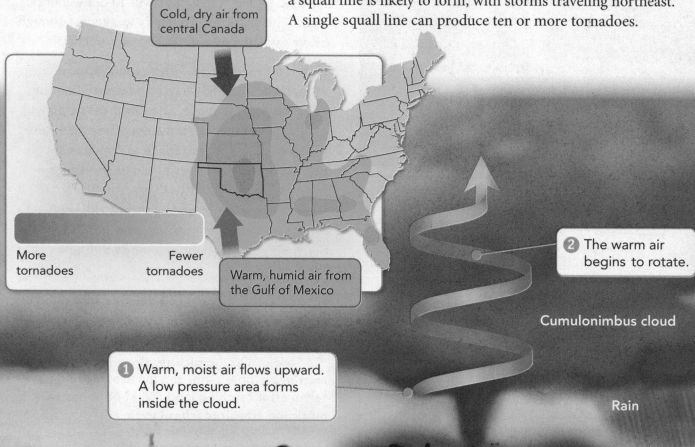

Cold, dry air from central Canada

More tornadoes　　　Fewer tornadoes

Warm, humid air from the Gulf of Mexico

① Warm, moist air flows upward. A low pressure area forms inside the cloud.

② The warm air begins to rotate.

Cumulonimbus cloud

Rain

Tornado Damage Tornado damage comes from both strong winds and flying debris. The low pressure inside the tornado sucks objects into the funnel. Tornadoes can move large objects and scatter debris many miles away. One tornado tore a sign off in Oklahoma and dropped it 50 km away in Arkansas! A tornado can level houses on one street but leave neighboring houses standing.

Tornadoes are ranked on the Enhanced Fujita scale by the amount of damage they cause. The scale was named for the scientist who devised the original scale, Dr. T. Theodore Fujita. As shown in **Figure 7,** the scale goes from light damage (EF0) to extreme damage (EF5). Only about one percent of tornadoes are ranked as EF4 or EF5.

FIGURE 7 ···

Tornado Damage

✏ CHALLENGE **How would you rank this tornado damage on the Enhanced Fujita scale? Why?**

_____

_____

_____

Enhanced Fujita Scale	Types of Damage
EF0	Branches broken off trees
EF1	Mobile homes overturned
EF2	Trees uprooted
EF3	Roofs and walls torn down
EF4	Houses leveled
EF5	Houses carried away

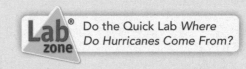

Do the Quick Lab *Where Do Hurricanes Come From?*

🔑 **Assess Your Understanding**

1a. Identify What is a hurricane?

_____

_____

_____

_____

b. Explain How do hurricanes form?

_____

_____

_____

_____

_____

c. Compare and Contrast How do hurricanes differ from tornadoes?

_____

_____

_____

_____

_____

_____

_____

_____

_____

_____

got it? ··

○ **I get it!** Now I know that the main kinds of storms are _____

_____

_____

_____

○ **I need extra help with** _____

_____

Go to MY SCIENCE ⓢ COACH *online for help with this subject.*

147

How Can You Stay Safe in a Storm?

A winter storm or a thunderstorm can be fun to watch if you're in a safe place. But you don't want to be near a hurricane or tornado if you can avoid it.

Winter Storm Safety Imagine being caught in a snowstorm when the wind suddenly picks up. High winds can blow falling snow sideways or pick up snow from the ground and suspend it in the air. This situation can be dangerous because the blowing snow limits your vision and makes it easy to get lost. Also, strong winds cool a person's body rapidly. 🗝 **If you are caught in a snowstorm, try to find shelter from the wind.** Cover exposed parts of your body and try to stay dry. If you are in a car, keep the engine running only if the exhaust pipe is clear of snow.

Thunderstorm Safety The safest place to be during a thunderstorm is indoors. Avoid touching telephones, electrical appliances, or plumbing fixtures. It is usually safe to stay in a car. The electricity will move along the metal skin of the car and jump to the ground. However, do not touch any metal inside the car. 🗝 **During thunderstorms, avoid places where lightning may strike. Also, avoid objects that can conduct electricity, such as metal objects and bodies of water.**

How can you remain safe if you are caught outside during a thunderstorm? Do not seek shelter under a tree, because lightning may strike the tree. Instead, find a low area away from trees, fences, and poles. Crouch with your head down. If you are swimming or in a boat, get to shore and find shelter away from the water.

Hurricane Safety Today, weather satellites can track the paths of hurricanes. So people now receive a warning well in advance of an approaching hurricane. A "hurricane watch" indicates that hurricane conditions are possible in an area within the next 36 hours. You should be prepared to **evacuate** (ee VAK yoo ayt), or move away temporarily. A "hurricane warning" means that hurricane conditions are expected within the next 24 hours. 🗝 **If you hear a hurricane warning and are told to evacuate, leave the area immediately.**

FIGURE 8 ······························

Evacuation Site
In September 2005, the city of Dallas opened up shelters such as the Reunion Arena for people who fled Hurricane Katrina.
✏ **Explain** What is the difference between a hurricane watch and a hurricane warning?

_____

_____

_____

_____

_____

_____

_____

_____

apply it!

The two signs in the pictures show warnings about possible storms.

1 **Infer** Match each safety sign to the appropriate storm.

2 In the space to the right, draw a sign to show how one could stay safe in a thunderstorm or winter storm.

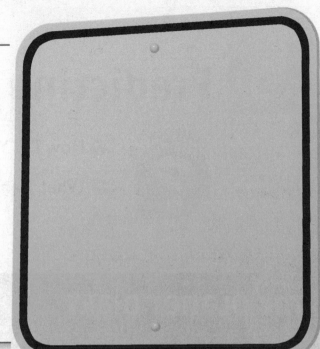

Tornado Safety A "tornado watch" is an announcement that tornadoes are possible in your area. A "tornado warning" is an announcement that a tornado has been seen in the sky or on weather radar. If you hear a tornado warning, move to a safe area as soon as you can. Do not wait until you actually see the tornado.

🗝 **The safest place to be during a tornado is in a storm shelter or a basement.** If there is no basement, move to the middle of the ground floor. Stay away from windows and doors. Lie under a sturdy piece of furniture. If you are outdoors, lie flat in a ditch.

Do the Quick Lab *Storm Safety.*

🗝 Assess Your Understanding

2a. List Based on the safety steps, list the four storms from least to most dangerous.

_____

_____

_____

b. Solve Problems How can a community make sure people stay safe in a storm?

_____

_____

_____

_____

got it?

○ **I get it!** Now I know that to stay safe in a storm I should either _____

or, in the case of a hurricane, I should _____

○ **I need extra help with** _____

Go to MY SCIENCE 🗨 COACH *online for help with this subject.*

Predicting the Weather

🔑 How Do You Predict the Weather?

🔑 What Can You Learn From Weather Maps?

MY PLANET DiARY

CAREERS

Meteorologist Mish Michaels

Mish Michaels uses computers in her work every day to sort data from weather satellites, radar, and weather stations from all over the world. Then she shares her weather forecasts with Boston television viewers.

Michaels became interested in weather while in kindergarten in Maryland. She watched a tornado damage her family's apartment complex. Since then, she has been fascinated by storms. Michaels went on to major in meteorology at Cornell University.

Michaels is devoted to educating others about weather. She supports the WINS program (Women in the Natural Sciences) of Blue Hill Weather Observatory in Milton, Massachusetts. The program inspires girls to pursue careers in math, science, and technology.

Communicate After you read about Mish Michaels, answer these questions with a partner.

1. Why do you think that meteorologists depend so heavily on computers?

_____

_____

_____

2. What subjects do you think future meteorologists need to study in school?

_____

_____

▷ **PLANET DIARY** Go to **Planet Diary** to learn more about predicting the weather.

Lab zone® Do the Inquiry Warm-Up *Predicting Weather.*

Vocabulary
- meteorologist
- isobar
- isotherm

Skills
- Reading: Compare and Contrast
- Inquiry: Predict

How Do You Predict the Weather?

The first step in weather forecasting is to collect data, either from direct observations or through the use of instruments. For example, if a barometer shows that the air pressure is falling, you can expect an approaching low-pressure area, possibly bringing rain or snow.

Making Simple Observations You can read weather signs in the clouds, too. Cumulus clouds often form on warm days. If they grow larger and taller, they can become cumulonimbus clouds, which may produce a thunderstorm. If you can see thin cirrus clouds high in the sky, a warm front may be approaching.

Even careful weather observers often turn to meteorologists for weather information. **Meteorologists** (mee tee uh RAHL uh jists) are scientists who study and try to predict weather.

Interpreting Complex Data Meteorologists interpret information from a variety of sources. 🔑 **Meteorologists use maps, charts, computers, and other technology to analyze weather data and to prepare weather forecasts.**

Weather reporters get their information from the National Weather Service, which uses balloons, satellites, radar, and surface instruments to gather data.

FIGURE 1 ....

Red Sky
Many people have their own weather sayings. Many of these sayings are based on long-term observations.

✏️ **Write your own weather poem in the space below.**

Red sky at night,
Sailors delight;
Red sky at morning,
Sailors take warning.

Evening red and morning gray
Will send the travelers on their way;
Evening gray and morning red
Will bring down rain upon their head.

151

Using Technology Techniques for predicting weather have changed dramatically in recent years. Short-range forecasts—forecasts for up to five days—are now fairly reliable. Meteorologists can also make somewhat accurate long-range predictions. Technological improvements in gathering weather data and using computers have improved the accuracy of weather forecasts.

FIGURE 2 ·······················
Weather Technology

✎ **Explain** why better technology leads to improved weather forecasting.

_____

_____

_____

Automated Weather Stations
Weather stations gather data from surface locations for temperature, air pressure, relative humidity, rainfall, and wind speed and direction. The National Weather Service has established a network of more than 1,700 surface weather observation sites.

Weather Balloons
Weather balloons carry instruments into the troposphere and lower stratosphere. The instruments measure temperature, air pressure, and humidity.

Weather Satellites
Satellites orbit Earth in the exosphere, the uppermost layer of the atmosphere. Cameras on weather satellites can make images of Earth's surface, clouds, storms, and snow cover. Satellites also collect data on temperature, humidity, solar radiation, and wind speed and direction.

Computer Forecasts
Computers process weather data quickly to help forecasters make predictions. The computer works through thousands of calculations using equations from weather models to make forecasts.

 Lab zone® Do the Quick Lab
Modeling Weather Satellites.

🔑 Assess Your Understanding

got it? ···

○ **I get it!** Now I know that meteorologists prepare weather forecasts using _____

_____

○ **I need extra help with** _____

Go to **MY SCIENCE COACH** *online for help with this subject.*

What Can You Learn From Weather Maps?

A weather map is a "snapshot" of conditions at a particular time over a large area. There are many types of weather maps.

Weather Service Maps Data from many local weather stations all over the country are assembled into weather maps at the National Weather Service. The way maps display data is shown in the Apply It feature below. The simplified weather map at the end of this lesson includes a key that shows weather station symbols.

On some weather maps you see curved lines. These lines connect places with similar conditions of temperature or air pressure. **Isobars** are lines joining places on the map that have the same air pressure. (*Iso* means "equal" and *bar* means "weight.") The numbers on the isobars are the pressure readings. These readings may be given in inches of mercury or in millibars.

Isotherms are lines joining places that have the same temperature. The isotherm may be labeled with the temperature in degrees Fahrenheit, degrees Celsius, or both.

Compare and Contrast
How are isobars and isotherms alike? How do they differ?

_____
_____
_____
_____
_____
_____

apply it!

The tables below show what various weather symbols represent.

1 Apply Concepts According to the weather map symbol below, what are the amount of cloud cover and the wind speed?

_____

2 Predict Would you expect precipitation in an area marked by this weather symbol? Why?

_____

Cloud Cover (%)	Symbol
0	○
10	◐
20–30	◔
40	◕
50	◑
60	◕
70–80	◕
90	◑
100	●

Weather Map Symbol

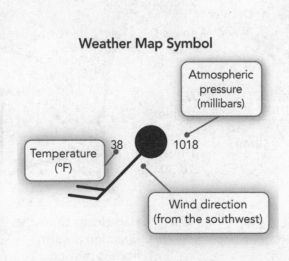

Temperature (°F) — 38
Atmospheric pressure (millibars) — 1018
Wind direction (from the southwest)

Wind Speed (mi/h)	Symbol
1–2	
3–8	
9–14	
15–20	
21–25	
26–31	
32–37	
38–43	
44–49	
50–54	
55–60	
61–66	
67–71	
72–77	

FIGURE 3 ·······················

Newspaper Weather Map

The symbols on this map show fronts, high- and low-pressure areas, the high and low temperature readings for different cities, and precipitation. The color bands indicate different temperature ranges.

✎ **Answer the questions below.**

1. **Interpret Maps** Identify the weather that will occur in Denver according to this map.

_____

_____

2. CHALLENGE Can you predict the weather in Denver a week later? Explain.

_____

_____

Newspaper Weather Maps

Maps in newspapers are simplified versions of maps produced by the National Weather Service. **Figure 3** shows a typical newspaper weather map. From what you have learned in this lesson, you can probably interpret most symbols on this map. 🗝 **Standard symbols on weather maps show fronts, areas of high and low pressure, types of precipitation, and temperatures.** Note that the high and low temperatures are given in degrees Fahrenheit instead of Celsius.

Limits of Weather Forecasts

As computers have grown more powerful, and new satellites and radar technologies have been developed, scientists have been able to make better forecasts. But even with extremely powerful computers, it is unlikely that forecasters will ever be able to predict the weather accurately a month in advance. This has to do with the so-called "butterfly effect." The atmosphere works in such a way that a small change in the weather today can mean a larger change in the weather a week later! The name refers to a scientist's suggestion that even the flapping of a butterfly's wings causes a tiny disturbance in the atmosphere. A tiny event might cause a larger disturbance that could—eventually—grow into a large storm.

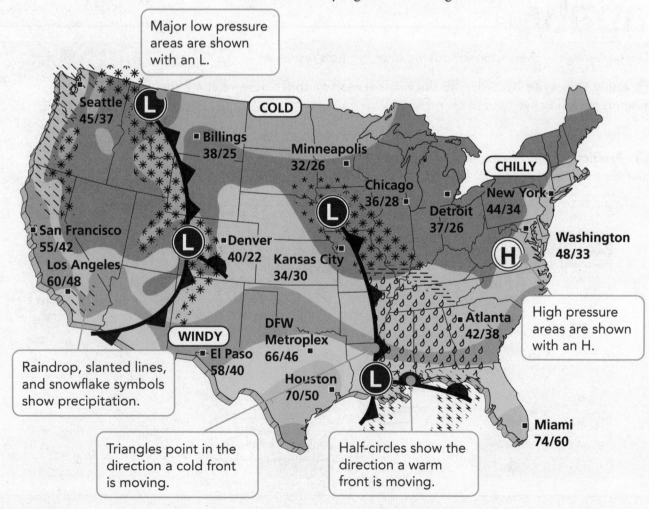

Major low pressure areas are shown with an L.

High pressure areas are shown with an H.

Raindrop, slanted lines, and snowflake symbols show precipitation.

Triangles point in the direction a cold front is moving.

Half-circles show the direction a warm front is moving.

Seattle 45/37 · COLD · Billings 38/25 · Minneapolis 32/26 · Chicago 36/28 · CHILLY · New York 44/34 · Detroit 37/26 · Washington 48/33 · San Francisco 55/42 · Denver 40/22 · Kansas City 34/30 · Los Angeles 60/48 · Atlanta 42/38 · WINDY · DFW Metroplex 66/46 · El Paso 58/40 · Houston 70/50 · Miami 74/60

Predicting the Weather

How do meteorologists predict the weather?

FIGURE 4 ....

▶ **REAL-WORLD INQUIRY** **Using a Weather Map**

✎ What would you tell the people of Miami, Kansas City, and Seattle about tomorrow's weather? Explain why.

_____

_____

_____

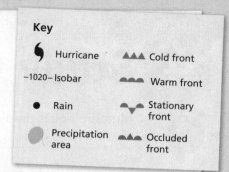

Key

〰 Hurricane	▲▲▲ Cold front
—1020— Isobar	︵︵︵ Warm front
● Rain	▲︵▲ Stationary front
Precipitation area	▲︵▲ Occluded front

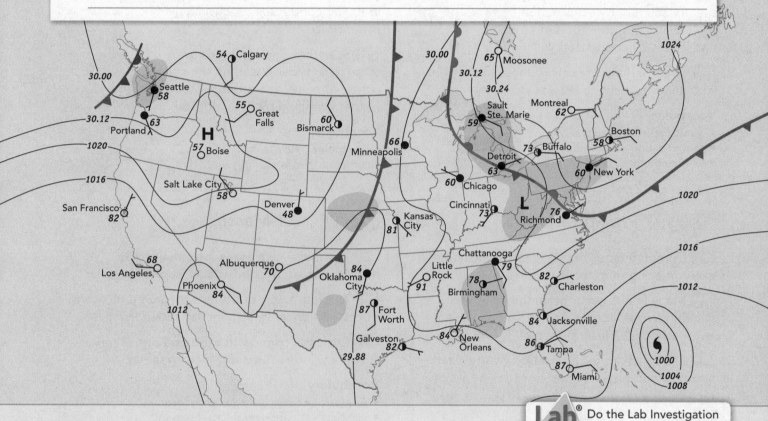

🔑 Assess Your Understanding

1a. Explain What is a weather map?

_____

_____

_____

_____

b. 🅰 **ANSWER** How do meteorologists predict the weather?

_____

_____

_____

_____

got **it?** ....

◯ **I get it!** Now I know that standard symbols on weather maps show _____

_____

◯ **I need extra help with** _____

Go to **MY SCIENCE** 🄢 **COACH** online for help with this subject.

Lab zone® Do the Lab Investigation *Reading a Weather Map.*

Meteorologists predict the weather by collecting data about _____,
_____ , _____ , and _____ .

LESSON 1 Water in the Atmosphere

🔑 In the water cycle, water vapor enters the atmosphere by evaporation from the oceans and other bodies of water and leaves by condensation.

🔑 Relative humidity can be measured with an instrument called a psychrometer.

Vocabulary
- water cycle • evaporation
- condensation • humidity
- relative humidity • psychrometer

LESSON 2 Clouds

🔑 Clouds form when water vapor in the air condenses to form liquid water or ice crystals.

🔑 Scientists classify clouds into three main types based on their shape: cirrus, cumulus, and stratus. Clouds are further classified by their altitude.

Vocabulary
- dew point • cirrus
- cumulus • stratus

LESSON 3 Precipitation

🔑 Common types of precipitation include rain, sleet, freezing rain, snow, and hail.

🔑 Many floods occur when the volume of water in a river increases so much that the river overflows its channel.

🔑 Droughts are usually caused by dry weather systems that remain in one place for weeks or months at a time.

Vocabulary
- precipitation • rain gauge • flood • drought

LESSON 4 Air Masses

🔑 The major air masses are classified as maritime or continental and as tropical or polar.

🔑 The four types of fronts are cold fronts, warm fronts, stationary fronts, and occluded fronts.

🔑 Cyclones come with wind and precipitation. An anticyclone causes dry, clear weather.

Vocabulary
- air mass • tropical • polar
- maritime • continental • jet stream
- front • occluded • cyclone • anticyclone

LESSON 5 Storms

🔑 Most precipitation begins in clouds as snow.

🔑 Thunderstorms and tornadoes form in cumulonimbus clouds.

🔑 A hurricane begins over warm ocean water as a low-pressure area, or tropical disturbance.

🔑 Always find proper shelter from storms.

Vocabulary
- storm • thunderstorm • lightning
- hurricane • storm surge • tornado • evacuate

LESSON 6 Predicting the Weather

🔑 Meteorologists use maps, charts, computers, and other technology to prepare weather forecasts.

🔑 Standard symbols on weather maps show fronts, air pressure, precipitation, and temperature.

Vocabulary
- meteorologist • isobar
- isotherm

Review and Assessment

LESSON 1 Water in the Atmosphere

1. Infer What is the energy source for the water cycle?

_____

2. math! At 3 P.M., a dry-bulb thermometer reading is 66°F. The wet-bulb reading is 66°F. What is the relative humidity? Explain.

_____
_____
_____
_____
_____
_____
_____
_____

LESSON 2 Clouds

3. What type of cloud forms at high altitudes and appears wispy and feathery?

  a. stratus   **b.** altocumulus

  c. cumulus   **d.** cirrus

4. One type of cloud is a nimbostratus, which is

_____
_____
_____

5. Infer Why do clouds usually form high in the air instead of near Earth's surface?

_____
_____
_____
_____

LESSON 3 Precipitation

6. What is the name for raindrops that freeze as they fall through the air?

  a. dew   **b.** sleet

  c. hail   **d.** frost

7. Rain and hail are both precipitation, which is

_____
_____
_____
_____

8. **Write About It** It is winter where Jenna lives. It's been snowing all day, but now the snow has changed to sleet and then to freezing rain. What is happening to cause these changes? In your answer, explain how snow, sleet, and freezing rain form.

LESSON 4 Air Masses

9. What do you call a hot air mass that forms over land?

_____

10. Predict What type of weather is most likely to form at the front shown below?

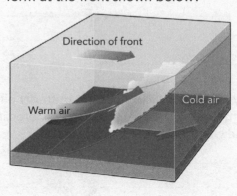

Direction of front

Warm air

Cold air

_____
_____

4 Review and Assessment

Storms

11. What are very large tropical cyclones with high winds called?

    a. storm surges   **b.** tornadoes

    c. hurricanes   **d.** thunderstorms

12. Thunderstorms usually contain lightning, which is _____

_____

_____

_____

13. Make Judgments What do you think is the most important thing people should do to reduce the dangers of storms?

_____

_____

_____

_____

LESSON 6 **Predicting the Weather**

14. On a weather map, lines joining places with the same temperature are called

    a. low-pressure systems.   **b.** isotherms.

    c. high-pressure systems.   **d.** isobars.

15. To predict weather, meteorologists use

_____

_____

_____

16. Apply Concepts How does the butterfly effect keep meteorologists from accurately forecasting the weather a month in advance?

_____

_____

_____

_____

_____

How do meteorologists predict the weather?

17. Meteorologists use information from many sources to make predictions about the weather. The weather map shows that right now it is sunny in Cincinnati, but the weather report for tomorrow shows a major snowstorm. Using the map, explain how a meteorologist is able to make this prediction. Include details on weather technology used and the atmospheric conditions that lead to a snowstorm. Make sure to discuss clouds, air masses, fronts, temperature, and pressure.

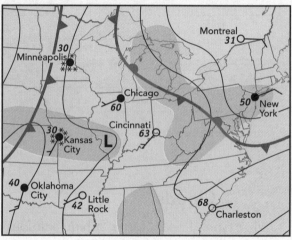

_____

_____

_____

_____

_____

_____

_____

_____

_____

_____

_____

_____

_____

_____

Standardized Test Prep

Multiple Choice

Circle the letter of the best answer.

1. The table below shows the amount of rainfall in different months.

Average Monthly Rainfall			
Month	**Rainfall**	**Month**	**Rainfall**
January	1 cm	July	49 cm
February	1 cm	August	57 cm
March	1 cm	September	40 cm
April	2 cm	October	20 cm
May	25 cm	November	4 cm
June	52 cm	December	1 cm

Which two months had the most rainfall?

A June and August   **B** January and March
C June and July   **D** August and May

2. When the temperature equals the dew point, what is the relative humidity?

A zero   **B** 10%
C 50%   **D** 100%

3. How are air masses classified?

A by temperature and pressure
B by pressure and humidity
C by temperature and density
D by temperature and humidity

4. What equipment would you need to design an experiment that measures relative humidity?

A a scale and a rain gauge
B a scale and a thermometer
C two thermometers or a psychrometer
D a rain gauge and a ruler

5. Which of the following map symbols identifies places with the same air pressure?

A jet streams   **B** isobars
C degrees   **D** isotherms

Constructed Response

Use the diagram below and your knowledge of science to help you answer Question 6. Write your answer on a separate piece of paper.

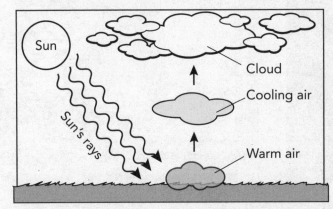

6. Describe the process by which a cloud forms. What two conditions are necessary for this process to occur? How does this process compare to the process by which dew or frost form?

The S'COOL Project

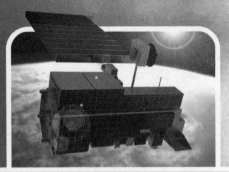

Schools around the world are teaming up to help scientists at the National Aeronautics and Space Administration (NASA). Since 1998, students have been helping NASA check satellite observations through a project called Students' Cloud Observations On-Line (S'COOL).

NASA tells schools in the program the date and time when the project satellites will be passing over different regions of the world. When a satellite passes over their school, students observe the clouds in the sky. Students can also measure weather data such as temperature and relative humidity. These observations are uploaded to the project Web site. Then NASA scientists compare the satellite data with the students' observations. This process, called ground truthing, helps scientists determine how accurate the satellite data are.

◀ Students' observations are compared to data collected by satellites like this one.

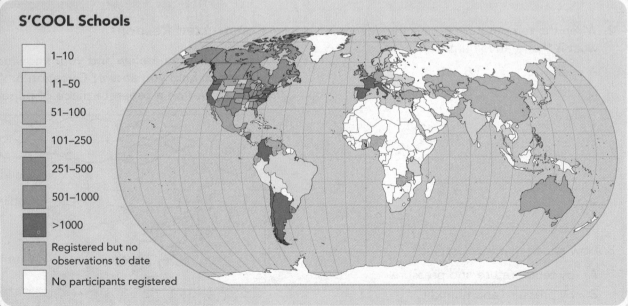

S'COOL Schools

- 1–10
- 11–50
- 51–100
- 101–250
- 251–500
- 501–1000
- >1000
- Registered but no observations to date
- No participants registered

▲ Schools around the world participate in the S'COOL program. The map above shows where they are. If you had to recruit schools to help NASA get complete data, where would you look for schools?

Research It Make a record book. Use it to keep a weeklong log of cloud formations and weather conditions, including photos or sketches, at a specific time each day.

Tracking Hurricanes
with Latitude and Longitude

Do you understand the important bulletin on the computer screen? Lines of latitude and longitude are imaginary lines that crisscross Earth's surface. Because the lines cross, they can help you describe any location on Earth, including the location of hurricanes. A location's latitude is always written before its longitude.

Hurricane Hilda is located in the Atlantic Ocean off the southeastern coast of the United States.

Write About It Assume that Hurricane Hilda is following a straight path. Using the information in the bulletin and the map, try to predict the path the hurricane will take to reach land, and how long it will take to get there. Compare your predicted path with the path of a real hurricane. Evaluate your prediction. Does the bulletin provide enough information for you to make a precise prediction? Write a paragraph explaining why or why not.

ATTENTION

HURRICANE HILDA IS CURRENTLY
LOCATED AT 30°N, 74°W.
IT IS MOVING 21 KM/H NW.
ALL RESIDENTS OF NEARBY
COASTAL AREAS ARE ADVISED
TO EVACUATE IMMEDIATELY.

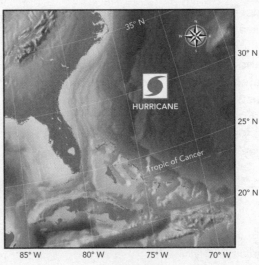

Hurricane Hilda is currently located at 30° N, 74° W. You can plot the hurricane's location on a map. What information do you need to predict where it will reach land? ▶

HOW
IS THIS
CLIMATE
DIFFERENT
FROM YOURS?

What factors affect Earth's climate?

On this icy, frozen island in Svalbard, Norway, the sun shines all day and night from mid-April to mid-August. Winter is long and cold, with three months of complete darkness. The average winter temperature is −12°C. But the average annual precipitation, mainly snow, is only about 20 centimeters. The island is located above the Arctic Circle, and scientists study glaciers, the environment, and meteorology there to detect climate changes.

Develop Hypotheses **How might this island climate in Norway be different from your climate?**

_____

_____

_____

_____

> **UNTAMED SCIENCE** Watch the **Untamed Science** video to learn more about Earth's climate.

Climate and Climate Change

5 Getting Started

Check Your Understanding

1. **Background** Read the paragraph below and then answer the question.

> Derek walks steadily up the path. As he climbs to a higher **altitude,** the air changes. He can feel the **temperature** get cooler. Soon, he puts up his hood to stay dry. At first the **precipitation** is rain, but as Derek gets higher up the mountain, it changes to snow.

Altitude is the height of a place above sea level.

Temperature is a measure of how hot or cold an object is compared to a reference point.

Precipitation is any form of water that falls from clouds and reaches Earth's surface.

- Why does the precipitation change to snow as Derek gets higher up the mountain?

_____

_____

> MY READING WEB If you had trouble completing the question above, visit **My Reading Web** and type in *Climate and Climate Change.*

Vocabulary Skill

High-Use Academic Words Learning high-use words will help you understand, discuss, and write about the science content in this chapter. These words differ from key terms because they appear in many other subject areas.

Word	Definition	Example
affect	*v.* to produce a change in or have an effect on	The actions of humans *affect* the environment.
distinct	*adj.* different; not the same	Each type of cloud is *distinct.*

2. **Quick Check** Choose the best word from the table to complete each sentence.

- Trees in the rain forest form several _____ layers.

- If you are high up on a mountain, the altitude can _____ how you breathe.

climate

aerosol

greenhouse gas

fossil fuel

Chapter Preview

LESSON 1

- climate
- tropical zone
- polar zone
- temperate zone
- marine climate
- continental climate
- windward
- leeward
- monsoon
- ↻ **Summarize**
- △ **Infer**

LESSON 2

- rain forest
- savanna
- steppe
- desert
- humid subtropical
- subarctic
- tundra
- permafrost
- ↻ **Identify the Main Idea**
- △ **Communicate**

LESSON 3

- ice age
- aerosol
- sunspot
- ↻ **Identify Supporting Evidence**
- △ **Interpret Data**

LESSON 4

- greenhouse gas
- fossil fuel
- global warming
- ↻ **Ask Questions**
- △ **Make Models**

> **VOCAB FLASH CARDS** For extra help with vocabulary, visit **Vocab Flash Cards** and type in *Climate and Climate Change.*

165

What Causes Climate?

🔑 What Factors Affect Temperature?

🔑 What Factors Affect Precipitation?

my planeT DiaRY

Changes in Climate

Misconception: Only changes in the atmosphere can affect climate.

Fact: As air moves, it's affected by sunlight, cloud cover, oceans, and even landforms such as mountains.

Evidence: The ocean plays a big role in shaping climate. For example, rain that falls in the mountains eventually runs into rivers and oceans. Then water evaporates from the oceans and forms clouds. Water in the oceans also absorbs heat. Ocean currents transfer thermal energy from the equator to cooler areas in the Northern and Southern hemispheres.

MISCONCEPTION

Think about your own observations of Earth's climate. Then answer these questions with a partner.

1. How does the ocean affect Earth's climate?

_____

_____

2. How do you think the climate in coastal areas differs from the climate farther inland?

_____

_____

> **PLANET DIARY** Go to **Planet Diary** to learn more about climate.

Lab® Do the Inquiry Warm-Up
zone *How Does Latitude Affect Climate?*

Vocabulary

- climate • tropical zone • polar zone • temperate zone
- marine climate • continental climate • windward
- leeward • monsoon

Skills

↻ **Reading:** Summarize

△ **Inquiry:** Infer

What Factors Affect Temperature?

No matter where you live, the weather changes every day. In some areas, the change might be as small as a 1-degree drop in temperature from one day to the next. In other areas, it can mean a cold, rainy day followed by a warm, sunny one. Climate, on the other hand, is the long-term weather pattern in an area. Specifically, **climate** refers to the average, year-after-year conditions of temperature, precipitation, wind, and clouds in an area.

The water cycle determines climate patterns. For example, in California's Mojave Desert, shown in **Figure 1,** there is more evaporation than precipitation. The climate there is hot and dry. If you moved west from the Mojave desert toward California's coast, you'd notice a different climate. It would be cooler and more humid. How is this possible? **⚷ Temperature is affected by latitude, altitude, distance from large bodies of water, and ocean currents.**

FIGURE 1 ···

Climate

✎ **List** Make a short list of words comparing the climate of the Mojave with the climate of the area in which you live.

Mojave's Climate:	Your Climate:

✏️ **Summarize** Read about latitude. Then summarize in your own words how latitude affects temperature.

_____

_____

_____

_____

_____

_____

Latitude

In general, areas near the equator have warmer climates than areas far from the equator. The reason is that the sun's rays hit Earth's surface more directly at the equator than at the poles. At the poles, the same amount of solar radiation is spread over a larger area, which brings less warmth.

Recall that latitude is the distance from the equator, measured in degrees, as shown in **Figure 2.** Based on latitude, Earth's surface can be divided into three types of temperature zones.

The **tropical zone** is the area near the equator, between about 23.5° north latitude and 23.5° south latitude. It receives direct or nearly direct sunlight all year, making climates there warm.

In contrast, the sun's rays always strike at a lower angle near the North and South poles, making climates there cold. These **polar zones** extend from about 66.5° to 90° north and 66.5° to 90° south latitudes.

Between the tropical zones and the polar zones are the **temperate zones.** In summer, the sun's rays strike the temperate zones more directly. In winter, the sun's rays strike at a lower angle. As a result, the weather in the temperate zones ranges from warm or hot in summer to cool or cold in winter.

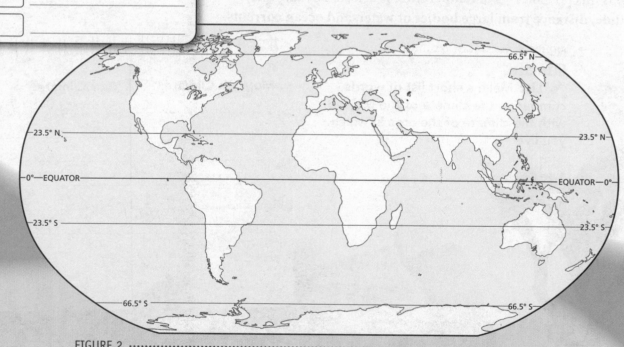

Key

FIGURE 2 ••

Latitude and Temperature

✏️ **Use the map above to complete the activity.**

1. **Relate Text and Visuals** Shade in the three temperature zones differently on the map and complete the key.

2. **Observe** In which temperature zone is most of the United States located?

_____

Altitude Standing at 6,309 meters high, Mount Chimborazo is Ecuador's tallest mountain. Its peak is covered in glaciers year-round, as shown in **Figure 3**. But at 1° south latitude, Chimborazo is located very close to the equator. How does the top of this mountain stay so cold?

In the case of high mountains, altitude is a more important climate factor than latitude. In the troposphere, temperature decreases about 6.5°C for every 1-kilometer increase in altitude. As a result, many mountainous areas have cooler climates than the lower areas around them. Chimborazo is just over 6 kilometers high. The air at the top of this mountain is about 39°C colder than the air at sea level at the same latitude.

did you know? ....
A species of *Polylepsis* tree in Bolivia grows at the highest altitude of any tree in the world—up to 5,200 m.

FIGURE 3 ....

> VIRTUAL LAB **Altitude and Temperature**
🖉 **Read about altitude and answer these questions.**

1. **Name** Use **Figure 2** to identify the temperature zone in which Ecuador is located. (*Hint:* Ecuador is in northwestern South America.)

   _____

2. **Calculate** If it was 30°C at the base of Mount Chimborazo, about how cold would it be at the peak?

   _____

3. **Interpret Photos** Use the photo below to compare the conditions at the base of Mount Chimborazo with the conditions at the peak.

   _____
   _____
   _____
   _____

Vocabulary High-Use Academic
Words Complete the sentence
to show you understand the
meaning of the word *affect*.
The ocean is too far from
the middle of North America
to _____

Distance From Large Bodies of Water Oceans
or large lakes can also affect temperatures. Oceans greatly moderate, or make less extreme, the temperatures of nearby land. Water
heats up about five times more slowly than land. It also cools down
more slowly. Therefore, winds off the ocean often prevent extremes
of hot and cold in coastal regions. Much of the west coasts of North
America, South America, and Europe have **marine climates.** These
climates have relatively mild winters and cool summers.

The centers of North America and Asia are too far inland to be
warmed or cooled by the ocean. Most of Canada, Russia, and the
central United States have **continental climates.** These climates
reach more extreme temperatures than marine climates. Winters
are cold, while summers are warm or hot.

apply it!

Alaska is about twice the size of Texas.
Factors influencing temperature, such as
distance from large bodies of water, affect
this big state in different ways.

1 Observe Where are Juneau and Fairbanks located in relation to each other?

_____

_____

_____

2 Infer Which climate data do you think
describe Juneau, A or B? Which describe
Fairbanks, A or B? Why?

_____

_____

_____

_____

_____

_____

	City A	City B	City C
Average Number of Days Below −17°C (0°F)	113	6	168
Average Number of Days Above 18°C (65°F)	82	40	2

3 CHALLENGE Which city on the map do you think represents the set of data for City C? Why?

_____

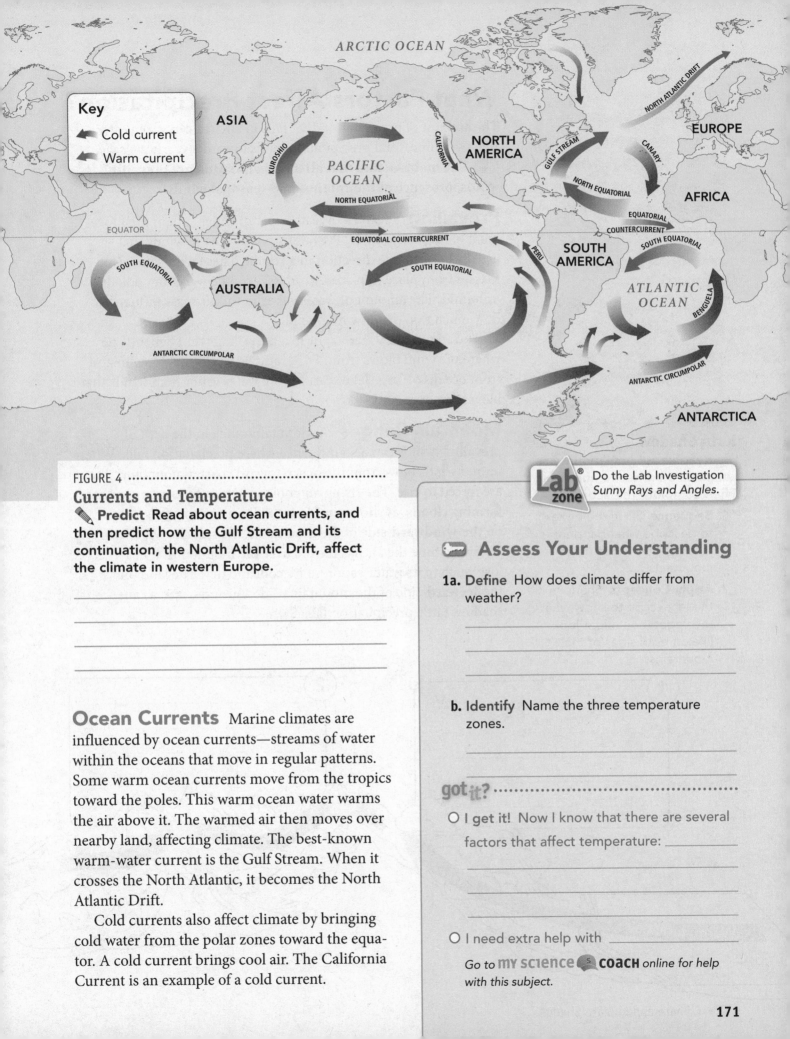

ARCTIC OCEAN

Key
← Cold current
← Warm current

ASIA

PACIFIC OCEAN

KUROSHIO

NORTH EQUATORIAL

CALIFORNIA

NORTH AMERICA

NORTH ATLANTIC DRIFT

EUROPE

GULF STREAM

CANARY

NORTH EQUATORIAL

AFRICA

EQUATOR

EQUATORIAL COUNTERCURRENT

EQUATORIAL COUNTERCURRENT

SOUTH EQUATORIAL

AUSTRALIA

SOUTH EQUATORIAL

PERU

SOUTH AMERICA

SOUTH EQUATORIAL

ATLANTIC OCEAN

BENGUELA

ANTARCTIC CIRCUMPOLAR

ANTARCTIC CIRCUMPOLAR

ANTARCTICA

FIGURE 4 ....
Currents and Temperature
✎ **Predict** Read about ocean currents, and then predict how the Gulf Stream and its continuation, the North Atlantic Drift, affect the climate in western Europe.

_____
_____
_____
_____

Ocean Currents
Marine climates are influenced by ocean currents—streams of water within the oceans that move in regular patterns. Some warm ocean currents move from the tropics toward the poles. This warm ocean water warms the air above it. The warmed air then moves over nearby land, affecting climate. The best-known warm-water current is the Gulf Stream. When it crosses the North Atlantic, it becomes the North Atlantic Drift.

Cold currents also affect climate by bringing cold water from the polar zones toward the equator. A cold current brings cool air. The California Current is an example of a cold current.

Lab zone ® Do the Lab Investigation
Sunny Rays and Angles.

🔑 Assess Your Understanding

1a. Define How does climate differ from weather?

_____
_____
_____

b. Identify Name the three temperature zones.

_____
_____

got it? ....

○ **I get it!** Now I know that there are several factors that affect temperature: _____

_____
_____

○ **I need extra help with** _____

Go to MY SCIENCE 🔍 COACH *online for help with this subject.*

171

What Factors Affect Precipitation?

The amount of precipitation that falls in an area can vary yearly. But, over time, total precipitation tends toward a yearly average. 🔑 **The main factors that affect precipitation are prevailing winds, presence of mountains, and seasonal winds.**

Prevailing Winds Weather patterns depend on the movement of huge air masses. Prevailing winds are the winds that usually blow in one direction in a region. These winds move air masses from place to place. Air masses can be warm or cool, dry or humid. The amount of water vapor in the air mass influences how much rain or snow might fall.

The amount of water vapor in a prevailing wind depends on where the wind blows from. For example, winds that blow inland from oceans or large lakes carry more water vapor than winds that blow from over land.

Mountain Ranges A mountain range in the path of prevailing winds can also influence where precipitation falls. When humid winds blow from the ocean toward coastal mountains, they are forced to rise. The rising air cools and its water vapor condenses, forming clouds, as shown in **Figure 5.** Rain or snow falls on the **windward** side of the mountains, the side the wind hits.

By the time the air has moved over the mountains, it has lost much of its water vapor, so it's cool and dry. The land on the **leeward** side of the mountains—downwind—is in a rain shadow. Little precipitation falls there.

FIGURE 5 ·······························
Rain Shadow

✏️ **Read about how mountains can form a barrier to humid air. Then complete the activity.**

1. **Sequence** Fill in the boxes to describe what happens as prevailing winds meet mountains.

2. **Apply Concepts** Shade in the landscape to show what the vegetation might look like on both sides of the mountains.

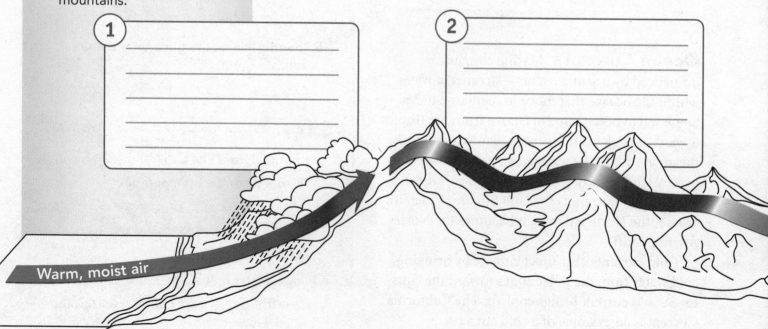

Warm, moist air

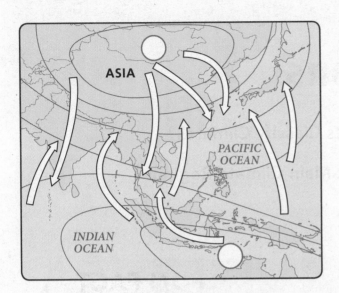

ASIA

PACIFIC OCEAN

INDIAN OCEAN

FIGURE 6 ··

Monsoons

Monsoons are seasonal winds that bring drastic changes in precipitation.

✎ **Read about seasonal winds below, and then complete the activity.**

1. **Relate Cause and Effect** Shade in the arrows that indicate a summer monsoon.

2. **Identify** Write an *H* or *L* in the circles on the map to indicate the areas of high pressure and low pressure during the summer monsoon.

Seasonal Winds In some parts of the world, a seasonal change in wind patterns can affect precipitation. Sea and land breezes over a large region that change direction with the seasons are called **monsoons.** What produces a monsoon? In the summer in South and Southeast Asia, the land gradually gets warmer than the ocean. A wind blows inland from the ocean all summer, even at night. Winds blow from areas of high pressure to areas of low pressure. The air blowing from the ocean during this season is very warm and humid. As the humid air rises over the land, the air cools. This cooling air causes water vapor to condense into clouds, producing heavy rains. In winter, the land becomes colder than the ocean. A wind blows from the land to the ocean. These winds carry little moisture.

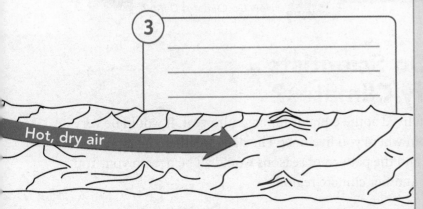

3 _____

Hot, dry air

Lab zone® Do the Quick Lab *Inferring United States Precipitation Patterns.*

⚷ **Assess Your Understanding**

2a. Define What is the leeward side of a mountain?

_____

_____

b. Summarize How do prevailing winds affect precipitation?

_____

_____

_____

_____

_____

got it? ···

I get it! Now I know three factors affect

precipitation: _____

_____

I need extra help with _____

_____

Go to my science ⓢ coach *online for help with this subject.*

Climate Regions

🔑 How Do Scientists Classify Climates?

🔑 What Are the Six Main Climate Regions?

MY PLANET DIARY

Rain, Rain Every Day

When you think of Hawaii, warm, sunny days spent surfing monster waves are probably the first thing that comes to mind. But Hawaii gets its fair share of rain, too. In fact, it's home to one of the wettest places on Earth—Mount Waialeale.

A lush mountain on the island of Kauai, Waialeale gets an average of 1,143 centimeters, or 450 inches, of rain every year. That's more than an inch of rain every day! Yet nearby parts of Kauai get only 10 inches of rain per year.

FUN FACT

Read about one of the rainiest places in the world and answer the questions.

1. Why do you think Mount Waialeale gets so much rain?

_____

_____

2. How much rain does your area get compared with Mount Waialeale?

_____

_____

_____

▶ PLANET DIARY Go to **Planet Diary** to learn more about climate regions.

Lab zone Do the Inquiry Warm-Up *How Do Climates Differ?*

How Do Scientists Classify Climates?

Suppose you lived at the equator for an entire year. It would be very different from where you live now. The daily weather, the amount of sunlight, and the pattern of seasons would all be new to you. You would be in another climate region.

Vocabulary

- rain forest • savanna • steppe • desert
- humid subtropical • subarctic • tundra
- permafrost

Skills

↻ Reading: Identify the Main Idea

△ Inquiry: Communicate

🔑 **Scientists classify climates according to two major factors: temperature and precipitation.** They use a system developed around 1900 by Wladimir Köppen (KEP un). Besides temperature and precipitation, Köppen also looked at the distinct vegetation in different areas. This system identifies broad climate regions, each of which has smaller subdivisions.

FIGURE 1 ....

Reading Climate Graphs

✏ **Interpret Graphs** A graph of temperature can be combined with a graph of precipitation to form a climate graph. The graphs below show climate data for Makindu, Kenya.

1. Look at the first graph. What is the average temperature in July?

_____

2. Look at the second graph. What is the average precipitation in July?

_____

3. Look at the climate graph. How much rain does Makindu get in its hottest month?

_____

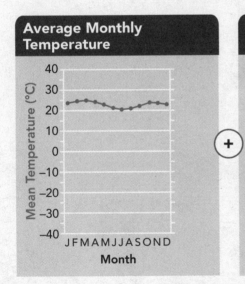

Average Monthly Temperature

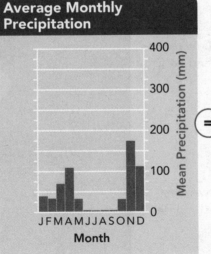

Average Monthly Precipitation

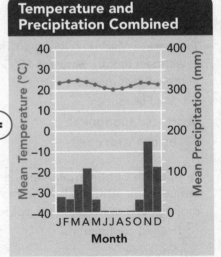

Temperature and Precipitation Combined

Lab zone ® Do the Quick Lab *Classifying Climates.*

🔑 Assess Your Understanding

got it? ....

○ I get it! Now I know that climates are classified using _____

_____

○ I need extra help with _____

Go to **my science** ⑤ **coach** online for help with this subject.

What Are the Six Main Climate Regions?

Maps can show boundaries between climate regions. But generally, in the real world, no clear boundaries mark where one climate region ends and another begins. In most cases, each region blends gradually into the next. 🔑 **The six main climate regions are tropical rainy, dry, temperate marine, temperate continental, polar, and highlands.** These climate regions are shown in **Figure 2**.

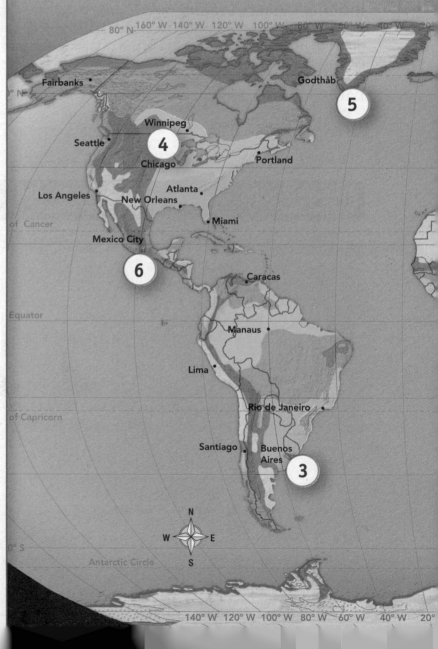

Key

Tropical Rainy: Temperature always 18°C or above
- Tropical wet
- Tropical wet-and-dry

Dry: Occurs wherever potential evaporation is greater than precipitation; may be hot or cold
- Semiarid
- Arid

Temperate Marine: Averages 10°C or above in warmest month, between −3°C and 18°C in the coldest month
- Mediterranean
- Humid subtropical
- Marine west coast

Temperate Continental: Average temperature 10°C or above in the warmest month, −3°C or below in the coldest month
- Humid continental
- Subarctic

Polar: Average temperature below 10°C in the warmest month
- Tundra
- Ice cap

Highlands: Generally cooler and wetter than nearby lowlands; temperature decreasing with altitude
- Highlands

FIGURE 2 ··

Climate Regions

✏️ **Identify** You've been selected by an Olympic committee to visit six cities this July and to choose one to host the next summer games.

1. On the map, draw a line connecting the stops on your itinerary.

2. List each city and its climate region.

1. Location: _____

   Climate Region: _____

2. Location: _____

   Climate Region: _____

3. Location: _____

   Climate Region: _____

4. Location: _____

   Climate Region: _____

5. Location: _____

   Climate Region: _____

6. Location: _____

   Climate Region: _____

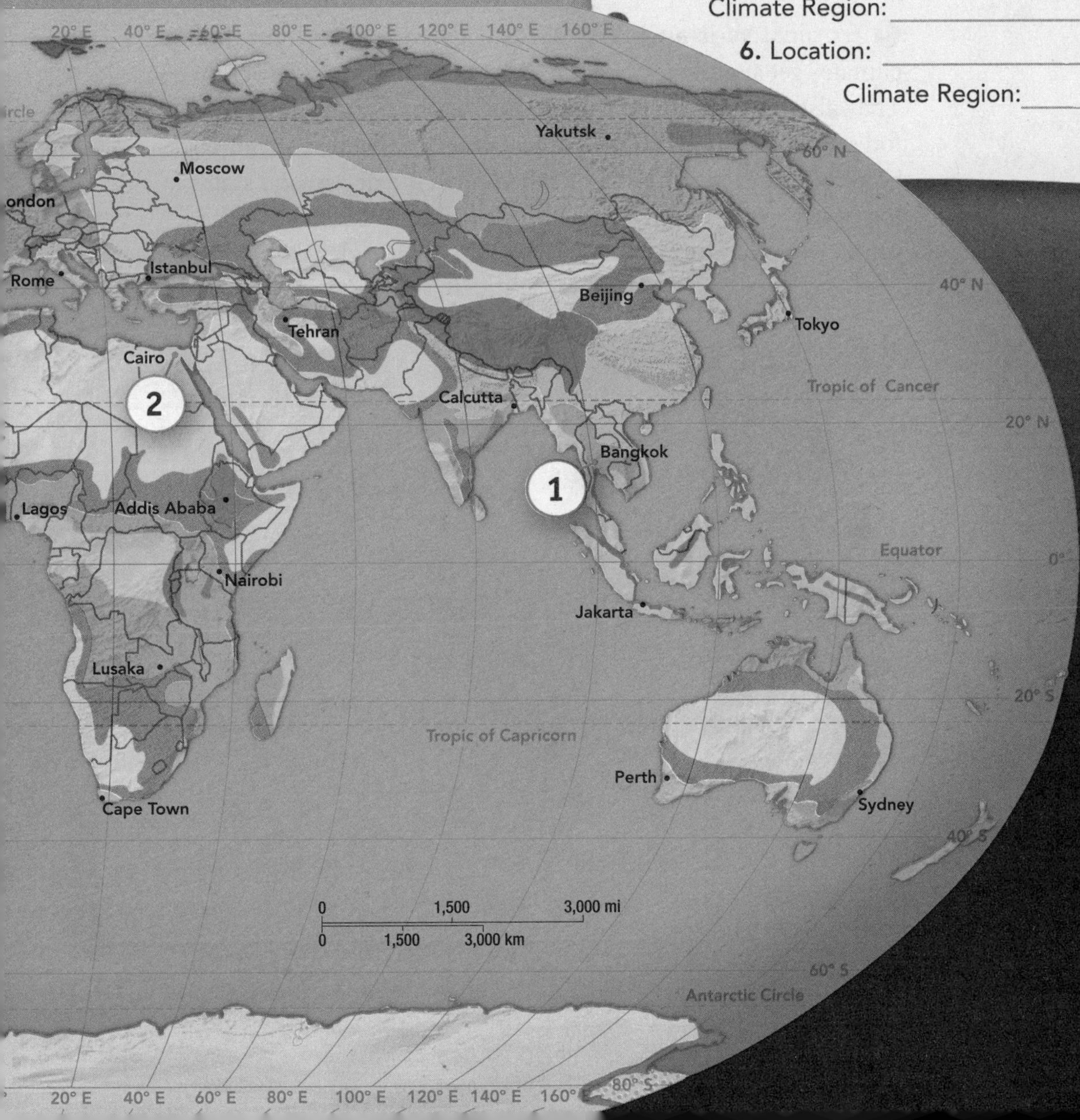

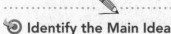
Identify the Main Idea
As you read, underline the main idea about tropical wet regions.

Tropical Rainy Climates Travel to Manaus, Brazil, or Bangkok, Thailand, and there's a good chance you might see some rain on your trip. Although continents apart, these two cities are both in the tropics. **The tropics are an area that have two types of rainy climates: tropical wet and tropical wet-and-dry.**

❶ **Tropical Wet** A tropical wet climate has many rainy days and frequent afternoon thunderstorms. These thunderstorms are triggered by midday heating. The trade winds also bring moisture from the oceans to some tropical wet areas. With year-round heat and heavy rainfall, vegetation grows lush and green. **Rain forests**—forests in which large amounts of rain fall year-round—are common. In the United States, only the windward sides of the Hawaiian Islands have a tropical wet climate.

❷ **Tropical Wet-and-Dry** Areas with tropical wet-and-dry climates get slightly less rain than areas with tropical wet climates. They also have distinct dry and rainy seasons. Instead of rain forests, these climates have tropical grasslands called **savannas.** Scattered clumps of trees that can survive the dry season stand in the coarse grasses. Only a small part of the United States—the southern tip of Florida—has a tropical wet-and-dry climate.

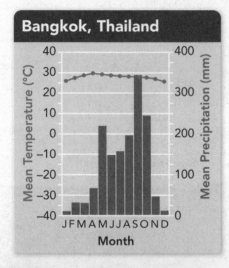

Bangkok, Thailand

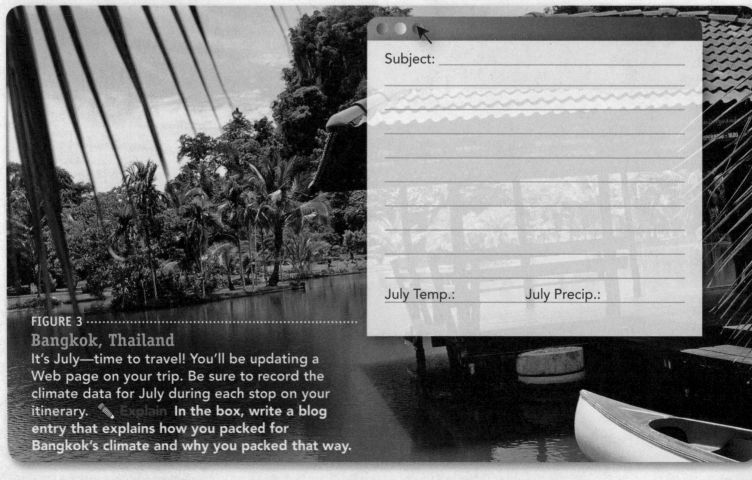

Subject: _____

July Temp.: _____ July Precip.: _____

FIGURE 3

Bangkok, Thailand
It's July—time to travel! You'll be updating a Web page on your trip. Be sure to record the climate data for July during each stop on your itinerary. ✎ Explain **In the box, write a blog entry that explains how you packed for Bangkok's climate and why you packed that way.**

Dry Climates A climate is dry if the amount of precipitation that falls is less than the amount of water that could potentially evaporate. 🔑 **Dry climates include semiarid and arid climates.**

❶ Semiarid Large semiarid areas are usually located on the edges of deserts. These semiarid areas are called steppes. A **steppe** is dry, but it gets enough rainfall for short grasses and low bushes to grow. For this reason, a steppe may also be called a prairie or grassland. The Great Plains are the steppe region in the United States.

❷ Arid When you think about **deserts,** or arid regions, you may picture blazing heat and drifting sand dunes. But deserts can actually be cold and rocky, too. On average, arid regions get less than 25 centimeters of rain a year. Some years may bring no rain at all. Only specialized plants such as cactus and yucca can survive the desert's dryness and extreme temperatures. In the United States there are arid climates in parts of California and the Southwest.

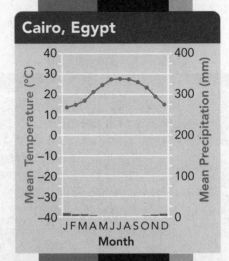

Cairo, Egypt

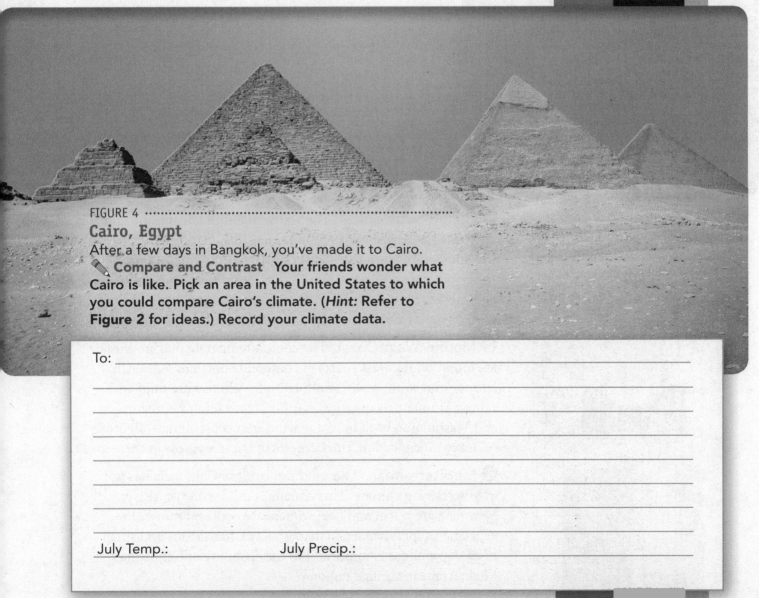

FIGURE 4 ························

Cairo, Egypt
After a few days in Bangkok, you've made it to Cairo.

✏️ **Compare and Contrast** Your friends wonder what Cairo is like. Pick an area in the United States to which you could compare Cairo's climate. (*Hint:* Refer to **Figure 2** for ideas.) Record your climate data.

To: _____
_____
_____
_____
_____
_____
_____
_____

July Temp.: _____   July Precip.: _____

Temperate Marine Climates Along the coasts of continents in the temperate zones, you can find the third main climate region, temperate marine. 🔑 **There are three kinds of temperate marine climates: humid subtropical, marine west coast, and Mediterranean.** Because of the moderating influence of oceans, all three are humid and have mild winters.

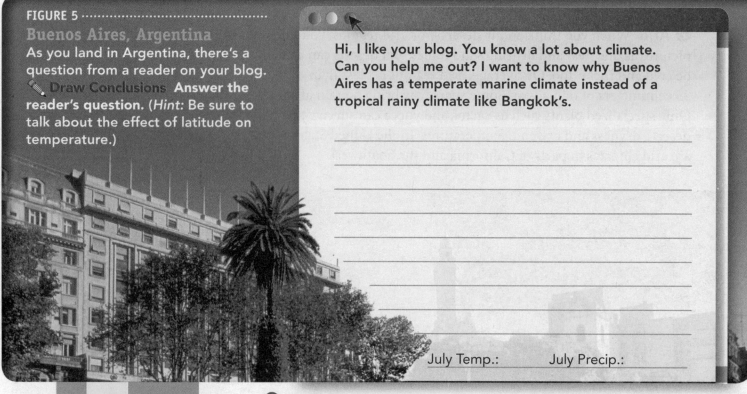

FIGURE 5 ·······

Buenos Aires, Argentina
As you land in Argentina, there's a question from a reader on your blog. ✏️ **Draw Conclusions** **Answer the reader's question.** (*Hint:* Be sure to talk about the effect of latitude on temperature.)

Hi, I like your blog. You know a lot about climate. Can you help me out? I want to know why Buenos Aires has a temperate marine climate instead of a tropical rainy climate like Bangkok's.

July Temp.: _____   July Precip.: _____

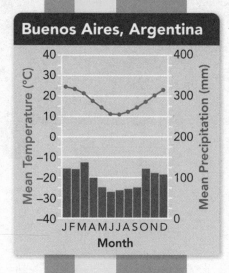

Buenos Aires, Argentina

❶ **Humid Subtropical** The warmest temperate marine climates are along the edges of the tropics. **Humid subtropical** climates are wet and warm, but not as constantly hot as the tropics. The South American city of Buenos Aires has a humid subtropical climate. Summers are hot, with much more rainfall than winters. Mixed vegetation of ceiba trees, rushes, and passionflowers grow here.

❷ **Marine West Coast** The coolest temperate marine climates are found on the west coasts of continents north of 40° north latitude and south of 40° south latitude. Winters are mild and rainy. Summer precipitation can vary considerably. Oregon and Washington both have a marine west coast climate. Because of heavy precipication, thick forests of tall trees grow in these areas.

❸ **Mediterranean** The southern coast of California has a Mediterranean climate. This climate is mild with two seasons. Summers are warm and dry; winters are cool and rainy. One vegetation type, chaparral (shap uh RAL), has shrubs and small trees. Agriculture is important to the economy of California's Mediterranean climate region.

Temperate Continental Climates

Temperate continental climates are not influenced very much by oceans, so they commonly have extremes of temperature. 🔑 **Temperate continental climates are only found on continents in the Northern Hemisphere, and include humid continental and subarctic. In the Southern Hemisphere there are no large land areas at the right latitude for this climate to occur.**

FIGURE 6 ···

Chicago, Illinois, U.S.

✏️ **Observe** One of your pen pals wants a picture of Illinois. But your digital camera is broken. Use the space below to draw a picture showing what the climate and vegetation of the Midwest look like in July. (*Hint:* Consult your climate graph.)

July Temp.: _____ July Precip.: _____

❶ **Humid Continental** Shifting tropical and polar air masses bring constantly changing weather to humid continental climates. In winter, continental polar air masses move south, bringing bitterly cold weather. In summer, tropical air masses move north, bringing heat and high humidity. In the United States, the eastern part of the climate region is the Northeast. There is a mixture of forest types in this area. Much of the western part of this climate region—the Midwest—was once tall grasslands, but is now farmland.

❷ **Subarctic** The **subarctic** climates lie north of the humid continental climates. Summers in the subarctic are short and cool. Winters are long and bitterly cold. In North America, coniferous trees such as spruce and fir make up a huge northern forest that stretches from Alaska to eastern Canada.

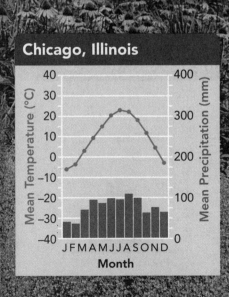

Chicago, Illinois

Godthåb, Greenland

Mean Temperature (°C) / Mean Precipitation (mm) vs Month (JFMAMJJASOND)

Polar Climates

Most polar climates are relatively dry, because the cold air contains little moisture. 🔑 **The polar climate is the coldest climate region and includes the tundra and ice cap climates.**

❶ Tundra The **tundra** climate region stretches across northern Alaska, Canada, and Russia. Short, cool summers follow bitterly cold winters. Because of the cold, some layers of tundra soil are always frozen. This permanently frozen soil is called **permafrost.** Because of the permafrost, water can't drain away, so the soil is wet and boggy in summer. It's too cold for trees to grow, but mosses, grasses, wildflowers, and shrubs grow during summer.

❷ Ice Cap With average temperatures always at or below freezing, the land in ice cap climate regions is covered with ice and snow. Intense cold makes the air dry. Lichens and a few low plants may grow on the rocks. Ice cap climates are found mainly in Greenland and Antarctica.

FIGURE 7 ....

Godthåb, Greenland

Your flight from Chicago to Greenland takes you to Godthåb, a city in the tundra. ✏️ **Identify Record the climate data for July.**

Temperature: _____ Precipitation: _____

Mexico City, Mexico

Mean Temperature (°C) / Mean Precipitation (mm) vs Month (JFMAMJJASOND)

Highlands

Why are highlands a distinct climate region? 🔑 **Temperature falls as altitude increases, so highland regions are colder than the regions that surround them.** Increasing altitude produces climate changes similar to the climate changes you would expect with increasing latitude.

The climate on the lower slopes of a mountain range is like that of the surrounding countryside. The Rocky Mountain foothills, for instance, share the semiarid climate of the Great Plains. But higher up into the mountains, temperatures become lower and precipitation increases. Climbing 1,000 meters up in elevation is like traveling 1,200 kilometers toward one of the poles. The climate high in the mountains is like the subarctic: cool with coniferous trees.

FIGURE 8 ....

Mexico City, Mexico

Finally, you've reached your last stop: Mexico City, Mexico. The surrounding highlands are very different from the tundra.

✏️ **Identify Record the climate data for July.**

Temperature: _____ Precipitation: _____

apply it!

You're home from your travel assignment. It's time to send your recommendation to the Olympic committee.

1 Graph Use the climate data you gathered for July to build a bar graph.

2 Communicate Write a letter to the committee explaining your choice of location. To support your answer, be sure to include information about the climate in the city you chose.

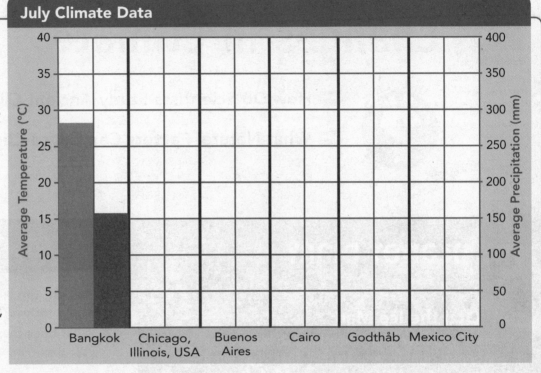

July Climate Data

Average Temperature (°C) — 0, 5, 10, 15, 20, 25, 30, 35, 40

Average Precipitation (mm) — 0, 50, 100, 150, 200, 250, 300, 350, 400

Bangkok · Chicago, Illinois, USA · Buenos Aires · Cairo · Godthåb · Mexico City

_____
_____
_____
_____
_____
_____

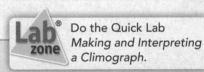

Lab zone® Do the Quick Lab _Making and Interpreting a Climograph._

🔑 Assess Your Understanding

1a. Sequence Place these climates in order from coldest to warmest: tundra, subarctic, humid continental, and ice cap.

_____
_____

b. [CHALLENGE] What place would have more severe winters: central Russia or the west coast of France?

_____
_____

got it?

○ **I get it!** Now I know where climate regions are found _____

I also know they change with latitude

and _____

○ **I need extra help with** _____

_____

_Go to_ **MY SCIENCE** 💬 **COACH** _online for help with this subject._

183

Changes in Climate

UNLOCK
THE BIG

🔑 **How Do Scientists Study Ancient Climates?**

🔑 **What Natural Factors Can Cause Climate Change?**

MY PLANET DIARY   DISCOVERY

Ötzi the Ice Man

Have you ever seen something so bizarre that you stopped right in your tracks? That's just what happened to a pair of hikers in 1991. During a hike in the Alps, they came across something strange. It was the 5,000-year-old mummified body of a man emerging from a melting glacier.

Archaelogists named the mummy Ötzi. After removing him from the ice, they began to study his weapons, clothes, and tools. What they found surprised them. There was evidence that early humans knew how to make warm, waterproof clothing. Ötzi's shoes were very complex. They had bearskin soles, top panels made of deerhide, and netting made of tree bark to give them traction on snow. Soft grass inside the shoes acted like a warm sock.

Read about the ice man and answer the questions below.

1. What does the discovery of Ötzi tell you about today's climate?

_____

_____

_____

2. What does Ötzi's clothing tell you about the climate during his time?

_____

_____

_____

_____

▷ **PLANET DIARY** Go to **Planet Diary** to learn more about ancient climates.

Lab zone Do the Inquiry Warm-Up *What Story Can Tree Rings Tell?*

Vocabulary
- ice age
- aerosol
- sunspot

Skills
- ↻ Reading: Identify Supporting Evidence
- △ Inquiry: Interpret Data

How Do Scientists Study Ancient Climates?

Think about a weather forecast that you've seen or heard. This forecast is a prediction about changes in upcoming weather. This prediction can help you plan your day. However, long-term changes in climate happen more slowly, and may not be apparent for years. Yet regardless of how slowly climate changes, the consequences can be great.

Take Greenland, for example. Today this large island is mostly covered by an ice cap. But 80 million years ago Greenland had a warm, moist climate. Fossils of magnolias and palm trees found in Greenland provide evidence for this climate change. Today magnolias and palm trees are native to warm, moist climates, like Florida. Scientists assume that the ancestors of these trees required similar conditions. 🔑 **In studying ancient climates, scientists follow an important principle: If plants or animals today need certain conditions to live, then similar plants and animals in the past also required those conditions.**

FIGURE 1 ·····················

Climate Change
Changes in climate happen gradually, but they have big effects on conditions in an area.
✎ **Develop Hypotheses** Why do you think Greenland's climate changed?

_____

_____

_____

_____

_____

_____

_____

_____

_____

_____

_____

Greetings from GREENLAND

Pollen One source of information about ancient climates is pollen records. Each type of plant has a particular type of pollen. Some lake bottoms have accumulated thick layers of mud and plant material, including pollen, over thousands of years. Scientists can drill down into these layers and bring up samples to examine. Using a microscope to look at the pollen in each layer, scientists can tell what types of plants lived there.

Tree Rings Tree rings also tell a story about ancient climates. Each summer, a tree grows a new layer of wood just under its bark. These layers form rings, as shown in **Figure 2.** Wide rings indicate a good growing season that was long or wet. Narrow rings indicate a dry year or a short growing season. Scientists study the patterns of thick or thin tree rings. From these data they can see if previous years were wet or dry, warm or cool.

Ice Cores Imagine drilling three kilometers down into ice and removing an ice core almost eight times longer than the Empire State Building! Ice cores have a layer for each year, just like tree rings. Scientists study these layers to find out about Earth's climate record. They can also analyze what's in the layers of ice, such as pollen and dust.

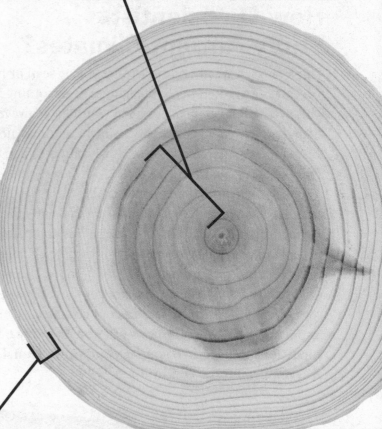

1. What was the climate like when the tree was young?

_____

_____

_____

_____

2. What was the climate like when the tree was older? How did the climate change over time?

_____

_____

_____

_____

FIGURE 2 ·······················
Evidence of Climate Change
Inner tree rings hold clues about a tree's early years. Outer rings hold clues about a tree's later years.

✏ **Infer** Look at the two sets of tree rings above, and answer the questions.

Do the Quick Lab *Climate Clues.*

🗝 **Assess Your Understanding**

got it? ···

O **I get it!** Now I know that scientists can learn about ancient climates from studying _____

_____

O **I need extra help with** _____

Go to **MY SCIENCE** 🔵ˢ **COACH** online for help with this subject.

What Natural Factors Can Cause Climate Change?

Why do climates change? 🔑 **Possible explanations for major climate changes include movement of the continents, variations in the position of Earth relative to the sun, major volcanic eruptions, and changes in the sun's energy output.**

Movement of Continents The continents have not always been located where they are now. Look at **Figure 3.** About 200 million years ago, most of the land on Earth was part of a single continent called Pangaea (pan JEE uh). At that time, most continents were far from their present positions. Continents that are now in the polar zones were once near the equator. This movement explains how tropical plants such as magnolias and palm trees could once have been native to Greenland.

The movements of continents over time changed the locations of land and sea. These changes affected the global patterns of winds and ocean currents, which slowly changed climates. As the continents continue to move, their climates will continue to change.

FIGURE 3 ···

> INTERACTIVE ART **Moving Continents**

✏️ **Use the maps to determine how continental movement has affected climate.**

1. **Interpret Maps** Look at the two maps. What happened to the location of Greenland over time?

_____

_____

_____

2. **Infer** How do you think the breakup of Pangaea affected Greenland's climate?

_____

_____

_____

_____

_____

_____

_____

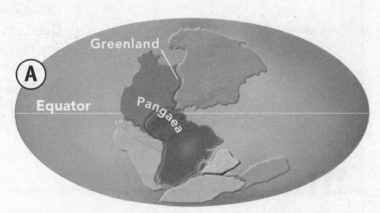

Earth 200 Million Years Ago

Earth Today

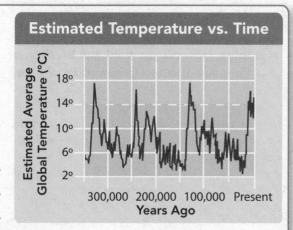

Identify Supporting Evidence Underline the changes in Earth's position that cause ice ages.

Earth's Position and Ice Ages

Earth's Position and Ice Ages The angle of Earth's axis and the shape of Earth's orbit affect Earth's climate. Earth travels in an elliptical orbit around the sun. But the shape of this ellipse varies over a period of about 100,000 years. When Earth's orbit is more elliptical, less sunlight reaches Earth during the year. This change causes Earth to experience an **ice age,** a period of glacial advance. Earth warms when its orbit is more circular. The angle at which Earth's axis tilts and the direction of the axis change over time as well. These changes in Earth's position affect the severity of ice ages. Altogether, these changes cause repeating 100,000-year cycles of ice ages interrupted by warm periods.

During each ice age, huge sheets of ice called continental glaciers covered large parts of Earth's surface. Glaciers transformed the landscape. They carved grooves in solid rock and deposited piles of sediment. They also moved huge boulders hundreds of kilometers. From this evidence, scientists have concluded that there were about 20 major ice ages in the last two million years. Brief, warm periods called interglacials occur between long, cold ice ages. The last ice age ended only about 10,000 years ago.

FIGURE 4

Glaciers in North America

The map shows the parts of North America that were covered by glaciers 18,000 years ago.

Observe Find and shade in your state. Was it covered with ice during the ice age? _____

Key

☐ Area covered by glaciers

■ Area not covered by glaciers

do the math!

Ice Ages and Temperature

The estimated average worldwide temperature for the past 350,000 years was about 14°C. Cold glacial periods have alternated with warm interglacial periods.

1 Interpret Data Explain the pattern you see in these data.

_____

_____

_____

2 CHALLENGE Based on the pattern in the graph, how might global temperature change in the future?

_____

FIGURE 5 ●●●●●●●●●●●●●●●●●●●●●●●●●●●●●●●●●●●

Volcanic Activity and Climate

The year 1816 is often called "the year without summer." A volcanic eruption in 1815 affected climates around the world.

✏ **Relate Cause and Effect** Write captions for the two photos to help tell the story of that summer.

Volcanic Activity Major volcanic eruptions release huge quantities of ash and aerosols into the atmosphere. **Aerosols** are solid particles or liquid drops in gas. Aerosols and ash can stay in the upper atmosphere for months or years. Scientists think that aerosols and ash reflect away some of the incoming solar radiation, and may lower temperatures. For example, the eruption of Mount Tambora in Indonesia in 1815 blasted about 100 cubic kilometers of ash into the atmosphere. Climates worldwide were dramatically colder the next few years, as shown in **Figure 5.**

Solar Energy Short-term changes in climate have been linked to changes in the amount of light given off by the sun. This amount changes over a regular 11-year cycle. It can also change over hundreds of years. The Little Ice Age was a period of cooling between about 1600 and 1850. It was caused by a decrease in the sun's energy output. The number of **sunspots,** dark, cooler regions on the surface of the sun, increases when the sun gives off more light. They can be used to measure solar output over the past 400 years.

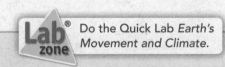
Do the Quick Lab *Earth's Movement and Climate.*

🔑 Assess Your Understanding

1a. Review What principle do scientists follow when studying ancient climates?

_____

_____

_____

b. Relate Cause and Effect How does a volcanic eruption affect climate?

_____

_____

got it?

○ **I get it!** Now I know that natural factors such as _____

_____

can cause climate change.

○ **I need extra help with** _____

Go to **MY SCIENCE COACH** *online for help with this subject.*

Human Activities and Climate Change

🔑 **How Are Human Activities Affecting Earth's Climate?**

MY PLANET DiARY

EVERYDAY SCIENCE

How Big Is Your Footprint?

Today people are measuring their effect on the environment by looking at their carbon footprint. Carbon is found in two of the greenhouse gases most responsible for warming Earth's climate. Your carbon footprint measures the total amount of greenhouse gases you emit directly and indirectly. Cars, factories, and home heating all rely on fuels that release carbon into the atmosphere. The manufacturing of products you use, like food and clothing, does, too. When people know how big their carbon footprints are, they can make changes that improve their own lives and the environment.

Brainstorm with a classmate and answer the questions below.

What activities affect your carbon footprint? How big is your carbon footprint?

_____

_____

_____

_____

_____

_____

▶ PLANET DIARY   Go to **Planet Diary** to learn more about global warming.

 Do the Inquiry Warm-Up
What Is the Greenhouse Effect?

How Are Human Activities Affecting Earth's Climate?

You may not realize it, but you are a powerful geologic force. Humans change the land, air, and water of Earth's surface faster than most geologic processes. In fact, human activities are causing a major change in the temperature of Earth's atmosphere. It's important to understand this impact because the atmosphere controls our climate and weather.

Vocabulary
- greenhouse gas
- fossil fuel
- global warming

Skills
- Reading: Ask Questions
- Inquiry: Make Models

Greenhouse Effect Outer space is incredibly cold: −270°C. If you were in a spaceship, you would rely on the insulated walls of the ship to keep you from freezing to death. Now think of Earth as a spaceship, moving through space as it orbits the sun. Earth's atmosphere is like the walls of the ship. It insulates us from the cold of space. How does it do this? The atmosphere keeps Earth's surface warm through a process called the greenhouse effect, as shown in **Figure 1.**

When the sun warms Earth's surface, this heat is radiated back to space as infrared waves. The infrared waves pass easily through nitrogen and oxygen, which make up 99 percent of Earth's atmosphere. However, **greenhouse gases,** such as water vapor, carbon dioxide, and methane, absorb the heat leaving Earth's surface. These gases then radiate some energy back toward Earth, trapping heat in the lower atmosphere. Greenhouse gases make up less than 1 percent of the atmosphere. But as you can see, it only takes a small amount of them to absorb heat, keeping Earth warm.

Ask Questions What questions do you have about the greenhouse effect? Before you read about it, write one question below. Try to answer your question after you read.

_____

_____

_____

_____

_____

FIGURE 1 ·············
ART IN MOTION **Greenhouse Effect**
Communicate Use the word bank to fill in the blanks. Then talk about the steps in the greenhouse effect with a classmate.

Word Bank
heated
radiated
absorbed

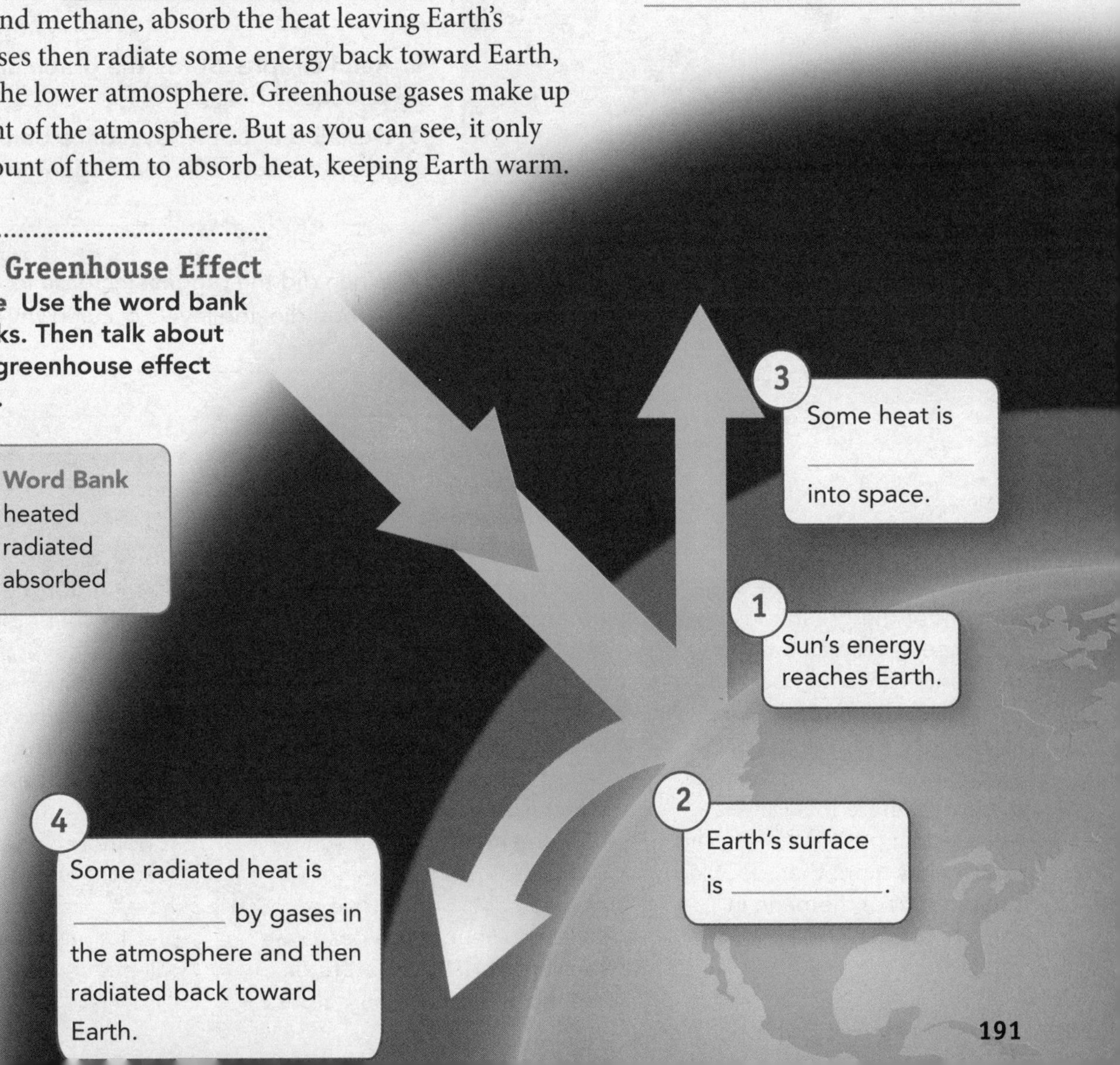

3 Some heat is _____ into space.

1 Sun's energy reaches Earth.

2 Earth's surface is _____.

4 Some radiated heat is _____ by gases in the atmosphere and then radiated back toward Earth.

Levels of Greenhouse Gases
We need the greenhouse effect, but you can have too much of a good thing. 🔑 **Many human activities are increasing the level of greenhouse gases in the atmosphere and producing changes in climate worldwide. This increase is causing global temperatures to rise.** This conclusion is based on our observations and measurements of the greenhouse gases humans release. It's also based on an understanding of how greenhouse gases affect the temperature at Earth's surface.

FIGURE 2 ·

Carbon Dioxide Levels
The graph shows the levels of carbon dioxide in the atmosphere over time.

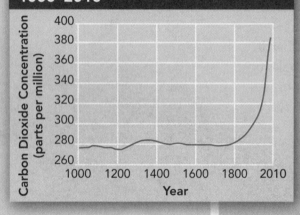

Atmospheric Carbon Dioxide, 1000–2010

Carbon Dioxide One of the most abundant greenhouse gases is carbon dioxide. Humans release billions of tons of it into the atmosphere each year. Most of this carbon dioxide is released by burning fossil fuels—energy-rich substances formed from the remains of organisms. Humans burn fossil fuels such as coal, natural gas, and gasoline to generate electricity, heat homes, and power cars.

· ·

✎ **Read Graphs** Study the graph and answer the questions below.

1. Describe what the level of carbon dioxide was like about 500 years ago.

   _____

2. When did the biggest increase in carbon dioxide levels occur? Why?

   _____

   _____

Methane

Human activities increase the amount of the greenhouse gas methane. Livestock emit methane. Large numbers of livestock, such as cattle, are raised for food production. As the population of livestock increases, more methane is released. In past centuries, this activity has more than doubled the amount of methane in the atmosphere.

Temperature Increase

Over the last 120 years, the average temperature of the troposphere has increased by about 0.7°C. This gradual increase in the temperature of Earth's atmosphere is called **global warming.** The effect is the same as it would be if the heat from the sun increased by about half of one percent. But increasing levels of greenhouse gases are causing global temperatures to rise more quickly than before.

Climate Models

Some models of climate change predict that global temperatures may rise several degrees over the next hundred years. Climate models are complex computer programs. They use data to predict temperature, precipitation, and other atmospheric conditions. Scientists are trying to improve climate models. They want to make more specific predictions about how warming will affect different regions.

Effects of Global Warming

Over the past 800,000 years, global temperatures have gone up and down. Scientists look at past events to predict the possible effects of global warming. 🔑 **The effects of global warming include melting glaciers, rising sea levels, drought, desertification, changes to the biosphere, and regional changes in temperature. Global warming is part of a larger set of changes to Earth's climate that together are called climate change.**

FIGURE 3 ·······························
Sea Level Rise
This satellite image shows how sea level rise could affect the eastern United States.

Key
- Low vulnerability
- Moderate vulnerability
- High vulnerability
- Very high vulnerability

USGS
science for a changing world

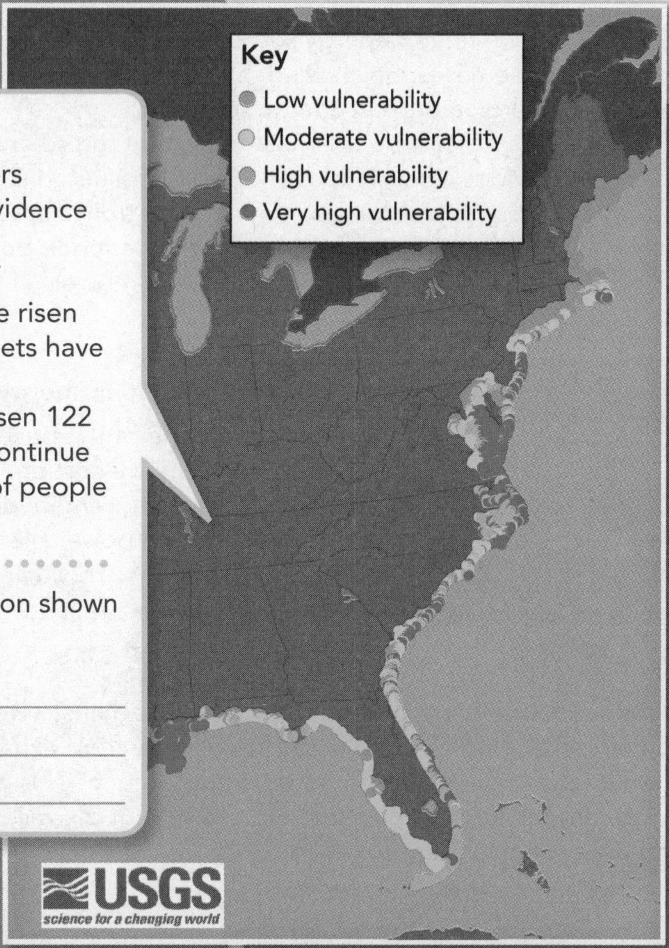

Melting Glaciers and Rising Sea Levels

Over the last century, scientists have observed glaciers retreating in many mountain regions. Now there is evidence that mountain glaciers are melting worldwide.

Records also indicate that temperatures in parts of Antarctica, which is covered by a thick ice sheet, have risen 6 degrees over 50 years. In fact, several giant ice sheets have collapsed and tumbled into the sea.

Since the end of the last ice age, sea levels have risen 122 meters. As glaciers continue to melt, sea levels will continue to rise. This rise poses a threat to the large number of people who live near the ocean.

✏️ **Interpret Data** How would the sea level prediction shown here affect people in the eastern United States?

_____

_____

_____

Droughts and Desertification

When global temperatures rise, some regions get very warm and dry. This can lead to water shortages or periods of drought. Today the southwestern United States is experiencing a severe drought at a time when global temperatures are warming. Severe droughts also cause some lands to become deserts. This process of desertification can lead to food shortages.

Changes to the Biosphere

Each climate region has its own communities of living organisms that are adapted to that climate. As global climates warm, organisms are often pushed to new locations to find familiar climates. Organisms that can't adapt may become extinct. Species that can adapt to warmer conditions will survive.

Regional Changes in Temperature

Global temperature changes affect regions differently. During the twentieth century, global temperatures increased by an average of less than one degree. Yet some parts of the world got warmer by more than five degrees, while others got cooler. In some areas, temperature changes have led to longer growing seasons.

193

Limiting Global Warming Scientists think human activities that release greenhouse gases are responsible for our recent episode of global warming. The solution might sound simple: Reduce greenhouse gas emissions. But how do we do that? **Solutions for limiting global warming and climate change include finding clean, renewable sources of energy, being more energy efficient, and removing carbon from fossil fuel emissions.**

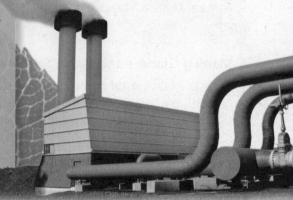

Clean Energy Sources

Clean energy refers to energy sources that release very small amounts of greenhouse gases. Solar, wind, hydroelectric, geothermal, nuclear, and tidal energy are clean energy sources.

Solar energy might be the most important future energy source. The sun provides a continuous and nearly unlimited supply of energy. In one hour, Earth receives as much energy from the sun as all humans use in one year. Solar energy drives the water cycle behind hydroelectric power and the air motions behind wind power.

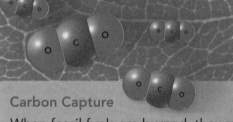

Efficient Energy

One of the best ways to reduce global warming is to develop more energy-efficient technologies. Clean energy power plants can power electric and hydrogen fuel cell cars. And factories can run on steam from power plants. People can also practice energy-efficient habits. They can turn off lights when they leave a room or use public transportation.

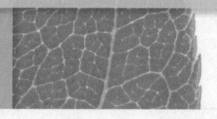

Carbon Capture

When fossil fuels are burned, they release exhaust. Technologies are being developed to remove carbon dioxide from exhaust. The carbon dioxide could then be buried underground. This process takes more energy and is a bit more expensive, but the result is that fewer greenhouse gases are released.

Make Models How can you help limit global warming? Pick one item from your home. Come up with a plan to make it more energy efficient. Use the space provided to draw or explain your idea.

CLIMATE IN THE MEDIA

What factors affect Earth's climate?

FIGURE 4 ···

> **INTERACTIVE ART** ✏ **Evaluate Science in the Media** Working with a group, choose at least three different media sources. Spend a week collecting stories about climate change from these sources. Discuss the stories with your group. Evaluate how they cover the topic of climate change. Present your findings to the class.

Lab zone® Do the Quick Lab *Greenhouse Gases and Global Warming.*

🔑 **Assess Your Understanding**

1a. Define What is a greenhouse gas?

_____

_____

b. List What are some solutions for reducing greenhouse gases?

_____

c. 🅰 **ANSWER THE BIG ?** What factors affect Earth's climate?

_____

_____

_____

_____

_____

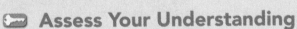

got it? ···

O **I get it!** Now I know that human activities can affect Earth's climate by _____

_____

O **I need extra help with** _____

Go to **MY SCIENCE** 🅢 **COACH** *online for help with this subject.*

Study Guide

Some factors that affect Earth's climate are _____, altitude, _____ _____, ocean currents, prevailing and _____ winds, and _____ .

LESSON 1 What Causes Climate?

🔑 Temperature is affected by latitude, altitude, distance from large bodies of water, and ocean currents.

🔑 Precipitation is affected by prevailing winds, presence of mountains, and seasonal winds.

Vocabulary
- climate • tropical zone • polar zone
- temperate zone • marine climate
- continental climate • windward
- leeward • monsoon

LESSON 2 Climate Regions

🔑 Scientists classify climates according to two major factors: temperature and precipitation.

🔑 The six main climate regions are tropical rainy, dry, temperate marine, temperate continental, polar, and highlands.

Vocabulary
- rain forest • savanna • steppe
- desert • humid subtropical • subarctic
- tundra • permafrost

LESSON 3 Changes in Climate

🔑 In studying ancient climates, scientists follow an important principle: If plants and animals today need certain conditions to live, then similar plants and animals in the past also required those conditions.

🔑 Possible explanations for major climate changes include movement of continents, variations in the position of Earth relative to the sun, major volcanic eruptions, and changes in the sun's energy output.

Vocabulary
- ice age • aerosol • sunspot

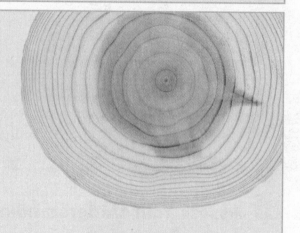

LESSON 4 Human Activities and Climate Change

🔑 Many human activities are increasing the level of greenhouse gases in the atmosphere, causing global temperatures to rise.

🔑 The effects of global warming include melting glaciers, rising sea levels, drought, desertification, changes in the biosphere, and regional changes in temperature.

🔑 Solutions for limiting global warming include finding clean, renewable sources of energy, being more energy efficient, and removing carbon from fossil fuel emissions.

Vocabulary
- greenhouse gas • fossil fuel • global warming

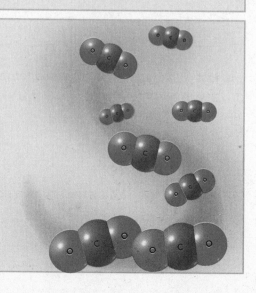

Review and Assessment

LESSON 1 What Causes Climate?

1. In which area do temperatures range from warm or hot summers to cool or cold winters?

   a. polar zone   **b.** temperate zone

   c. tropical zone   **d.** tundra zone

2. The long-term weather in an area is its climate, which includes _____

_____

Use the map of world temperature zones to answer Question 3.

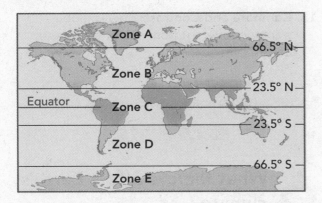

3. Interpret Maps Which zone has the highest average temperatures all year? Why?

_____

4. Relate Cause and Effect Explain how distance from large bodies of water can affect the temperature of nearby land areas.

_____

_____

_____

5. Compare and Contrast How are summer monsoons different from winter monsoons?

_____

_____

_____

LESSON 2 Climate Regions

6. What do we call a climate region that is semiarid with short grasses and low bushes?

   a. tundra   **b.** savanna

   c. desert   **d.** steppe

7. Rain forests are common in tropical wet regions because _____

_____

_____

_____

8. Explain Why are highland regions considered a climate region?

_____

_____

_____

_____

_____

_____

_____

9. Calculate Suppose a city receives an average of 35 centimeters of precipitation in November. If an average of 140 centimeters of precipitation falls there in a year, what percentage falls in November?

_____

_____

10. **Write About It** Suppose you live in Location A, a part of the United States with a semiarid climate. You travel to Location B, which is in a neighboring area. There you find a humid continental climate. In which direction is Location B likely to be, relative to Location A? What is the best explanation for the difference? (*Hint:* Read the section on humid continental climates.)

Changes in Climate

11. Which of the following is probably the main cause of ice ages?

   a. Earth's orbit

   b. volcanic activity

   c. continental movement

   d. solar energy

12. Define Some climate changes are correlated

with sunspots, which are _____

_____

_____

13. Relate Cause and Effect How does the movement of continents explain changes in climate over millions of years?

_____

_____

_____

_____

_____

14. Infer How is Earth's climate affected by major volcanic eruptions?

_____

_____

_____

_____

15. Draw Conclusions Thick tree rings in a cool climate suggest a longer warm season. Thick tree rings in a dry climate suggest a rainier wet season. What conclusions can you draw about the effect of climate on tree growth?

_____

_____

_____

_____

Human Activities and Climate Change

16. Which change in the atmosphere appears to contribute to global warming?

   a. decreased moisture

   b. decreased heat

   c. increased oxygen

   d. increased carbon dioxide

17. Identify Greenhouse gases absorb _____

_____

18. Compare and Contrast How is global warming different from earlier changes in Earth's climate?

_____

_____

_____

_____

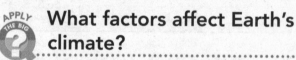

What factors affect Earth's climate?

19. You've been asked to give a report about global warming at your next school meeting. As you prepare your report, be sure to mention what you think the town can do to reduce its carbon footprint.

_____

_____

_____

_____

_____

_____

_____

_____

_____

_____

_____

_____

Standardized Test Prep

Multiple Choice

Circle the letter of the best answer.

The graph below shows average monthly precipitation for a location in Arizona. Use the graph to answer Question 1.

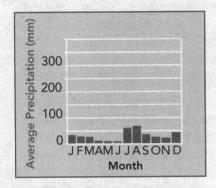

1. During which period does this location get the most precipitation?

   A   January–March   C   July–September

   B   April–June   D   October–December

2. What kind of climate would you expect to find in an area with these features: interior of a large continent, east side of a major mountain range, and winds usually from west to east?

   A   polar

   B   temperate marine

   C   tropical rainy

   D   dry

3. What two major factors are usually used to classify climate?

   A   altitude and precipitation

   B   precipitation and temperature

   C   air pressure and humidity

   D   temperature and air pressure

4. Which of the following is an effect of global warming?

   A   increased frequency of droughts

   B   falling sea levels

   C   decreased coastal flooding

   D   spreading glaciers

5. Which climate is warm, wet, and located on the edges of the tropics?

   A   humid continental

   B   subarctic

   C   semiarid

   D   humid subtropical

Constructed Response

Use the map and your knowledge of science to answer Question 6. Write your answer on a separate piece of paper.

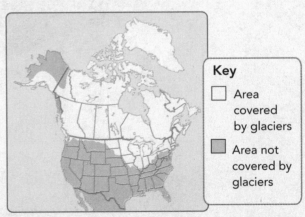

Key

☐ Area covered by glaciers

▨ Area not covered by glaciers

6. Ice ages have occurred at several times during Earth's history. What is an ice age, and how does it affect the land surface and the oceans?

TRACKING EARTH'S GASES FROM SPACE

Our planet has gas. In fact, it is surrounded by gas. Satellites help us measure this gassy envelope.

Specifically, these satellites measure greenhouse gases. The Japanese satellite GOSAT was launched on January 23, 2009. Its main job is to measure the levels of two major greenhouse gases—carbon dioxide (CO_2) and methane (CH_4). Watching changes in the concentrations of these gases all over the world will help scientists learn about climate change.

Scientists already use 282 land-based observation sites, but GOSAT will gather data from 56,000 locations! In 44 orbits, GOSAT will map all of Earth every three days. GOSAT will also record greenhouse gas concentrations over remote areas like the ocean and help every country keep track of its greenhouse gas emissions.

As Earth gets gassier, satellites are helping us get a clearer picture.

The GOSAT satellite's mission is to record the concentration of greenhouse gases on Earth. ▼

Research It The levels of CO_2 have been increasing, but not all scientists agree on the best solutions for reducing CO_2 emissions. Research different ways of reducing or combating greenhouse gas emissions, and participate in a class debate about the costs and benefits of different approaches.

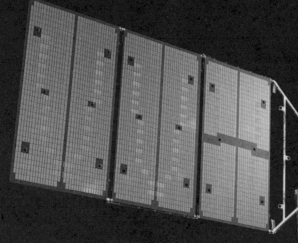

Museum of Science

Bacterial RAINMAKERS

Could bacteria influence the weather? Some scientists think that some bacteria can! Researchers have found rainmaking bacteria in samples of rainwater throughout the world. These bacteria are also found in the clouds that produce rain.

The cycle that carries bacteria from Earth to the clouds and back, known as bioprecipitation, begins at Earth's surface. The bacteria reproduce on the leaves of plants, often damaging their hosts. Then wind currents carry the bacteria high into the atmosphere. If conditions are right, water vapor freezes on the bacteria, forming rain. Rain carries the bacteria back to Earth's surface and the bioprecipitation cycle repeats.

Understanding the role of bacteria in weather patterns could be important for predicting or even preventing droughts. In the future, scientists may be able to increase the chance of rain by seeding clouds with rainmaking bacteria.

Research It Find out more about bioprecipitation. Make a presentation that shows how rainmaking bacteria may influence weather patterns as part of their life cycle.

▲ Rainmaking bacteria, carried into the atmosphere by Earth's winds, may play a role in Earth's patterns of rain and drought.

GLOSSARY

A

abyssal plain A smooth, nearly flat region of the deep ocean floor. (p. 45)
llanura abisal Región llana, casi plana, de la cuenca oceánica profunda.

aerosols Solid particles or liquid droplets in the atmosphere. (p. 189)
aerosoles Partículas sólidas o gotas de líquido en la atmósfera.

air mass A huge body of air that has similar temperature, humidity, and air pressure at any given height. (p. 133)
masa de aire Gran cuerpo de aire que tiene temperatura, humedad y presión similares en todos sus puntos.

air pressure The pressure caused by the weight of a column of air pushing down on an area. (p. 79)
presión de aire Presión causada por el peso de una columna de aire en un área.

altitude Elevation above sea level. (p. 82)
altitud Elevación sobre el nivel del mar.

anemometer An instrument used to measure wind speed. (p. 102)
anemómetro Instrumento que se usa para medir la velocidad del viento.

aneroid barometer An instrument that measures changes in air pressure without using a liquid. (p. 81)
barómetro aneroide Instrumento que mide los cambios en la presión del aire sin usar líquidos.

anticyclone A high-pressure center of dry air. (p. 138)
anticiclón Centro de aire seco de alta presión.

aquifer An underground layer of rock or sediment that holds water. (p. 21)
acuífero Capa subterránea de roca o sedimento que retiene agua.

artesian well A well in which water rises because of pressure within the aquifer. (p. 23)
pozo artesiano Pozo por el que el agua se eleva debido a la presión dentro del acuífero.

atmosphere The envelope of gases that surrounds Earth. (p. 74)
atmósfera Capa de gases que rodea la Tierra.

B

barometer An instrument used to measure changes in air pressure. (p. 80)
barómetro Instrumento que se usa para medir cambios de la presión del aire.

benthos Organisms that live on the bottom of the ocean or another body of water. (p. 62)
bentos Organismos que viven en el fondo del océano u otro cuerpo de agua.

C

cirrus Wispy, feathery clouds made of ice crystals that form at high levels. (p. 124)
cirros Nubes que parecen plumas o pinceladas y que están formadas por cristales de hielo que se crean a grandes alturas.

climate The average annual conditions of temperature, precipitation, winds, and clouds in an area. (pp. 56, 167)
clima Condiciones promedio anuales de temperatura, precipitación, viento y nubosidad de un área.

condensation The change of state from a gas to a liquid. (p. 118)
condensación Cambio del estado gaseoso al estado líquido.

conduction 1. The transfer of thermal energy from one particle of matter to another. 2. A method of charging an object by allowing electrons to flow by direct contact from one object to another object. (p. 98)
conducción 1. Transferencia de energía térmica de una partícula de materia a otra 2. Método por el cual se carga un objeto al permitir el flujo de electrones por contacto directo entre objetos.

continental (air mass) A dry air mass that forms over land. (p. 133)
masa de aire continental Masa de aire seco que se forma sobre la Tierra.

continental climate The climate of the centers of continents, with cold winters and warm or hot summers. (p. 170)
clima continental Clima del centro de los continentes, con inviernos fríos y veranos templados o calurosos.

continental shelf A gently sloping, shallow area of the ocean floor that extends outward from the edge of a continent. (p. 44)
plataforma continental Área poco profunda con pendiente suave en la cuenca oceánica que se extiende desde los márgenes de un continente.

continental slope A steep incline of the ocean floor leading down from the edge of the continental shelf. (p. 44)
talud continental Región de la cuenca oceánica con pendiente empinada que baja del borde de la plataforma continental.

convection The transfer of thermal energy by the movement of a fluid. (p. 98)
convección Transferencia de energía térmica por el movimiento de un líquido.

convection current The movement of a fluid, caused by differences in temperature, that transfers heat from one part of the fluid to another. (p. 99)
corriente de convección Movimiento de un líquido ocasionado por diferencias de temperatura, y por medio del cual se transfiere calor de un punto del líquido a otro.

Coriolis effect The effect of Earth's rotation on the direction of winds and currents. (pp. 55, 105)
efecto Coriolis Efecto de la rotación de la Tierra sobre la dirección de los vientos y las corrientes.

cumulus Fluffy, white clouds, usually with flat bottoms, that look like rounded piles of cotton. (p. 124)
cúmulos Nubes blancas, normalmente con la parte inferior plana, que parecen grandes masas de algodón esponjosas y redondas.

current A large stream of moving water that flows through the oceans. (p. 55)
corriente Gran volumen de agua que fluye por los océanos.

cyclone A swirling center of low air pressure. (p. 138)
ciclón Centro de un remolino de aire de baja presión.

D

density The ratio of the mass of a substance to its volume (mass divided by volume). (p. 79)
densidad Relación entre la masa y el volumen de una sustancia (la masa dividida por el volumen).

desert A dry region that on average receives less than 25 centimeters of precipitation per year. (p. 179)
desierto Región seca en la que se registra un promedio menor de 25 centímetros de precipitación anual.

dew point The temperature at which condensation begins. (p. 123)
punto de rocío Temperatura a la que comienza la condensación.

divide A ridge of land that separates one watershed from another. (p. 13)
divisoria Elevación de terreno que separa una cuenca hidrográfica de otra.

drought A long period of low precipitation. (p. 131)
sequía Período prolongado de baja precipitación.

E

El Niño An abnormal climate event that occurs every two to seven years in the Pacific Ocean, causing changes in winds, currents, and weather patterns for one to two years. (p. 57)
El Niño Suceso climático anormal que se presenta cada dos a siete años en el océano Pacífico y que causa cambios de vientos, corrientes y patrones meteorológicos que duran uno o dos años.

electromagnetic wave A wave that can transfer electric and magnetic energy through the vacuum of space. (p. 90)
onda electromagnética Onda que puede transferir energía eléctrica y magnética a través del vacío del espacio.

eutrophication The buildup over time of nutrients in freshwater lakes and ponds that leads to an increase in the growth of algae. (p. 16)
eutroficación Acumulación gradual de nutrientes en lagos y estanques de agua dulce que produce un aumento en el crecimiento de algas.

evacuate Moving away temporarily from an area about to be affected by severe weather. (p. 148)
evacuar Desalojar temporalmente un área que será afectada por mal tiempo.

evaporation The process by which molecules at the surface of a liquid absorb enough energy to change to a gas. (pp. 8, 118)
evaporación Proceso mediante el cual las moléculas en la superficie de un líquido absorben suficiente energía para pasar al estado gaseoso.

GLOSSARY

exosphere The outer layer of the thermosphere. (p. 89)
  exósfera Capa externa de la termósfera.

---- **F** ----

flood An overflowing of water in a normally dry area. (p. 130)
  inundación Ocupación de agua en un área que habitualmente permanece seca.

food web The pattern of overlapping feeding relationships or food chains among the various organisms in an ecosystem. (p. 63)
  red alimentaria Patrón de las relaciones de alimentación intercruzadas o de cadenas alimentarias entre los diferentes organismos de un ecosistema.

fossil fuel Coal, oil, or natural gas that forms over millions of years from the remains of ancient organisms; burned to release energy. (p. 192)
  combustible fósil Carbón, petróleo o gas natural que se forma a lo largo de millones de años a partir de los restos de organismos antiguos; se queman para liberar energía.

frequency The number of complete waves that pass a given point in a certain amount of time. (p. 48)
  frecuencia Número de ondas completas que pasan por un punto dado en cierto tiempo.

front The boundary where unlike air masses meet but do not mix. (p. 135)
  frente Límite donde se encuentran, pero no se mezclan, masas de aire diferentes.

---- **G** ----

global warming A gradual increase in the average temperature of the atmosphere, thought to be caused by an increase in greenhouse gases from human activities. (p. 192)
  calentamiento global Aumento gradual de la temperatura promedio de la atmósfera cuya causa se piensa que es el aumento de emisiones de gases de efecto invernadero ocasionados por actividades humanas.

global winds Winds that blow steadily from specific directions over long distances. (p. 104)
  vientos globales Vientos que soplan constantemente desde direcciones específicas por largas distancias.

greenhouse effect The trapping of heat near a planet's surface by certain gases in the planet's atmosphere. (p. 95)
  efecto invernadero Retención de calor cerca de la superficie de un planeta debido a la presencia de ciertos gases en la atmósfera.

greenhouse gases Gases in the atmosphere that trap energy. (p. 191)
  gases de efecto invernadero Gases presentes en la atmósfera que atrapan la energía.

groin A wall made of rocks or concrete that is built outward from a beach to reduce erosion. (p. 53)
  escollera Pared de piedra o concreto que se construye perpendicularmente a una playa para reducir la erosión.

groundwater Water that fills the cracks and spaces in underground soil and rock layers. (p. 7)
  aguas freáticas Agua que llena las grietas y huecos de las capas subterráneas de tierra y roca.

---- **H** ----

habitat An environment that provides the things a specific organism needs to live, grow, and reproduce. (p. 5)
  hábitat Medio que provee lo que un organismo específico necesita para vivir, crecer y reproducirse.

heat The transfer of thermal energy from one object to another because of a difference in temperature. (p. 98)
  calor Transferencia de energía térmica de un cuerpo más cálido a uno menos cálido.

humidity The amount of water vapor in a given volume of air. (p. 120)
  humedad Cantidad de vapor de agua en cierto volumen de aire.

humid subtropical A wet and warm climate found on the edges of the tropics. (p. 180)
  subtropical húmedo Clima húmedo y templado que se encuentra en los límites de los trópicos.

hurricane A tropical storm that has winds of about 119 kilometers per hour or higher. (p. 144)
  huracán Tormenta tropical que tiene vientos de cerca de 119 kilómetros por hora o más.

I

ice ages Times in Earth's history during which glaciers covered large parts of the surface. (p. 188)
edades de hielo Períodos en la historia de la Tierra durante los cuales gran parte de la superficie terrestre estaba cubierta por glaciares

impermeable A characteristic of materials, such as clay and granite, through which water does not easily pass. (p. 19)
impermeable Característica de los materiales, como la arcilla y el granito, que no dejan pasar fácilmente el agua.

infrared radiation Electromagnetic waves with wavelengths that are longer than visible light but shorter than microwaves. (p. 91)
radiación infrarroja Ondas electromagnéticas con longitudes de onda más largas que la luz visible, pero más cortas que las microondas.

intertidal zone An area between the highest high-tide line on land and the point on the continental shelf exposed by the lowest low-tide line. (p. 61)
zona intermareal Área entre el punto más alto de la marea alta y el punto más bajo de la marea baja.

ionosphere The lower part of the thermosphere. (p. 89)
ionósfera Parte inferior de la termósfera.

isobar A line on a weather map that joins places that have the same air pressure. (p. 153)
isobara Línea en un mapa del tiempo que une lugares que tienen la misma presión de aire.

isotherm A line on a weather map that joins places that have the same temperature. (p. 153)
isoterma Línea en un mapa del tiempo que une lugares que tienen la misma temperatura.

J

jet streams Bands of high-speed winds about 10 kilometers above Earth's surface. (p. 135)
corrientes de viento en chorro Bandas de vientos de alta velocidad a unos 10 kilómetros sobre la superficie de la Tierra.

L

La Niña A climate event in the eastern Pacific Ocean in which surface waters are colder than normal. (p. 57)
la Niña Fenómeno climático que ocurre en la parte este del océano Pacífico, en el cual las aguas superficiales están más fías que lo normal.

land breeze The flow of air from land to a body of water. (p. 103)
brisa terrestre Flujo de aire desde la tierra a una masa de agua.

latitude The distance in degrees north or south of the equator. (p. 106)
latitud Distancia en grados al norte o al sur del ecuador.

leeward The side of a mountain range that faces away from the oncoming wind. (p. 172)
sotavento Lado de una cadena montañosa que está resguardado del viento.

lightning A sudden spark, or energy discharge, caused when electrical charges jump between parts of a cloud, between nearby clouds, or between a cloud and the ground. (p. 143)
rayo Chispa repentina o descarga de energía causada por cargas eléctricas que saltan entre partes de una nube, entre nubes cercanas o entre una nube y la tierra.

local winds Winds that blow over short distances. (p. 103)
vientos locales Vientos que soplan en distancias cortas.

longshore drift The movement of water and sediment down a beach caused by waves coming in to shore at an angle. (p. 52)
deriva litoral Movimiento de agua y sedimentos paralelo a una playa debido a la llegada de olas inclinadas respecto a la costa.

M

marine climate The climate of some coastal regions, with relatively warm winters and cool summers. (p. 170)
clima marino Clima de algunas regiones costeras, con inviernos relativamente templados y veranos fríos.

maritime (air mass) A humid air mass that forms over oceans. (p. 133)
masa de aire marítima Masa de aire húmedo que se forma sobre los océanos.

GLOSSARY

mercury barometer An instrument that measures changes in air pressure, consisting of a glass tube partially filled with mercury, with its open end resting in a dish of mercury. (p. 80)
barómetro de mercurio Instrumento que mide los cambios de presión del aire; es un tubo de vidrio parcialmente lleno de mercurio con su extremo abierto posado sobre un recipiente con mercurio.

mesosphere The layer of Earth's atmosphere immediately above the stratosphere. (p. 88)
mesósfera Capa de la atmósfera de la Tierra inmediatamente sobre la estratósfera.

meteorologists Scientists who study the causes of weather and try to predict it. (p. 151)
meteorólogos Científicos que estudian las causas del tiempo e intentan predecirlo.

mid-ocean ridge An undersea mountain chain where new ocean floor is produced; a divergent plate boundary under the ocean. (p. 45)
cordillera oceánica central Cadena montañosa submarina donde se produce el nuevo suelo oceánico; borde de placa divergente bajo el océano.

monsoon Sea or land breeze over a large region that changes direction with the seasons. (p. 173)
monzón Vientos marinos o terrestres que soplan en una región extensa y cambian de dirección según las estaciones.

N

nekton Free-swimming animals that can move throughout the water column. (p. 62)
necton Animales que nadan libremente y pueden desplazarse por la columna de agua.

neritic zone The area of the ocean that extends from the low-tide line out to the edge of the continental shelf. (p. 61)
zona nerítica Área del océano que se extiende desde la línea de bajamar hasta el borde de la plataforma continental.

O

occluded Cut off, as in a front where a warm air mass is caught between two cooler air masses. (p. 137)
ocluido Aislado o cerrado, como un frente donde una masa de aire cálido queda atrapada entre dos masas de aire más frío.

open-ocean zone The deepest, darkest area of the ocean beyond the edge of the continental shelf. (p. 61)
zona de mar abierto Zona más profunda y oscura del océano, más allá de la plataforma continental.

P

permafrost Permanently frozen soil found in the tundra biome climate region. (p. 182)
permagélido Suelo que está permanentemente congelado y que se encuentra en el bioma climático de la tundra.

permeable Characteristic of a material that contains connected air spaces, or pores, that water can seep through easily. (p. 19)
permeable Característica de un material que contiene diminutos espacios de aire, o poros, conectados por donde se puede filtrar el agua.

plankton Tiny algae and animals that float in water and are carried by waves and currents. (p. 62)
plancton Algas y animales diminutos que flotan en el agua a merced de las olas y las corrientes.

polar (air mass) A cold air mass that forms north of 50° north latitude or south of 50° south latitude and has high air pressure. (p. 133)
masa de aire polar Masa de aire frío que se forma al norte de los 50° de latitud norte o al sur de los 50° de latitud sur y que tiene presión alta.

polar zones The areas near both poles from about 66.5° to 90° north and 66.5° to 90° south latitudes. (p. 168)
zona polar Áreas cercanas a los polos desde unos 66.5° a 90° de latitud norte y 66.5° a 90° de latitud sur.

precipitation Any form of water that falls from clouds and reaches Earth's surface as rain, snow, sleet, or hail. (pp. 9, 127)
precipitación Cualquier forma del agua que cae de las nubes y llega a la superficie de la tierra como lluvia, nieve, aguanieve o granizo.

psychrometer An instrument used to measure relative humidity. (p. 120)
psicrómetro Instrumento que se usa para medir la humedad relativa.

R

radiation The transfer of energy by electromagnetic waves. (p. 91)
radiación Transferencia de energía por ondas electromagnéticas.

rain forest A forest that receives at least 2 meters of rain per year, mostly occurring in the tropical wet climate zone. (p. 178)
selva tropical Bosque donde caen al menos 2 metros de lluvia al año, principalmente en la zona climática tropical húmeda.

rain gauge An instrument used to measure precipitation. (p. 127)
pluviómetro Instrumento que se usa para medir la precipitación.

relative humidity The percentage of water vapor in the air compared to the maximum amount of water vapor that air can contain at a particular temperature. (p. 120)
humedad relativa Porcentaje de vapor de agua del aire comparado con la cantidad máxima de vapor de agua que puede contener el aire a una temperatura particular.

reservoir A lake that stores water for human use. (p. 15)
embalse Lago que almacena agua para el uso humano.

rip current A strong, narrow current that flows briefly from the shore back toward the ocean through a narrow opening. (p. 52)
corriente de resaca Corriente fuerte que fluye por un canal estrecho desde la costa hacia el mar abierto.

S

salinity The total amount of dissolved salts in a water sample. (p. 41)
salinidad Cantidad total de sales disueltas en una muestra de agua.

saturated zone The area of permeable rock or soil in which the cracks and pores are totally filled with water. (p. 20)
zona saturada Área de roca o suelo permeable cuyas grietas y poros están totalmente llenos de agua.

savanna A grassland located close to the equator that may include shrubs and small trees and receives as much as 120 centimeters of rain per year. (p. 178)
sabana Pradera que puede tener arbustos y árboles pequeños, ubicada cerca del ecuador y donde pueden caer hasta 120 centímetros de lluvia al año.

scattering Reflection of light in all directions. (p. 93)
dispersión Reflexión de la luz en todas las direcciones.

sea breeze The flow of cooler air from over an ocean or lake toward land. (p. 103)
brisa marina Flujo de aire frío procedente de un océano o lago hacia la costa.

seamount A steep-sided volcanic mountain rising from the deep-ocean floor. (p. 44)
montaña marina Montaña muy inclinada de origen volcánico cuya base es el fondo del mar.

sonar A system that uses reflected sound waves to locate and determine the distance to objects under water. (p. 44)
sonar Sistema que emite ondas ultrasonoras para determinar la distancia y localizar objetos bajo el agua.

steppe A prairie or grassland found in semiarid regions. (p. 179)
estepa Pradera o pastizal que se encuentra en las regiones semiáridas.

storm A violent disturbance in the atmosphere. (p. 141)
tormenta Alteración violenta en la atmósfera.

storm surge A "dome" of water that sweeps across the coast where a hurricane lands. (p. 145)
marejadas "Cúpula" de agua que se desplaza a lo largo de la costa donde aterriza un huracán.

stratosphere The second-lowest layer of Earth's atmosphere. (p. 87)
estratósfera Segunda capa de la atmósfera de la Tierra.

stratus Clouds that form in flat layers and often cover much of the sky. (p. 125)
estratos Nubes que aparecen como capas planas y que a menudo cubren gran parte del cielo.

subarctic A climate zone that lies north of the humid continental climates. (p. 181)
subártico Zona climática situada al norte de las regiones de clima continental húmedo.

GLOSSARY

sunspots Relatively dark, cool regions on the surface of the sun. (p. 189)
manchas solares Regiones relativamente frías y oscuras de la superficie solar.

T
---

temperate zones The areas between the tropical and the polar zones. (p. 168)
área templada Áreas ubicadas entre las zonas tropical y polar.

temperature How hot or cold something is; a measure of the average energy of motion of the particles of a substance. (p. 96)
temperatura Cuán caliente o frío es algo; medida de la energía de movimiento de las partículas de una sustancia.

thermal energy The total energy of all the particles of an object. (p. 97)
energía térmica Energía total de las partículas de un objeto.

thermometer An instrument used to measure temperature. (p. 97)
termómetro Instrumento que se usa para medir la temperatura.

thermosphere The outermost layer of Earth's atmosphere. (p. 89)
termósfera Capa exterior de la atmósfera de la Tierra.

thunderstorm A small storm often accompanied by heavy precipitation and frequent thunder and lightning. (p. 142)
tronada Pequeña tormenta acompañada de fuertes precipitaciones y frecuentes rayos y truenos.

tornado A rapidly spinning column of air that reaches down to touch Earth's surface. (p. 146)
tornado Columna de aire que gira rápidamente y que alcanza y toca la superficie de la Tierra.

transpiration The process by which water is lost through a plant's leaves. (p. 8)
transpiración Proceso por el que las plantas pierden agua a través de sus hojas.

trench A deep, steep-sided canyon in the ocean floor. (p. 44)
fosa Cañón profundo, de lados empinados, en el suelo oceánico.

tributary A stream or river that flows into a larger river. (p. 11)
afluente Río o arroyo que desemboca en un río más grande.

tropical (air mass) A warm air mass that forms in the tropics and has low air pressure. (p. 133)
masa de aire tropical Masa de aire templado que se forma en los trópicos y cuya presión atmosférica es baja.

tropical zone The area near the equator between about 23.5° north latitude and 23.5° south latitude. (p. 168)
zona tropical Área cercana al ecuador entre aproximadamente los 23.5° de latitud norte y los 23.5° de latitud sur.

troposphere The lowest layer of Earth's atmosphere. (p. 86)
troposfera Capa más inferior de la atmósfera de la Tierra.

tsunami A giant wave usually caused by an earthquake beneath the ocean floor. (p. 51)
tsunami Ola gigantesca, generalmente provocada por un sismo que ocurrió debajo de la cuenca oceánica.

tundra An extremely cold, dry biome climate region characterized by short, cool summers and bitterly cold winters. (p. 182)
tundra Bioma de la región climática extremadamente fría y seca, que se caracteriza por veranos cortos y frescos e inviernos sumamente fríos.

U
---

ultraviolet radiation Electromagnetic waves with wavelengths that are shorter than visible light but longer than X-rays. (p. 91)
radiación ultravioleta Ondas electromagnéticas con longitudes de onda más cortas que la luz visible, pero más largas que los rayos X.

unsaturated zone The layer of rocks and soil above the water table in which the pores contain air as well as water. (p. 20)
zona insaturada Capa de rocas y suelo encima del nivel freático en la que los poros contienen aire además de agua.

W

water cycle The continual movement of water among Earth's atmosphere, oceans, and land surface through evaporation, condensation, and precipitation. (pp. 8, 118)
ciclo del agua Circulación continua del agua por la atmósfera, los océanos y la superficie de la Tierra mediante la evaporación, la condensación y la precipitación.

water table The top of the saturated zone, or depth to the groundwater under Earth's surface. (p. 20)
nivel freático Límite superior de la zona saturada, es decir de la profundidad de las aguas freáticas del subsuelo.

water vapor Water in the form of a gas. (p. 76)
vapor de agua Agua en forma de gas.

watershed The land area that supplies water to a river system. (p. 12)
cuenca hidrográfica Área de terreno que suministra agua a un sistema fluvial.

wave 1. A disturbance that transfers energy from place to place. **2.** The movement of energy through a body of water. (p. 47)
onda 1. Perturbación que transfiere energía de un lugar a otro. **2.** Movimiento de energía por un fluido.

wave height The vertical distance from the crest of a wave to the trough. (p. 48)
altura de una ola Distancia vertical desde la cresta de una ola hasta el valle.

wavelength The distance between two corresponding parts of a wave, such as the distance between two crests. (p. 48)
longitud de onda Distancia entre dos partes correspondientes de una onda, por ejemplo la distancia entre dos crestas.

weather The condition of Earth's atmosphere at a particular time and place. (p. 74)
tiempo meteorológico Condición de la atmósfera terrestre en un momento y lugar determinado.

wetland A land area that is covered with a shallow layer of water during some or all of the year. (p. 25)
tierra cenagosa Terreno cubierto por una capa poco profunda de agua durante todo el año o parte de éste.

wind The horizontal movement of air from an area of high pressure to an area of lower pressure. (p. 101)
viento Movimiento horizontal de aire de un área de alta presión a una de menor presión.

wind-chill factor A measure of cooling combining temperature and wind speed. (p. 102)
factor de enfriamiento por viento Medida del enfriamiento que combina la temperatura y la velocidad del viento.

windward The side of a mountain range that faces the oncoming wind. (p. 172)
barlovento Lado de una cadena montañosa donde pega el viento de frente.

INDEX

Page numbers for key terms are printed in **boldface** type.

A

Abyssal plain, **44–45**
Air. *See* Atmosphere
Air masses, **133**–139
    cyclones and anticyclones, **138**
    fronts, **135**, 136–137
    movement of, 135
    types of, 133–134
Air pressure, 78, **79**–83
    and altitude, 82
    in different atmospheric layers, 85–89
    effect on wind, 101
    mass and density of, 78–79
    measuring, 80–81
Altitude
    effect on atmosphere, **82**–83
    effect on climate, 169, 176–177, 182
Altocumulus clouds, 124
Anemometer, **102**
Aneroid barometers, **81**
Animals
    and water, 5, 119
    in wetlands, 28
Anticyclones, **138**
Application of skills
    Apply It!, 9, 14, 26, 43, 48, 56, 61, 76, 82, 93, 98, 105, 125, 129, 139, 149, 153, 183, 194
    Do the Math!, 6, 21, 59, 87, 121, 188
    interactivities, 8–9, 11, 12, 13, 15, 17, 20, 22, 42, 44–45, 50, 52, 61, 62–63, 75, 79, 80, 83, 91, 95, 98, 103, 104, 106, 107, 119, 125, 133, 138, 139, 145, 149, 151, 172–173, 176–177, 181, 189
    Science Matters
        Aquanauts, 69
        Aura Mission, 112
        Bacterial Rainmakers, 201
        Miami Fort, 35
        Pearl of a Solution, 34
        Plugging into the Jet Stream, 113
        S'Cool Project, 160
        Sustainable Shrimp Farms, 68
        Tracking Earth's Gasses from Space, 200
        Tracking Hurricanes, 161
Apply It!. *See* Application of skills
Aquifers, **21**–22
Arid climate, 176–177, 179
Artesian well, **23**
Assessment
    Assess Your Understanding, 5, 7, 9, 13, 15, 17, 20, 23, 27, 29, 43, 45, 51, 53, 57, 59, 63, 76, 77, 79, 81, 83, 85, 89, 91, 95, 97, 99, 102, 107, 119, 121, 123, 125, 129, 131, 135, 137, 139, 147, 149, 152, 155, 171, 173, 175, 183, 186, 189, 195
    Review and Assessment, 31–32, 65–66, 109–110, 157–158, 197–198
    Standardized Test Prep, 33, 67, 111, 159, 199
    Study Guide, 30, 64, 108, 156, 196
Atmosphere, **74**–113
    air masses, 132–139
    air pressure, 78–83
    composition of, 74–77
    energy absorption by, 92–95
    heating, 98–99
    layers of, 85–89
    mesosphere, **88**
    ozone layer, 87, 92
    stratosphere, **87**, 92
    studying, 74, 112
    thermosphere, **89**
    troposphere, **86**, 93, 99
    water in, 118–122
    winds, 100–106, 113

B

Barometers, **80–81**
Barrier beaches, 53
Beach erosion, 53
Benthos, **62**–63
Big Idea, xx–xxi
Big Question
    Answer the Big Question, 17, 45, 107, 155, 195
    Apply the Big Question, 32, 66, 110, 158, 198
    chapter opener, 1, 37, 71, 114, 163
    Explore the Big Question, 17, 45, 107, 155, 195
    Review the Big Question, 30, 64, 108, 156, 196
    Unlock the Big Question, 4, 10, 18, 24, 40, 46, 54, 60, 74, 78, 84, 90, 96, 100, 118, 122, 126, 132, 140, 150, 166, 174, 184, 190
Bogs, 26
Breezes, sea and land, **103**

C

Carbon capture, 194
Carbon dioxide, 74–75, 191–194
Carbon footprint, 190
Celsius scale, 97
Cirrocumulus clouds, 125
Cirrus clouds, **124**
Climate, **56**, **167**
    classifying, 174–177
    and ocean currents, 56–57, 170
    precipitation factors, 172–173, 201
    temperature factors, 167–171
Climate change, **185**–195
    effect of oceans on, 166
    effect of volcanoes and sunspots on, 189
    greenhouse effect, 191–194, 200
    ice ages, **188**
    measuring, 185–186, 200
    models, 192
Climate regions and features, 174–182
    desert, 176–177, 179
    dry (arid and semiarid), 176–177, 179
    highlands, 176–177, 182
    humid continental, 181
    humid subtropical, **180**
    marine west coast, 180
    Mediterranean, 180
    permafrost, **182**
    polar, 176–177, 182
    rain forests, **178**
    savannas, **178**
    steppes, **179**
    subarctic, **181**
    temperate continental, **170**, 176–177, 181
    temperate marine, **170**, 176–177, 180
    tropical rainy (wet and wet-and-dry), 176–177, 178
    tundra, **182**
Clouds, 122–125
    and absorption of radiation, 92
    formation of, 76, 119, 122–123
    seeding, 126
    types of, 124–125
    in water cycle, 119
Coastal wetlands, 27
Cold fronts, 136
Condensation, 9, 17, **118**–119, 122–123
Conduction, **98**–99
Continental air masses, **133**–134
Continental climate, **170**, 176–177, 181
Continental shelf, **44–45**
Continental slope, **44–45**
Continents, movement of, 187

Convection, **98**–99
Convection currents, **99**
   global, 104
Coriolis effect, **55, 105**–106
Cumulonimbus clouds, 142
Cumulus clouds, **124**
Currents, 54, **55**–59
   Coriolis effect, **55**
   deep, 58–59
   effect on climate, 56–57, 171
   surface, 55–57
   thermohaline circulation, 58–59
Cyclones, 132, **138**

———————— **D** ————————

Dams, 15, 130
Density of air, **79**
   and altitude, 82–83
   in different atmospheric layers,
   85–89
   and wind, 101
Desert, 176–177, 179
Desertification, 193
Dew point, **123**
Did You Know?, 22, 43, 88, 142,
   169
Digital Learning
   Apply It!, 9, 15, 25, 75, 83, 93,
   99, 103, 125, 131, 139, 149, 153
   Art in Motion, 19, 20, 55, 57, 93,
   95, 127, 128, 191
   Do the Math!, 7, 21, 87, 121
   Interactive Art, 8, 9, 28, 29, 45,
   47, 49, 61, 62, 80, 81, 103, 106,
   119, 136, 137, 141, 146, 187
   My Reading Web, 2, 3, 38, 39,
   72, 73, 116, 117, 164, 165
   My Science Coach, 5, 7, 9, 11,
   13, 15, 17, 20, 21, 23, 27, 29, 31,
   43, 45, 51, 53, 57, 59, 63, 65, 76,
   77, 79, 81, 83, 85, 87, 89, 91, 95,
   97, 99, 101, 102, 107, 119, 121,
   123, 125, 129, 131, 133, 135,
   137, 139, 147, 149, 151, 152,
   155, 157, 171, 173, 175, 177,
   183, 185, 186, 189
   Planet Diary, 4, 5, 10, 11, 18, 19,
   24, 25, 40, 41, 46, 47, 54, 55, 60,
   61, 74, 75, 78, 79, 84, 85, 90, 91,
   96, 97, 100, 101, 118, 119, 122,
   123, 126, 127, 132, 133, 140,
   141, 150, 151, 166, 167, 174,
   175, 184, 185, 190, 191
   Real-World Inquiry, 17, 153, 155
   Untamed Science, xxii, 1, 36, 37,
   70, 71, 114, 115, 162, 163
   Virtual Lab, 41, 83, 167, 169

   Vocab Flash Cards, 3, 39, 73,
   117, 165
Divide, **13**
Do the Math!. *See* Application of
   skills
Doldrums, 106
Drought, **131**
   and global warming, 193
Dry climate, 176–177, 179

———————— **E** ————————

El Niño, **57**
Electromagnetic waves, **90**
   See also Radiation
Energy, clean and efficient, 194
Energy, solar
   absorption of, 92–95
   effect on climate, 189
   from electromagnetic waves,
   90–91
   from radiation, **91**
   from visible light, 91
Energy, thermal, **97**–99
Erosion, beach, 53
Eutrophication, **16**
Evacuation, **148**
Evaporation, **8**, 17, **118**–119
Exosphere, **89**

———————— **F** ————————

Fahrenheit scale, 97
Floods, 29, **130**, 143
Fog, 124
Food web, marine, **63**
Fossil fuels, **192**
Fossils, 185
Freezing rain, 128
Fresh water
   location of, 6–7
   source of, 9
   See also Water
Freshwater wetlands, 26
Fronts, **135**, 136–137

———————— **G** ————————

Gases
   in atmosphere, 74–75
   greenhouse, **191**–194, 200
Geysers, 22
Glaciers, 193
Global warming, **192**–194

Global winds, **104**–106
Gravity, in river systems, 11
Great Divide, 13
Greenhouse effect, **95**, 191–194
Greenhouse gases, **191**–194, 200
Groin (beach), **53**
Groundwater
   in aquifers, 21–23
   movement of, 19–20, 22
   and ponds and lakes, 14
   under pressure, 22, 23
   as source of water, **7**
   use of, 21–23
   in water cycle, 9
   See also Water

———————— **H** ————————

Habitat, **5**
   ocean, 60–63
   wetlands, 25
Hail, 128
Heat, **98**
Heat transfer, 96–99
Highlands climate region,
   176–177, 182
Horse latitudes, 106
Human activities, impact of
   on aquifers, 21–23
   on drought, 131
   greenhouse effect, 95, 191–194
   on lakes and ponds, 16
   seafood farming, 68
Humid continental climate, 181
Humid subtropical climate, **180**
Humidity, **120**
Hurricanes, **144**–145, 149, 161

———————— **I** ————————

Ice, 6
Ice ages, **188**
Ice cores, 186
Impermeable materials, **19**
Infrared radiation, **91**
Inquiry Skills. *See* Science Inquiry
   Skills; Science Literacy Skills
Interactivities. *See* Application of
   skills
Intertidal zone, **61**
Ionosphere, **89**
Isobars and isotherms, **153**

INDEX

Page numbers for key terms are printed in **boldface** type.

J

Jet stream, 113, **135**

L

La Niña, **57**
Lab Zone
 Inquiry Warm-Up, 4, 10, 18, 24, 40, 46, 54, 60, 74, 78, 84, 90, 96, 100, 118, 122, 126, 132, 140, 150, 166, 174, 184, 190
 Lab Investigation, 9, 57, 95, 155, 171
 Quick Lab, 5, 7, 13, 15, 17, 20, 23, 27, 29, 43, 45, 51, 53, 59, 63, 76, 77, 79, 81, 83, 85, 89, 91, 97, 99, 102, 107, 119, 121, 123, 125, 129, 131, 135, 137, 139, 147, 149, 152, 173, 175, 183, 186, 189, 195
Lake-effect snow, **141**
Lakes and ponds, **14**–16
 eutrophication, 16
 formation, 15
 impact on temperature, 170
 as source of water, 6–7
 in water cycle, 9
Land breeze, **103**
Latitude
 and temperature, 168
 and wind, **106**
Leeward, **172**
Lightning, **143**
Local winds, **103**
Longshore drift, **52**

M

Marine climate, **170**, 176–177, 180
Marine west coast climate, 180
Maritime air masses, **133**–134
Marshes, 26
Mass of air, 78, 80, 84–85
Math. *See* Application of skills
Measuring
 air pressure, 80–81
 greenhouse gases, 200
 humidity, 120
 rain, 127
 temperature, 97
 wind, 102
Mediterranean climate, 180
Mercury barometers, **80**
Mesosphere, **88**
Meteoroids, 88

Meteorologists, **151**
Methane, 191–192
Mid-ocean ridge, **44**–45
Monsoons, **173**
Mountains
 and precipitation, 172
 temperature of, 169
 See also Altitude
My Planet Diary
 Blogs, 90, 122
 Careers, 18, 150
 Disasters, 46, 140
 Discovery, 78, 184
 Everyday Science, 54, 190
 Extreme Sports, 100
 Fun Facts, 10, 118, 174
 Misconceptions, 84, 132, 166
 Profile, 24
 Science in the Kitchen, 96
 Science Stats, 5
 Science Today, 60
 Technology, 40, 126
 Voices from History, 74

N

Nekton, **62**–63
Neritic zone, **61**
Nitrogen, 74–75

O

Occluded fronts, **137**
Oceans, 36–69
 currents, 54, **55**–59, 171
 exploring, 42, 44, 69
 and global warming, 193–194
 habitats, 60–63
 impact on climate, 170–171
 ocean floor features, 44–45
 organisms, 62–63
 salinity, **41**, 58
 temperature and depth, 42
 waves, 46, **47**–53
 zones, 60–61
Open-ocean zone, **61**
Oxygen, 74–75
Ozone layer, 87, 92

P

Particles
 in atmosphere, 76
 and cloud formation, 123
Permafrost, **182**

Permeable materials, **19**
 in aquifers, 21
Photosynthesis, **5**
 and eutrophication, 16
Plankton, **62**–63
Plants
 in water cycle, 8, 119
 and water use, 5
 in wetlands, 26–27
Polar air masses, **133**–134
Polar climate, **176**–177, 182
Polar easterlies, **106**
Polar zone, **168**
Pollen records, **186**
Pollution
 of fresh water, 34
 of ocean water, 68
Ponds. *See* Lakes and ponds
Precipitation, **9**, 126, **127**–131
 in different climate regions, 178–182
 effect of bacteria on, 201
 effect of winds and mountains on, 172–173
 floods and drought, 130–131
 types of, 127–129
 in water cycle, 14, 17, 19, 118–119
Predicting weather
 methods and technology, 151–152, 160–161
 using weather maps, 153–155
Pressure
 air, 78–83
 water, 42
Prevailing westerlies, **106**, 135
Prevailing winds, **172**
Process Skills. *See* Science Inquiry Skills; Science Literacy Skills
Psychrometer, **120**
Pumps, 23

R

Radiation, **91**
 absorption of, 92–95
 and heat transfer, 98–99
Rain. *See* Precipitation
Rain forests, **178**
Rain gauge, **127**
Reading Skills
 graphic organizers
  Venn Diagram, 14

reading/thinking support strategies
> apply concepts, 8, 28, 49, 65, 66, 79, 80, 99, 109, 135, 153, 158, 172
> define, 57, 76, 83, 102, 129, 137, 171, 195, 198
> describe, 23, 29, 57, 79, 125, 137
> explain, 15, 17, 20, 27, 45, 59, 99, 101, 131, 147, 148, 155, 178, 197
> identify, 9, 13, 48, 61, 81, 91, 94, 98, 102, 107, 139, 147, 171, 173, 177, 182, 198
> interpret data, 6, 21, 43, 87, 188, 193
> interpret diagrams, 13, 20, 50, 62, 65, 95, 104, 123, 138, 142, 144
> interpret graphs, 175
> interpret maps, 12, 141, 146, 154, 187, 197
> interpret photos, 169
> list, 7, 45, 76, 77, 89, 149, 167, 173, 195
> make generalizations, 13
> make judgments, 7, 11, 22, 32, 131, 158
> mark text, 5, 6, 7, 42, 47, 50, 55, 83, 85, 105, 128, 141, 178, 188
> name, 27, 81, 169
> read graphs, 6, 21, 41, 87, 192
> relate text and visuals, 42, 44
> review, 20, 59, 63, 97, 121, 128, 135, 189
> solve problems, 23, 149

target reading skills
> ask questions, 29, 62, 93, 191
> compare and contrast, 15, 19, 27, 48, 56, 65, 66, 76, 92, 109, 110, 121, 139, 147, 153, 179, 197, 198
> identify supporting evidence, 85, 105, 188
> identify the main idea, 6, 42, 99, 178
> outline, 144
> relate cause and effect, 23, 31, 50, 52, 65, 66, 83, 102, 110, 131, 173, 189, 197, 198
> relate text and visuals, 103, 106, 120, 134, 135, 139, 168
> sequence, 9, 16, 31, 63, 65, 95, 109, 119, 172, 183
> summarize, 13, 16, 50, 66, 77, 83, 95, 99, 107, 119, 123, 168, 173, 189

Relative humidity, 120

Reservoir, 15
Rip currents, 52
Rivers
> and floods, 130
> river systems, 10–13
> as source of water, 6–7
Runoff, 9, 17
> and ponds and lakes, 14

S

Salinity, ocean, 41
Salt water. See Oceans
Sand dunes, 53
Saturated zone, 20
Savannas, 178
Scattering, 93
Science Inquiry Skills
> basic process skills
>> calculate, 21, 59, 97, 109, 121, 127, 129, 169, 197
>> classify, 7, 15, 26, 31, 32, 63, 89, 125, 133, 134, 135, 137, 139
>> communicate, 18, 51, 107, 122, 140, 150, 183, 191
>> graph, 75, 93, 183
>> infer, 20, 23, 32, 55, 56, 63, 76, 98, 109, 130, 136, 143, 149, 157, 170, 186, 187, 198
>> make models, 83, 194
>> observe, 9, 25, 26, 82, 86, 114, 125, 168, 170, 181, 188
>> predict, 21, 32, 45, 47, 58, 61, 83, 95, 125, 145, 153, 157, 171

Science Literacy Skills
> integrated process skills
>> develop hypotheses, xxii, 29, 36, 70, 82, 162, 185
>> draw conclusions, 57, 94, 105, 109, 129, 180, 198
>> evaluate science in the media, 195
>> form operational definitions, 14, 48
>> interpret data, 43, 87, 121, 188, 193
>> make generalizations, 13
>> relate evidence and explanation, 83

Science Matters. See Application of skills
Sea breeze, 103
Sea levels, rising, 193–194
Semiarid climate, 176–177, 179
Sleet, 128
Snow, 128, 140, 141, 148

Soil
> and groundwater, 7, 19
> in water cycle, 8
Sonar, 44
Springs, 21
Stationary fronts, 137
Steppes, 179
Storm surge, 145
Storms, 141–149
> cyclones, 132, 138
> floods, 29, 130, 143
> hurricanes, 144–145, 149, 161
> lightning, 143
> monsoons, 173
> safety precautions, 148–149
> thunderstorms, 142–143, 149
> tornadoes, 114, 132, 146–147, 149
> winter storms, 140, 141, 148
Stratosphere, 87, 92
Stratus clouds, 125
Streams. See Rivers
Subarctic climate, 181
Sunspots, 189
Surface water
> ponds and lakes, 14–16
> river systems, 10–13
Swamps, 26

T

Temperate continental climate, 170, 176–177, 181
Temperate marine climate, 170, 176–177, 180
Temperate zone, 168
Temperature, 96–97
> and altitude, 169
> of atmospheric layers, 85–89, 169
> and cloud formation, 122–123
> in different climate regions, 170, 178–182
> and global warming, 191–193
> of oceans, 42
> of tropical, polar, and temperate zones, 168
> and wind, 101–104
Thermal energy, 97–99
Thermometer, 97
Thermosphere, 89
Thunderstorms, 142–143, 149
> in tropical climates, 178
Tornadoes, 114, 132, 146–147, 149
Trade winds, 106
Transpiration, 8, 17
Tree rings, 186

INDEX

Page numbers for key terms are printed in **boldface** type.

Trenches, 44–**45**
Tributaries, **11**
Tropical air masses, **133**–134
Tropical rainy climates (wet and wet-and-dry), 176–177, 178
Tropical zone, **168**
Troposphere, **86**, 93
Tsunami, **51**
Tundra, **182**

U

Ultraviolet radiation, **91**
Underground water. *See* Groundwater
Unsaturated zone, **20**

V

Vocabulary Skills
   high-use academic words, 164, 170
   prefixes, 116, 138
   suffixes, 38, 41
   word origins (Greek or Latin), 2, 8, 21, 72, 80
Volcanic activity, 189

W

Warm fronts, 136
Water, 1–34
   importance and usefulness, 4, 5, 21–23, 28–29
   location, 6–7, 18
   management, 35
   ocean currents, 54–59
   ocean features, 41–45
   ocean habitats, 60–63
   ocean waves, 46–53
   pollution, 34, 68
   ponds and lakes, 14–16
   river systems, 10–13
   surface water, 10–17
   underground water, 19–23
   wetlands, 24–29
Water cycle, 8–9, 17, **118**–119
   condensation, 9, **118**
   evaporation **8, 118**
   transpiration, **8**
Water table, **20**–21

Water vapor, 6, 9, **76**
   in atmosphere, 74, 76
   and greenhouse effect, 191
   in water cycle, 118–119, 122–123
Watersheds, **12**
Waves, **47**–53
   breakers, 50
   deep currents, 58–59
   energy and motion, 49
   erosion, 53
   formation of, 47
   longshore drift and rip currents, **52**
   size, 46–47
   surface currents, 54–57
   tsunami, **51**
   wavelength, wave height, and frequency, **48**
Weather, **74,** 114–161
   air masses, 132–139
   and atmospheric layers, 86
   clouds, 122–125
   humidity, 120–121
   precipitation, 126–131
   predicting, 150–155, 160–161
   storms, 140–149
   and water cycle, 118–119
   and water vapor, 76
   See also Precipitation; Temperature
Wells, 22
Wetlands, **25**–29
   coastal, 27
   freshwater, 26
   importance of, 28–29
Wildlife. *See* Animals
Wind, 100, **101**–106
   and air pressure and temperature, 101
   Coriolis effect, **105**–106
   effect on temperature, 172
   effect on water currents, 55
   energy from, 113
   global, 104–106
   jet stream, 113
   local, 103
   measuring, 102
   studying, 113
Windchill factor, **102**
Windward, **172**

ACKNOWLEDGMENTS

Staff Credits

The people who made up the *Interactive Science* team—representing composition services, core design digital and multimedia production services, digital product development, editorial, editorial services, manufacturing, and production—are listed below.

Jan Van Aarsen, Samah Abadir, Ernie Albanese, Zareh MacPherson Artinian, Bridget Binstock, Suzanne Biron, MJ Black, Nancy Bolsover, Stacy Boyd, Jim Brady, Katherine Bryant, Michael Burstein, Pradeep Byram, Jessica Chase, Jonathan Cheney, Arthur Ciccone, Allison Cook-Bellistri, Rebecca Cottingham, AnnMarie Coyne, Bob Craton, Chris Deliee, Paul Delsignore, Michael Di Maria, Diane Dougherty, Kristen Ellis, Theresa Eugenio, Amanda Ferguson, Jorgensen Fernandez, Kathryn Fobert, Julia Gecha, Mark Geyer, Steve Gobbell, Paula Gogan-Porter, Jeffrey Gong, Sandra Graff, Adam Groffman, Lynette Haggard, Christian Henry, Karen Holtzman, Susan Hutchinson, Sharon Inglis, Marian Jones, Sumy Joy, Sheila Kanitsch, Courtenay Kelley, Chris Kennedy, Toby Klang, Greg Lam, Russ Lappa, Margaret LaRaia, Ben Leveillee, Thea Limpus, Dotti Marshall, Kathy Martin, Robyn Matzke, John McClure, Mary Beth McDaniel, Krista McDonald, Tim McDonald, Rich McMahon, Cara McNally, Melinda Medina, Angelina Mendez, Maria Milczarek, Claudi Mimo, Mike Napieralski, Deborah Nicholls, Dave Nichols, William Oppenheimer, Jodi O'Rourke, Ameer Padshah, Lorie Park, Celio Pedrosa, Jonathan Penyack, Linda Zust Reddy, Jennifer Reichlin, Stephen Rider, Charlene Rimsa, Stephanie Rogers, Marcy Rose, Rashid Ross, Anne Rowsey, Logan Schmidt, Amanda Seldera, Laurel Smith, Nancy Smith, Ted Smykal, Emily Soltanoff, Cindy Strowman, Dee Sunday, Barry Tomack, Patricia Valencia, Ana Sofia Villaveces, Stephanie Wallace, Christine Whitney, Brad Wiatr, Heidi Wilson, Heather Wright, Rachel Youdelman

Photography

Cover, Front and Back
Mark A. Johnson/Corbis.

Front Matter
Page vi, Pete Saloutos/Corbis; **vii,** Kirstin Scholtz/ASP/Getty Images; **viii,** LOOK Die Bildagentur der Fotografen GmbH/Alamy; **ix,** Eric Nguyen/Photo Researchers, Inc.; **x,** Ralph Lee Hopkins/Getty Images; **xi all,** iStockphoto.com; **xiii tr,** iStockphoto.com; **xv br,** JupiterImages/Getty Images; **xviii laptop,** iStockphoto.com; **xx,** Roel Dijkstra/Sunshine/Zuma Press; **xxi l,** UIG via Getty Images; **xxi r,** Jeremy Woodhouse/Photodisc/Getty Images.

Chapter 1
Pages xxii–1, Pete Saloutos/Corbis; **3,** Les David Manevitz/SuperStock; **4 t,** Milos Luzanin/iStockphoto.com; **4 m,** Jorge Salcedo/iStockphoto.com; **4 b,** Steve Jacobs/iStockphoto.com; **5,** Gerald Hinde/Getty Images; **9,** Tiburonstudios/iStockphoto.com; **14 r,** Philip Kramer/Getty Images; **14 l,** Halina/Alamy; **15 l,** Alison Wright/Getty Images; **15 inset,** NASA/Courtesy of Jeff Schmaltz; **15 r,** Ralph Lee Hopkins/Photo Researchers, Inc.; **16,** North Wind Picture Archives/Alamy; **17,** David Noton Photography/Alamy; **18 r,** Ted Spiegel/Corbis; **19 bkgrnd,** Stock photo/iStockphoto.com; **21 tl,** Inga Spence/Photo Researchers, Inc.; **21 r,** Theodore Clutter/Photo Researchers, Inc.; **21 m,** Peter Bowater/Photo Researchers, Inc.; **21 bl,** Photoroller/Dreamstime.com; **22,** Photodisc/SuperStock; **24 bl,** Neil Hardwick/Alamy; **24 br,** age fotostock/SuperStock; **25,** Jim Zipp/Photo Researchers, Inc.; **26 t,** North Wind Picture Archives/Alamy; **26 inset,** Thomas R. Fletcher/Alamy; **26 b,** Michael P. Gadomski/Science Source; **26–27,** Paula Stephens/iStockphoto.com; **27 l,** Fletcher & Baylis/Photo Researchers, Inc.; **27 r,** Alberto Pomares/iStockphoto.com; **28–29,** Karen Huntt/Getty Images; **29 t,** Howie Garber/Mira.com; **29 m,** Herbert Phillips/iStockphoto.com; **29 b,** Nancy Camel/Alamy; **30,** Jim Zipp/Photo Researchers, Inc.

Interchapter Feature
Page 34 bkgrnd, George Grall/National Geographic Stock; **34 inset,** Ian O'Leary/Dorling Kindersley; **35 b,** Melanie Cannon, University of Cincinnati.

Chapter 2
Pages 36–37, Kirstin Scholtz/ASP/Getty Images; **39 t,** SPL/Science Source; **39 bm,** NASA/Goddard Space Flight Center Scientific Visualization Studio; **39 b,** M. I. Walker/Science Source; **40 inset,** Mass Communication Specialist Seaman Luciano Marano/U.S. Navy; **40–41,** Marevision Marevision/age Fotostock/Photolibrary New York; **43 tl,** Fotolia; **43 tr,** Courtesy of Deep Flight Hawkes Ocean Technologies; **43 bl,** Emory Kristof and Alvin Chandler/National Geographic Society; **45,** U.S. Navy News Photo; **46,** Commander Richard Behn, NOAA Corps/National Oceanic and Atmospheric Administration; **48 b,** Arnulf Husmo/Getty Images; **48–49,** iStockphoto.com; **51 bl,** Dita Alangkara/AP Images; **53 t,** Steve Dunwell/age Fotostock; **53 m,** Imagebroker/age Fotostock; **53 b,** Jim Wark/Airphoto; **53 bkgrnd,** Sven Zacek/Oxford Scientific/Photolibrary; **54 both,** Dr. W. James Ingraham, Jr./National Oceanic and Atmospheric Administration (NOAA); **55 both,** Dr. W. James Ingraham, Jr./National Oceanic and Atmospheric Administration (NOAA); **56 l,** Eitan Simanor/ Robert Harding World Imagery; **56 r,** Chris Wattie/Reuters; **57 t,** NASA/Goddard Space Flight Center Scientific Visualization Studio; **57 b,** NASA/Goddard Space Flight Center Scientific Visualization Studio; **58–59,** Photo courtesy of Argonne National Laboratory; **59 t,** SPL/Science Source; **60,** Kim Briers/Shutterstock; **61,** Ernest A. Janes/Bruce Coleman, Inc.; **62 l,** M. I. Walker/Science Source; **62 m,** FLPA/Alamy; **62 r,** Georgie Holland/Photolibrary New York; **64 t,** Arnulf Husmo/Getty Images. **64 b,** Ernest A. Janes/Bruce Coleman, Inc.

Interchapter Feature
68 bkgrnd, Kevin Schafer/Alamy; **68 shrimp,** Dave King/Dorling Kindersley; **69** Brian J. Skerry/National Geographic Stock.

Chapter 3
Pages 70–71, Corbis/Kevin Fleming; **73 t,** Bettmann/Corbis; **73 tm,** Van D. Bucher/Photo Researchers, Inc.; **73 bm,** David Wall/Alamy; **73 b,** Norma Cornes/Shutterstock, Inc.; **74,** Charles D. Winters/Photo Researchers, Inc.; **75,** Bettmann/Corbis; **76 t,** Sean Randall/iStockphoto.com; **76 b,** Digital Vision/Alamy; **77,** NASA/GSFC Lab for Atmospheres;

78, HIGH-G Productions/Stocktrek Images/Getty Images; 81, Van D. Bucher/Photo Researchers, Inc.; 84, Melissa McManus/Getty Images; 85, David Wall/Alamy; 88, LOOK Die Bildagentur der Fotografen GmbH/Alamy; 91, Aqua Image/Alamy; 93 l, Ermin Gutenberger/iStockphoto.com; 93 ml, Mark Yuill/iStockphoto.com; 93 mr, Ideeone/iStockphoto.com; 93 r, Jason Major/iStockphoto.com; 96, Helle Bro Clemmensen/iStockphoto.com; 98, Mikhail Kokhanchikov/iStockphoto.com; 98–99, Xavi Arnau/iStockphoto.com; 100–101, Norma Cornes/Shutterstock, Inc.; 102, Kruwt/Fotolia; 103, Harris Shiffman Shutterstock; 108, NASA/GSFC Lab for Atmospheres.

Interchapter Feature
Page 112, NASA; 113 t, Stefano Bianchetti/Corbis; 113 b, LPI/NASA.

Chapter 4
Pages 114–115, Eric Nguyen/Photo Researchers, Inc.; 117 t, John Howard/Photo Researchers, Inc.; 117 b, Gene Rhoden/Still Pictures; 119, Jeremy Horner/Corbis; 122 r, Reimar/Alamy; 126, Ng Han Guan/AP Images; 128 tl, Don Johnston/age Fotostock/Photolibrary New York; 128 tr, Tom King/Alamy; 128 bl, Liz Leyden/iStockphoto.com; 128 br, John Howard/Photo Researchers, Inc.; 129, Matthias Hauser/Imagebroker/Alamy; 130, Stephen Morton/Stringer/Getty Images; 131, Paul S. Howell/Getty Images; 132, Digital Vision/Getty Images; 135, Gene Rhoden/Still Pictures; 139, NASA; 140, AP Images; 142, Peter Menzel/Photo Researchers, Inc.; 143, King Wu/iStockphoto.com; 145 tl and bl, NASA/Goddard Space Flight Center Scientific Visualization Studio; 145 tr, Joe Raedle/Getty Images; 147, Kansas City Star/MCT/Getty Images; 148, Donna McWilliam/AP Images; 149, Chris Mampe/iStockphoto.com; 150 inset, imac/Alamy; 150 bkgrnd, Tom Sibley/Corbis; 151, Fitzsimage/Shutterstock; 152 l, NASA/Photo Researchers, Inc.; 152 m, Paul Rapson/Science Photo Library; 152 r, David Parker/Photo Researchers, Inc.; 156 br, David Parker/Photo Researchers, Inc.

Interchapter Feature
Page 160 bkgrnd, Brian Cosgrove/Dorling Kindersley; 160 inset, NASA.

Chapter 5
Pages 162–163, Ralph Lee Hopkins/Getty Images; 165 t, Mark A. Johnson/Corbis; 165 m, Steve Allen/Getty Images; 165 b, Andrew Penner/iStockphoto.com; 166, Duncan Shaw/SPL/Photo Researchers, Inc.; 167, Mark A. Johnson/Corbis; 169 t, Emmanuel Lattes/Alamy; 169 b, Steve Allen/Getty Images; 174, Douglas Peebles Photography/Alamy; 175, Joseph Sohm-Visions of America/Getty Images; 178, image100/Corbis; 179, Jennifer Trenchard/iStockphoto.com; 180, Dave G. Houser/Corbis; 181 inset, wwwoland/iStockphoto.com; 181 bkgrnd, Kim Karpeles/Alamy; 182 t, Robert Landau/Getty Images; 182 b, THesIMPLIFY/Fotolia; 184 tr, Rebecca Paul/iStockphoto.com; 184 bl, Vienna Report Agency/Corbis; 184 br, Petr David Josek/AP Images; 185, Atlantide Phototravel/Corbis; 186, GYRO PHOTOGRAPHY/amanaimages/Corbis; 189 t, Krafft/Photo Researchers, Inc.; 189 b, *The Snowstorm* (1786–87), Francisco Jose de Goya y Lucientes. Oil on canvas, 275 x 293 cm/Prado, Madrid/Bridgeman Art Library/Getty Images; 190 bkgrnd, Andrew Penner/iStockphoto.com; 190 inset, Kazberry/Shutterstock, Inc.; 193, Courtesy of USGS; 194 bkgrnd, Long Tran The/iStockphoto.com; 194 t, Alistair Baker/Getty Images; 195, Rudi Sebastian/Getty Images; 196 t, Joseph Sohm Visions of America/Getty Images; 196 b, GYRO PHOTOGRAPHY/amanaimages/Corbis.

Interchapter Feature
Page 200, Japan Aerospace Exploration Agency, HO/AP Images; 201, Joe Tree/Alamy.

take note

this space is yours—great for drawing diagrams and making notes

this is your book

you can write in it